# Knock Me Up, Knock Me Down

# Knock me up, Knock me down

IMAGES

OF

PREGNANCY

IN

HOLLYWOOD

FILMS

## Kelly Oliver

COLUMBIA UNIVERSITY PRESS / NEW YORK

Columbia University Press
*Publishers Since 1893*
New York    Chichester, West Sussex
cup.columbia.edu
Copyright © 2012 Columbia University Press

*Cover image: Courtesy of Universal Studios Licensing LLC*

Library of Congress Cataloging-in-Publication Data
Oliver, Kelly, 1958–
Knock me up, knock me down : images of pregnancy in Hollywood film /
Kelly Oliver.
p. cm.
Includes bibliographical references and index.
ISBN 978-0-231-16108-4 (cloth : alk. paper) — ISBN 978-0-231-16109-1
(pbk : alk. paper) — ISBN 978-0-231-53070-5 (ebook)
1. Pregnancy in motion pictures.    2. Motion pictures—United States.
3. Feminist theory.      I. Title

PN1995.9.P66045     2012
791.43'654—dc23                    2012014208

Columbia University Press books are printed on permanent and durable
acid-free paper.

This book is printed on paper with recycled content.
Printed in the United States of America

c 10 9 8 7 6 5 4 3 2 1
p 10 9 8 7 6 5 4 3 2 1

*Cover design: Lisa Hamm*

References to Internet Web sites (URLs) were accurate at the time of writing.
Neither the author nor Columbia University Press is responsible for URLs
that may have expired or changed since the manuscript was prepared.

TO MY MOM,
WHO GAVE UP (ALMOST) EVERYTHING ELSE TO HAVE A FAMILY

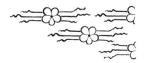

# CONTENTS

# ACKNOWLEDGMENTS

I WOULD LIKE TO THANK audiences at various conferences and universities where I presented parts of this book for their helpful feedback and suggestions. Also, I would like to thank my graduate and undergraduate students who discussed these issues and films with me in several courses at Vanderbilt University. I am especially grateful to comments made by Kalpana Rahita Seshadri, Pleshette D'Armitt, Melinda Hall, Alison Suen, and Erin Tarver, who read the entire manuscript, which is better for their suggestions. Thanks to Wendy Lochner at Columbia University Press for her encouragement and support throughout the publishing process. Thanks to my friends and family who watched films with me (especially my dad, Glen, and Beni, who were subjected to most of them), gave me suggestions for other films to watch (especially film-buffs Harvey and Ruthy), and helped me formulate my ideas. As always, Benigno Trigo was a provocative interlocutor, who is game for talking criticism and theory; I couldn't have done it without him. And, Yuki, Huri, and Mayo were always great company when we watched movies at home.

# Knock Me Up, Knock Me Down

# INTRODUCTION: FROM SHAMEFUL TO SEXY

## PREGNANT BELLIES EXPLODING ONTO THE SCREEN

Images of pregnancy, once scarce, now proliferate as a powerful technological imperative drives the disembodiment of reproduction and secures its manipulation at a genetic level. The pregnant icon demands to be examined, for what it pictures and for what it leaves out.

—SANDRA MATTHEWS AND LAURA WEXLER (2000:218)

**FROM THE MID-NINETEENTH CENTURY** until the late twentieth century, pregnancy was considered a medical condition that should be hidden from public view. Even prior to the medicalization of pregnancy, the pregnant body was considered a private affair and certainly not for public display. When not pathologized, the pregnant body was hidden from view because it was considered ugly, even shameful. Women were advised to "lay-in," which meant not leaving their homes or even their beds. In recent years this view has changed dramatically. Now, women's pregnant bodies are exhibited in ways that could not have been imagined just a few decades ago. Pregnancy has become an obsession in popular culture where paparazzi are constantly on the lookout for celebrities' telltale "baby bumps" and heavily pregnant bellies, and reality television shows and tabloid magazines parade teen pregnancies, sexy "momshells," and celebrity baby woes and triumphs. Pregnancy and pregnant bodies have gone from shameful and hidden to sexy and spectacular.

This book sprang from puzzlement over this drastic change in popular conceptions of pregnancy. In just a couple of decades, how did we go from abject pregnancy to pregnant glam, from pregnancy as shameful to pregnancy as sexy? How can we interpret what appears to be such a dramatic shift in ideals of pregnancy and women's roles in reproduction? Is it true that "we've come a long way baby" to get to the ideal of a woman having a family and a successful career while keeping her knockout figure and sexy good looks? Or do these images of women's seemingly newfound freedom to be pregnant, sexy, and financially independent cover up deeper desires and fears? This book is an attempt to interpret recent Hollywood representations of pregnancy in order to diagnose the ways in which these images open up new possibilities for conceiving of pregnancy and women's role in reproduction, but also continue to reinforce old stereotypes and restrictions on women.

Certainly, positive and desirable images of pregnant women are a step forward. But if we look closer, we can see how these seemingly new stories repeat traditional ideas about abject maternal bodies, conventional notions of family values, familiar anxieties over women's role in reproduction, and fears of miscegenation. In addition, current ideals that promote pregnancy and maternity as desirable, especially for career women, bring new expectations that often require heroic efforts and large doses of caffeine, antidepressants, and sleeping pills—not to mention Mama Spanx maternity wear, "mommy-tucks," diet fads, and taxing workouts at the gym. Today, women are not only responsible for the health and welfare of their babies but also expected to stay beautiful and fit while pregnant and to lose their "baby fat" as soon as possible in order to "get their bodies back" (as one tabloid put it, suggesting that their pregnant bodies are not their *real* bodies). Pregnancy has become like an accessory worn by the rich and famous, an adornment that can be removed. Pregnant celebrities go from lack to excess and back again, from anorexic to sporting the telltale "baby bump," so popular in the media. Now, rather than laying in or staying at home, pregnant women are expected to exercise, continue working, and still be beautiful and sexy for their male partners. In the words of Wenda Wardell Morrone, "We can all recognize the successful pregnant working woman: she is the one in the maternity jogging suit running a marathon on her way to chairing a business meeting; she'll give birth in her lunch hour without even smudging her eye shadow. She is also a fantasy" (1984:1).

If Hollywood did not create this fantasy, it continues to feed it. Indeed, in recent years Hollywood has helped revive the fantasy of women "having it all"—babies, careers, sexy bodies, and the freedom to enjoy them. Pregnancy has become as desirable as ever, now fueled by images of "knocked-up knockouts," "momshells," and pregnant celebrities. Hollywood is giving birth to new images of sexy, cute, and attractive pregnancies offscreen and on. This book is concerned with representations of pregnancy on screen, and although there is some discussion of other popular media and a few independent and foreign films, its primary subject is mainstream Hollywood film. While there have been interesting developments on television and the internet, in order to limit its focus the purview of this book is Hollywood films, which not only provide plenty of images to analyze but also, insofar as they are marketed to a wider audience than any particular television or internet show, may give us the big picture, so to speak. And while over the years there have been many films about the travails, joys, and comedy of motherhood, this book examines the use of pregnancy as a central plot device, which unlike motherhood is a relatively recent phenomenon.

Big-screen representations of pregnant bellies give us new romcoms—*momcoms*—that promise women romance, love, and sex, all through the transformative power of pregnancy. Popular curiosity about pregnancy has given birth to a new subgenre of romantic comedy, in which pregnancy is not only the main theme but also the central plot device. These films display bare pregnant bellies, water breaking, vaginal birth, and show pregnancy as never before seen in popular film. Alien birth continues to be a popular subgenre of horror and science fiction films. In addition, new reproductive technologies, especially assisted reproductive technologies (ARTs), genetic engineering, and cloning, have become themes in comedies as well as the horror and science fiction genres. To interpret the meaning of the relatively sudden appearance of the pregnant belly on the Hollywood scene, this book studies Hollywood films ranging from romantic comedies such as *Juno* and *Knocked Up* or *The Back-up Plan* and *The Switch*, to horror and science fiction such as *Rosemary's Baby* and *The Astronaut's Wife* or *Grace* and *Splice*.

Interest in these films, with their exposed cute and sexy pregnant bellies, is heightened when we consider some of the first American reactions to "French Feminist" theory in the 1970s and 1980s, just before Hollywood's embrace of pregnancy as entertainment. At the vanguard of this French Feminist thought were attempts to rearticulate and revalue the pregnant maternal body, which had been heretofore considered shameful and hidden, into something desiring, desirable, and even the basis for a newly conceived ethics. Luce Irigaray, Julia Kristeva, and their American readers, including Iris Marion Young and Cynthia Willett, described pregnancy and the maternal body in positive terms, and in various ways suggested that a desiring and desirable maternal body with its doubleness and literal openness to the Other might be a more productive model for ethical relationships than traditional antagonistic models such as the master-slave relationship or the Sartrian notion that "hell is other people."

Following Kristeva and Irigaray, Iris Young went so far as to say that, "Patriarchy is founded on the border between motherhood and sexuality. . . . Freedom for women involves dissolving this separation" (Young 1990:166). By motherhood, Young specifically meant pregnant embodiment. What, then, are we to make of pregnant celebrities as cover girls, internet sites devoted to knocked-up knockouts, and popular fascination with pregnant teenagers? Has the border between pregnancy and sexuality that was once on the frontier now familiar territory? In the 2008 presidential election, with Sarah Palin and her daughter Bristol's status as "MILFs" ("mothers I would like to fuck") and momshells, we seemed to have crossed a boundary between motherhood, pregnancy, sexuality, and politics. And if the separation between sexuality and pregnancy or maternity has been dissolved, then following Young's logic, has the foundation of patriarchy been broken and are women free from patriarchal restrictions and stereotypes? Are women freer now than they were when Young wrote those words? Do patriarchal values have any less of a hold on us than they did on her when she wrote her seminal essays on pregnant embodiment and breasted experience? In popular media, has the sexuality of pregnant women been recognized and legitimated? Or, rather, have women's pregnant bodies become sexual objects?

We might answer that while the pregnant body has become desirable, and therefore another way in which women's bodies can be objectified, pregnant women have not become desiring subjects. Given recent representations of women's bodies and desires in Hollywood films, this may be true but it is not the end of the story by any means. Indeed, some of the most recent pregnant Hollywood films are stories of career women who have waited to have babies and now race against their biological clocks aided by new reproductive technologies. Do these new technologies give women more freedom? Or do they merely multiply the difficulties and disappointments of women's reproductive choices, such as they are in today's technologically mediated world? Clearly, women who use assisted reproductive technologies want babies. And in Hollywood films some go to extremes to get them. Indeed, if Hollywood's representations of career women trying to beat the clock (*Miss Conception, Baby Mama, The Back-up Plan, The Switch*) are any indication, women want babies more than anything else. Their desire is fierce and urgent.

The urgency of images of women racing against their biological clocks in these films is fascinating as seen against the backdrop of the feminism of the 1970s, 1980s, and 1990s. For example, Julia Kristeva's most famous essay amongst American audiences is

"Women's Time," in which she argues that the time of women's bodies cannot be measured in linear time; rather, it is cyclical and monumental, even eternal. The time that Kristeva describes is not a race; it is neither urgent nor a ticking time bomb. Rather, it is an expansive time, the time that Iris Young goes on to associate with pregnant embodiment, a time that gives women a special link both to the past, especially their own mothers, and to the future, through the generation of offspring. The urgent time of recent representations of women's desires for babies seems at odds with these academic feminist articulations of women's time. We might wonder whether this trend in feminism from the 1970s through the 1990s is out of touch with Hollywood and therefore out of date, perhaps even out of sync with the time of new reproductive technologies; or, whether a return to that academic feminism might provide a counterbalance to the desperation of Hollywood's "baby hunger."

The first chapter, "Academic Feminism Versus Hollywood Feminism: How Modest Maternity Becomes Pregnant Glam," traces the parallel trajectories of some feminists' revaluations of pregnant embodiment and Hollywood's changing representations of pregnancy. While many feminists discuss motherhood and the mother-child relationship—and there have been lots of films about motherhood—this book takes up representations of pregnancy itself and not the motherhood that follows. This chapter weaves together developments in feminist thought, medicine, science, and popular film to begin to sketch changing attitudes toward pregnant bodies and desires, including desires of, and for, that body and for the babies it births. Pregnancy is no longer in the shadows. But many of the emotions and stigmas attached to it still exist, sometimes in more subterranean forms. Moreover, the way that pregnancy has become a hot image for Hollywood and the tabloids continues a long tradition of objectifying and sexualizing women's bodies. In addition to the objectification of the pregnant body as a sex object, another effect of making pregnancy glamorous and the stuff of celebrity has been to put more pressure on women to "have it all"—babies, careers, the man of their dreams, and sexy bodies.

Nonetheless, can attractive images of pregnancy also be empowering to women even as they promote conventional family values?

We can interpret the meaning of changing representations of pregnant bodies in Hollywood film both in terms of their implications for thinking about women's "freedom," in the words of Young, and new forms of disciplinary expectations levied on pregnant bodies. This chapter is an overview of trends in both feminist theory and Hollywood film for representing pregnant bodies. It traces images of pregnant bodies from 1930s and 1940s Hollywood films through the present in relation to both their changing historical contexts, particularly developments in feminist theory, and the women's movement. The aim of the first chapter, and this book generally, is to explore shifting ideals of pregnancy and how they are shaped through complex interrelations between feminism, popular culture, medicine, science, and filmic discourses.

While a developed theory of filmic representation is beyond the scope of this book, its analysis challenges any simple attempts to answer the question of which comes first, filmic representations or cultural attitudes. In the words of film theorist Frank Krutnik, "in general one can see generic forms as a functional interface between the cinematic institution, audiences and the wider realm of culture. Films never spring magically from their cultural context, but they represent instead much more complex activities of negotiation, addressing cultural transformation in a highly compromised and displayed manner" (1990:57). In the case of pregnancy, Hollywood films mediate between cultural norms and changing notions of the pregnant body influenced by political and technological developments in medicine, media, and feminism. Its claim is not that films mirror so-called "reality"— indeed the relationship is much more productive—but they do tell us something about our values, norms, expectations, and dreams for the future. In these films the pregnant body has become a screen onto which various desires and fears are projected. Indeed, in *Once Around* (1991), this is literally the case when Renata (Holly Hunter) and her husband Sam (Richard Dreyfus) watch home videos of her childhood projected onto her bare, heavily pregnant belly.

Situating Hollywood films within their cultural contexts, including academic feminism, brings into stark relief the ways in which our desires and fears over new reproductive technologies and women's role in reproduction are projected onto pregnant bodies. This ambivalence is obvious in late-nineteenth to mid-twentieth-century expectations regarding pregnancy and maternity, which are driven by notions that women are first and foremost mothers whose duty is to reproduce the species and the nation, and by seemingly conflicting notions that pregnancy and childbirth are abject and should remain hidden from public view. But this ambivalence seems less obvious in current celebrations of pregnancy that make pregnancy a public media spectacle; yet, it is still here, perhaps in more discreet forms.

Pregnancy is one of the most obvious physical and emotional transformations that a human being can undergo. In Hollywood film, pregnancy has become a metaphor for other types of transformations, particularly in the romantic comedy genre that traditionally relies on transformation in one or more characters to enable the sparring couple to be united in the end. In the last decade, year after year we have seen more romantic comedies that make pregnancy and having babies attractive on many levels, including physically, emotionally, psychologically, and in terms of the meaning of life itself and even faith in God. From the beginnings of screwball romantic comedy through more neurotic contemporary forms of the genre, the boy-meets-girl formula necessitates changes, usually a combination of the maturation of one partner and the loosening up of the other, to bring the unlikely couple together. Pregnancy has recently taken the place of adventure on the high seas or cross-dressing masquerades to bring our protagonists together. "First comes love, then comes marriage, then comes Suzy with a baby carriage" has been replaced by *The Back-up Plan*'s tagline: "Fall in Love.* Get Married. Have a Baby. *Not Necessarily in that Order.*"

The second chapter, "MomCom as RomCom: Pregnancy as a Vehicle for Romance," traces the history of the romantic comedy genre in terms of elements that continue or are transformed in pregnant romcom or *momcom*. Momcom is a new subgenre of romcom in which pregnancy is the vehicle for the couple—a man and a woman—to get together. This new pregnant subgenre of romantic comedy has many of the traditional elements of romantic comedy, most especially transformation and reconciliation. Romantic comedies in which pregnancy becomes a new form of romance that brings heterosexual couples together include *Look Who's Talking* (1989), *Junior* (1994), *Fools Rush In* (1997), *Home Fries* (1998), *Saved!* (2004), *Bella* (2006), *Juno* (2007), *Knocked Up* (2007), *Miss Conception* (2008), *Labor Pains* (2009), *The Back-up Plan* (2010), and *The Switch* (2010). These films run the gamut from celebrating teenage pregnancies as cute to celebrating ARTs, which allow increasingly older women to give birth. From teen pregnancy to career women's "baby hunger," these films make pregnancy look sexy, attractive, and, most of all, romantic and funny.

In many of these films, however, the pregnant woman is the butt (sometimes literally!) of the joke. Pregnancy is funny because the pregnant woman's body is out of control, which is especially funny if the woman in question is a neurotic control freak, a common trope in recent *momcoms*. Laughing at the pregnant woman's bodily emissions, growing proportions, and cravings, including sexual appetite (or lack of it), are staples of the momcom genre. In this regard, pregnant romantic comedies continue traditional conceptions of the pregnant body as gross and abject. More accurately, these films display ambivalence about pregnant embodiment that continues earlier ambivalences over the maternal body. If pregnancy was once considered obscene and shameful, now its obscenities and pregnant women's embarrassment about their lack of control are played for laughs.

Pregnancy in these films is funny, but it is also romantic. Pregnancy is the means through which both the male and female characters grow and mature as individuals, and thereby become suitable partners and parents. By turning what is usually an unwanted pregnancy into a wanted baby, these characters learn to want each other. They come to love each other as they prepare themselves to love the future baby. In some of these films—*Saved!* (2004) and *Waitress* (2007)—the unwanted pregnancy not only becomes a wanted baby, but this beloved baby also becomes the solution to the woman's troubles, which have occupied her during the course of the film. Curiously, these happy endings in which the baby is the answer to all of a woman's problems is not far from Freud's seemingly outdated idea that a woman needs a baby for fulfillment (and to resolve what he calls "penis-envy"—even a successful career is not enough).

Although in most of these films (except the more recent variety about career women using Assisted Reproductive Technologies to satisfy their "baby hunger") these women become pregnant "by accident," none of them seriously consider abortion. While it has become more open about pregnancy, Hollywood remains relatively mute on the issue of abortion. Abortion may be the "elephant in the room" in many mainstream Hollywood pregnant romantic comedies, but the issue of choice is central. It is fascinating that the language of choice used by the pro-choice movement is co-opted in these films and put in the service of justifying the woman's "right to choose to have her baby," in spite of what others may think, and although the conception was the result of a one-night stand with a stranger (*Fools Rush In*, *Knocked Up*). Even Arnold Schwarzenegger's character in *Junior* uses pro-choice rhetoric ("my body, my choice") when defending *his* right to have *his* baby, which started as merely an experiment. In most of these films, there is a choice after the fact, which seems to reassure us that although pregnancy may be an "accident," babies are not. An interesting side effect of pro-choice rhetoric as it has made its way into popular culture is that if a woman does not choose abortion, then she has *chosen* pregnancy.

The focus of chapter 3, "Accident and Excess: The 'Choice' to Have a Baby," is the ways in which the language of choice is recuperated in these films and put into the service of *pro-life* family values. Even while these films embrace a woman's right to choose, they still expect women to choose babies and not abortions. In a telling scene that exemplifies Hollywood's attitude toward women's choice, *Fools Rush In* "plays" the audience when the male protagonist Alex (Matthew Perry) uses the phrase "I believe in a woman's right to choose" (suggesting but not mentioning abortion) and the female protagonist Isabel (Selma Hayek) turns his pro-choice rhetoric into a woman's right to choose to have her baby by responding "good, because I choose to have this baby!" And while the runaway indie hit *Juno* has a brief comic visit to the abortion clinic, once her schoolmate tells her that her fetus already has fingernails, she can't go through with it. For all of its candor and gross-out humor, *Knocked Up* can't even say the word "abortion"; instead one of Ben's (Seth Rogan) friends asks why they don't get a "shmushorshon."

Other pregnancy films are even more explicitly anti-abortion in their approach to turning unwanted pregnancies into wanted babies. In *Bella*, a coworker José (played by Eduardo Verástegui, a handsome real-life pro-life activist) talks Nina (Tammy Blanchard) out of having an abortion and raises her child for her until she is ready to meet the beautiful little Bella. Teenager Mary runs away rather than have the abortion suggested by her mother in *Expecting Mary* (2010); and so does teen Aviva in *Palindromes* (2004). Abortion never comes up in *Saved!* (2004), *Quinceñera* (2006), or *Waitress* (2007), even though these girls and women do not want to be pregnant. And in *Waitress* and *Saved!* the arrival of the baby is what saves our female protagonists. Although in these films women have the right to choose, they are expected to make the *right* choice, which is always to have their baby. Given that in these films unwanted pregnancies become adorable babies that change girls' and women's lives for the better, Hollywood seems to both promote and reflect conservative family values that insist on women becoming mothers in order to live valuable or happy lives.

The issue of women's reproductive choice—particularly in terms of the ideal of "having it all" and using technology to get it—points to class differences that leave many women without any such choice. Most of the people living in poverty in the United States, and the world, are women with children, women with few choices; they do not have the choice of careers, let alone jobs that give them a decent standard of living for themselves and their children. Moreover, it is not a coincidence that these films show primarily middle-class white women having babies, since in the United States, birthrates for middle-class white women have declined. In this context, Hollywood's preference for middle-class white women choosing to have babies rather than abortions could be interpreted as a racist anxiety over the "browning of America" (cf. Sundstrom 2008). Certainly, the expensive reproductive technologies that promise to extend women's fertility later in life are marketed and sold primarily to middle- and upper-class white women. Pregnancy films in general, and those that exploit themes of new reproductive technologies in particular, are fraught with anxieties over both men and women's roles in reproduction, worries that heterosexual sex is no longer necessary for reproduction, and fears of miscegenation, which is manifest in recent romantic comedies and science fiction films.

The question of how to interpret Hollywood's anxieties over women's reproductive choices is complex and striated. Certainly, pregnancy films reflect, amplify, and perpetuate ambivalent attitudes toward women's role in reproduction. Which means that we can study these films as artifacts that give clues to mainstream culture's desires and fears regarding pregnant embodiment. We can look to these films to appreciate how contemporary anxieties over reproduction both inherit older preoccupations (such as fears of miscegenation and the desire for eugenics) and signal new ones (fears of new reproductive technologies and the desire for "green" babies). But Hollywood's fantasies of pregnancy are multifaceted, contradictory, and ambivalent.

We could interpret Hollywood's return to family values as a response to the women's movement and the language of pro-choice essential to it. Or we could see it as a reaction to ever-increasing choices about how to have a family, choices ranging from what to name the child, what kind of stroller to get, how to have a "green" baby, what kind of birth to have, what technologies to use, what drugs to take, what exercises to do, and/or what not to drink, eat, or smoke, and so on. Alternatively, Hollywood's recent focus on women's reproductive choices signals a renewed commitment to women "having it all"—family, meeting "the one," a career, and a sexy body. Yet, at the same time, it seems to be a reaction to more (middle-class white) women delaying or not having children. It could be interpreted as anxiety over decreasing numbers of college-educated white women choosing to have babies; so, idealizing the white pregnant body as cute or sexy in the service of conventional family values makes having babies attractive in new ways that might lure white college-educated women back into the fold, so to speak. In various ways, Hollywood's representations of pregnant embodiment and women's role in reproduction can be interpreted as all of the above.

What are we to make of the fact that even as teen pregnancy is called an "epidemic," it is also celebrated in film and popular media? According to some news media these idealized images of teenage pregnancies in Hollywood are causing more teenage girls to try to get pregnant like the girls in the so-called "pregnancy pact" in Massachusetts. At the same time, older women (some almost 70 years old) are giving birth, and popular books such as *Baby Hunger* (2002) and *Everything Conceivable* (2008) are warning college-educated women to have babies before their "biological clocks" turn into "time bombs" that require risky and problematic medical interventions. Even as teenage pregnancy is figured as out of control and excessive, it is captivating entertainment. So while career women's "baby hunger" is represented as desperate and out of control, its fulfillment is a celebratory feast. At both ends of the spectrum, pregnancy is figured as excessive and out of control, particularly in Hollywood birth scenes that typically feature violent, screaming, and sometimes bloody women out of control.

The imagined threat of pregnant excess is no more evident than in horror films. Since *Rosemary's Baby* (1968), women giving birth to demonic and alien spawn is a common trope in the horror genre. Chapter 4, "Pregnant Horror: Gestating the Other(s) Within," examines various horror fantasies of women's role in reproduction and their reproductive choices as abject and dangerous. Pregnant horror films display anxieties over women's reproductive desires and capacities, particularly the fantasy of women's wombs as harboring evil and spewing multiple inhuman spawn that threaten the extinction of the human race. These anxieties can be linked to unease over women's reproductive choices, especially abortion and new ARTs, which lead to more multiple births, and anxieties over hybridity and species miscegenation.

Many of these films are haunted by dead or unborn babies (e.g., *The Unborn*, *Stephanie Daley*, *Grace*) that, within a culture still gripped by debates over abortion, can be interpreted as the dangerous consequence of abortion, or more recently new reproductive technologies that require "selective reduction" of fetuses. Films that feature incomplete or monstrous fetus-like creatures (e.g., *The Brood*, *Aliens*) can be read as cautionary tales about abortion and new technology. In most of these films, in one way or another, the mother is to blame for her offspring's evil. Indeed, many of these films present the mother as a morally ambiguous character whose desire to reproduce is excessive and whose responsibility for evil is often the result of her weakness, passive receptivity, and her mental instability, if not outright insanity.

*Rosemary's Baby*, *The Astronaut's Wife* (1999), *Stephanie Daley* (2006), and *Splice* (2009) are evidence of a continued association between pregnancy and insanity. In all of these films, the pregnant protagonists are mentally unstable in ways that suggest their complicity with evil and danger. Some of the crazy pregnant women of horror take "baby hunger" to its literal extreme. In one Hong Kong horror film called *Dumplings* (*Gaau ji*, 2004), women eat aborted fetuses because they have rejuvenating power that keep them young and beautiful. Hollywood also has its share of rich beautiful women who use cannibalism—or skin cream versions of it—to stay young (e.g., *The Wasp Woman* [1959 & 1995], *Catwoman* [2004]). On the flip side, there are the mothers who will stop at nothing to have babies and keep them alive. Madeline in *Grace* (2009) is a vegan mother who feeds blood to her "undead" baby and resorts to killing first animals and then humans to feed baby Grace. Elsa in *Splice* is another vegetarian mother who is appalled when her genetically engineered "daughter" Dren kills and devours a rabbit. A leitmotif of these films is nature's bloody resurgence as carnivores make a spectacle of eating meat and blood, to the point of cannibalism. *Species*'s beautiful alien Sil takes "baby hunger" to an extreme when, desperate to have a baby, she seduces men and then kills them in her attempts to get pregnant. Even horror and sci-fi's more ambivalent mothers like Rosemary, Jillian in *The Astronaut's Wife*, and Elsa in *Splice* embrace their unholy, alien, or monstrous offspring in the end. But, like Madeline's relation to her undead baby in *Grace*, their maternal love is represented as excessive and dangerous to society. Indeed, their maternal love is associated with the instinct to reproduce that not only drives these women mad but also threatens humanity. In many of these films the association of women and dangerous animal instincts is explicit. For example, in *Species*, Sil is described as an animal hunting prey, who lives to reproduce; she, in turn, is hunted down like an animal. Madeline kills animals to feed baby Grace. Even the drama (cum horror film) *Stephanie Daley* makes a parallel between women and animals, especially dead animals. And *Splice* features a human-animal hybrid that kills its "father" and rapes its "mother."

The proximity of women and animals and the possibility that women may give birth to nonhuman species threatens not only the family and civil society but also the human race. The fear of animality in these films and the association of animality with women play on traditional stereotypes of both. In these films, the threat of species mixing or hybridization is even creepier than an outright alien invasion. In most of these films (*Rosemary's Baby*, *The*

*Astronaut's Wife*, *The Brood*, *Species*, *Splice*) it is the combination of human and inhuman elements that threaten the human race. It is seemingly innocent and pretty women betraying their species by giving birth to something other than human that we find fascinatingly horrible. The common fantasy of women or female aliens giving birth to broods, hordes, or litters of multiple offspring that threaten to overrun or outrun the human race (e.g., *Aliens*, *The Brood*) now displaces worries about new reproductive technologies producing "Octomoms" that spew spawn rather than having babies, and who reproduce at accelerated and therefore dangerous rates. The threat of animality and hybridity imagined in these films display anxieties about new reproductive technologies and fears of miscegenation.

The fifth and final chapter, " 'What's the Worst That Can Happen?': Techno-Pregnancies Versus *Real* Pregnancies," continues the analysis of anxieties over new reproductive technologies as they appear in Hollywood film. "What's the worst that can happen?" is the last line spoken by pregnant Elsa in *Splice*. She is pregnant by her genetically engineered daughter, who has changed sexes and rapes her. In the horror genre, this question is ominous as Elsa looks out the window onto a bleak world awaiting the future beyond humankind, her human-hybrid baby. In melodrama the worst that can happen pulls at the heartstrings. For example, in *My Sister's Keeper* (2009), the worst that can happen is that a child is genetically engineered to save her sister and her sister dies anyway. In another pregnant melodrama, *Precious* (2009), the protagonist is raped and pregnant by her father, abused by her mother, and if that is not enough, has AIDS. And, in the ART comedy-drama *The Kids Are All Right* (2010), the worst that can happen is that the kids find their sperm-donor dad and he nearly breaks up their parents' marriage by having an affair with one of their mothers.

In the romantic comedy or comedy genres, however, the worst that can happen is funny. For example, in *The Back-up Plan*, the worst that can happen is that a woman meets the man of her dreams on her way out of a fertility clinic wherein she has been artificially inseminated. In *Due Date* (2010), the worst that can happen is a white man's nightmare that his wife will give birth to a black baby. And in *The Solomon Brothers* (2007), the worst that can happen is that the dumb and dumber white brothers are duped by a black man when the surrogate they hire really does give birth to a black baby. As we learn from psychoanalysis, however, jokes are often ways of displacing anxieties, fears and desires. Hollywood's "worst that can happen" displays anxieties about new reproductive technologies decoupling sex and reproduction, replacing romance and love with test tubes and turkey basters, making heterosexual sex obsolete, risking miscegenation or hybrid babies, leading to inhuman multiple births, and turning babies into the products of big business. Pregnancy films ranging from horror, sci-fi, drama, and comedy to documentary show how Hollywood is fascinated with, yet afraid of, new reproductive technologies. Echoing fears over ART mix-ups that lead to racially mixed babies, some of these films manifest anxieties over miscegenation. Others seem to signal the fear that men or heterosexual sex might become irrelevant to reproduction. And most favor "good old fashioned" ways to make babies that involve sex, love, and romance rather than risk turning babies, or human beings, into products.

Most of the films that explicitly take up new reproductive technologies are comedies that feature uptight career women who decide to use assisted reproductive technology because their "biological clocks" are ticking down. What is striking about these films is that although our protagonists use technology to try to get pregnant, they end up pregnant through "good old fashioned" heterosexual sex (*Baby Mama*, 2008) or they end up having sex with the sperm donor (*The Switch, The Kids Are All Right*). Against all odds, they end up having more "romantic" pregnancies that are not mediated by technology but are the result of heterosexual sex and love (*Baby Mama, The Back-up Plan, Miss Conception*). It is as if artificial insemination produces artificial babies and Hollywood prefers the real thing, babies produced "the old fashioned way"—in the words of Chaffee Bicknell, Sigourney Weaver's character *in Baby Mama*—through sex with men.

Even though the myth of "having it all" is still alive and well, as evidenced by these Hollywood films in which career women get babies, find "the one," remain sexy, and apparently live happily ever after, real women continue to grapple with how to juggle career and family in the face of ever-shrinking social services and support. Hollywood attempts to quell these anxieties with reassuring tales of white career women getting babies before it's too late and of girls and women turning unwanted pregnancies into wanted babies. Or it terrorizes us with horror and sci-fi fantasies in which abject monstrous hybrid offspring—usually the result of technological mediation and human hubris—threaten the end of the human race as we know it. In either case, Hollywood's recent fascination with pregnancy displays continued anxieties about women's role in reproduction and continued ambivalence about pregnant embodiment. Even as Hollywood films present pregnant bodies in ways unimaginable only a couple of decades ago, they continue to picture conventional attitudes toward women, pregnancy, and childbirth. Even while they attempt to grapple with new reproductive technologies and women's expanding choices regarding reproduction, they manifest fears and anxieties that surround them.

Although recent Hollywood films show us some of the difficulties of reproductive choice, they usually end with resolutions that cover over, if not openly disavow, the ambiguities of women's desires and freedoms. For the most part, they do not engage the complexities of reproductive freedom in a culture where women's value is still seen, at least in part, in terms of having and raising babies. Although the debates over motherhood and feminism have changed—with Sarah Palin we supposedly have a new brand of "rogue feminism"—the culture that inspires them has not changed as dramatically as we might think. If pregnant Hollywood films are any indication, above all, women are still expected to reproduce, only now they are also expected to freely choose to do so and to do it the old-fashioned way lest they risk giving birth to monsters. If they do give birth to monsters, they are expected to love them anyway with the ferocity of the mother-love that any female should feel, whether human or animal. Like most women expecting babies, however, Hollywood prefers that their offspring have ten (human) fingers and ten (human) toes. But even if they don't, the little monsters provide good entertainment by giving life to latent desires and fears, both old and new. In spite of their tendency to simplify and resolve the ambiguities and ambivalences of women's choices about issues of motherhood, sexuality, and pregnancy, recent Hollywood films also show us characters struggling with them. Pregnancy films show us women refusing the either/or of traditions that make them choose career over family and relationships. Today, questions of family and career are no longer necessarily simple either/or choices. Beyond the myth of "having it all," (middle-class) women are trying to figure out how to have both/and. Even as they create new myths of "having it all," recent Hollywood pregnancy films also display deep-seated anxieties about women's reproductive choices and the "accident" that is pregnancy in an age of changing technologies.

# ACADEMIC FEMINISM VERSUS HOLLYWOOD FEMINISM

## HOW MODEST MATERNITY BECOMES PREGNANT GLAM

The sex/gender system as we know it, then, enacts a border between motherhood and sexuality. . . . Freedom for women involves dissolving this separation.

—IRIS YOUNG (2005:87–88)

Matricide is our vital necessity, the sine-qua-non condition of our individuation, provided that it takes place under optimal circumstances and can be eroticized.

—JULIA KRISTEVA (1989:27–28)

ONE OF THE MOTIVATIONS for this book is to explore and interpret changing representations of pregnancy. Filmic images of cute girls and beautiful women sporting large bare pregnant bellies seem at odds with second wave feminism and its insistence that the separation between maternity and sexuality is a cornerstone of patriarchy, upon removal of which, patriarchy would fall. While women have achieved many "firsts" since the 1970s and 1980s when this wave of feminism was in its heyday, and women have made inroads into politics and business (although most of the world's poor remain women, and the salary gap between men and women is still significant, and men still greatly outnumber women at higher levels of politics and business, and women are still responsible for the majority of childcare and nursing duties), we can hardly say that patriarchy has fallen. Perhaps this suggests that the cornerstone identified by earlier feminists—the separation between maternity and sexuality—still stands. But if Hollywood is any indication, it is also undeniable that our attitudes toward pregnant embodiment and maternal sexuality have changed dramatically since the 1980s. Of course, just because the pregnant body has become an *object* of desire does not mean that it has become a *subject* of desire.

In different ways, Continental feminists such as Julia Kristeva, Luce Irigaray, and Angela Davis in the 1970s and 1980s, and following them in the 1990s Iris Young and Cynthia Willett, argued that women, like men, are desiring subjects, and pregnant women above all embody the split between nature and culture and makes all human beings desiring beings. When they attempted to articulate a positive account of pregnancy and of the maternal body, one that could provide a new understanding of the human condition, could they have imagined that pregnancy would become a cultural obsession such that "baby bumps" and "hot mamas" appear weekly on magazine stands? Although, in various ways, they suggested that the pregnant body had been desexualized and insisted on resexualizing it as a step toward women's freedom, their elaborations of pregnant embodiment and the ethics that might result from considering primary to human existence cannot be reduced to making pregnancy sexy or cute. Still, there is something uncanny in returning to their texts in light of recent representations of pregnancy in Hollywood film and popular media.

By tracing the parallel trajectories of Continental feminist theory and Hollywood film in terms of representations of pregnancy, we can begin to see how Hollywood incorporated feminism and puts its demands into the service of traditional family values. Starting with Simone de Beauvoir's advice that women should avoid pregnancy and motherhood altogether and Hollywood's ban on even saying the word *pregnancy* let alone showing a pregnant body, in the 1940s and 1950s pregnancy was considered abject and shameful. In the 1960s and 1970s with the women's movement, attitudes toward pregnancy and reproduction began to shift. The publication of *Our Bodies, Ourselves* (New England Free Press

1971) featured pictures of pregnant women as beautiful. Pregnant embodiment became a topic in academic feminism when, with Julia Kristeva, Luce Irigaray, Adrienne Rich, Audre Lorde, Sara Ruddick, and others, there was not only an embrace of women's sexuality but also a revaluation of women's role in reproduction. In Hollywood, however, as women gained more reproductive freedom with access to birth control and abortion, the preoccupation was with sexual liberation rather than reproduction. And in the 1960s and 1970s, reproduction was seen for the most part in horror films such as the classic *Rosemary's Baby* (1968), where the pregnant body continued to be represented as abject.

Advances in new reproductive technology and more social acceptance of women's bodies led to more openness in Hollywood to pregnancy and motherhood, as evidenced by the films of the 1980s and especially the 1990s, which began to feature pregnancy as a main theme. In feminist theory, the work of Kristeva and Irigaray had significant impact on the thinking of American feminists such as Iris Young, Cynthia Willett, and others, who continued to develop models of ethical relations based on the maternal body. With Demi Moore's nude glistening pregnant belly on the cover of *Vanity Fair* in 1991, a new era of sexy glamour pregnancy began. The decades that followed showed increasing interest in the pregnant body, which was displayed on magazine covers, in films, and in beauty contests. In the 2000s, Hollywood's "baby boom" began outright. Now, every year sees increasing numbers of Hollywood films and television shows about pregnancy and new reproductive technologies. The meaning of pregnancy has changed dramatically from a few decades ago when it was considered abject and shameful to today when it is considered fascinating entertainment, if not also sexy and cute. But, as we will see throughout this book, behind the embrace of pregnant embodiment is often a resurgence of the nineteenth-century cult of motherhood or what Erica Jong calls "an orgy of motherphilia" that perpetuates conventional and conservative attitudes toward women's role in reproduction and family (Jong 2010).

## WHAT IS A PREGNANT WOMAN?

> Woman experiences a more profound alienation when fertilization has occurred . . . gestation is a fatiguing task of no individual benefit to the woman but on the contrary demanding heavy sacrifices. . . . The conflict between species and individual, which sometimes assumes dramatic force as childbirth, endows the feminine body with a disturbing frailty . . . it is the species gnawing at their vitals.
>
> —SIMONE DE BEAUVOIR (1949:29–30)

Simone de Beauvoir opens her 1949 treatise *The Second Sex* with the question "What is a woman?" She acknowledges that traditionally the answer has been "woman is a womb" (1949:xxv). Yet she insists that although biology cannot be denied, it never completely defines human beings for whom the meaning of even physical existence is a matter of interpretation. Discussing the fact that women give birth while men do not, she says, "the body of woman is one of the essential elements in her situation in the world. But that body is not enough to define her as woman. . . . It is not merely [as] a body, but rather [as] *a body subject to taboos*" (1949:36–37; my emphasis). Even while emphasizing that women cannot be reduced to their capacity for reproduction, de Beauvoir repeatedly warns that women's reproductive function limits them and prevents their true participation in the social and political spheres. At the extreme, her manifesto could be read as much against childbirth and motherhood as it is against the patriarchal notions and institutions that circumscribe them. Even while acknowledging the taboos that stigmatize pregnancy, childbirth, and motherhood, de Beauvoir does not suggest revaluing these activities as much as avoiding them altogether.

De Beauvoir's views on pregnancy and maternity are complex and have been the subject of ongoing feminist interpretation, including attempts to revalue motherhood (cf. Adams 2009).

We have not "outgrown" de Beauvoir's deep-seated ambivalence about pregnancy and maternity, which continues into the present, although in newly technological mediated forms. Today, some past taboos surrounding pregnancy discussed by de Beauvoir seem old-fashioned, even laughable. Yet new taboos and changing recursions of old ones are not always easy to detect. They are normalized within medical practice and popular culture so that they become as familiar to us as the air that we breathe. By looking to past conceptions of pregnancy and transformations in the meaning of the pregnant body, however, we can begin to understand recent images in film, images that define our era in terms of the history of hopes and fears that surround pregnancy.

In the mid-twentieth century, pregnancy was a private, even shameful, affair hidden from public view. At that time, although pregnant women could still smoke and drink (drinking wine was considered especially relaxing for pregnant women), they were advised to discontinue exercise and physical activities in favor of bed rest. Even though pregnancy has "come out of the closet," so to speak, today doctors and myriad books prescribe various regimens for prenatal care, including moderate to vigorous exercise and abstinence from smoking, alcohol, and caffeine. While for centuries women have been held responsible for the detrimental effects of their imaginings on their developing fetuses, recently they have been held criminally responsible for physical "abuse" to "unborn children," and there are various pressures on pregnant women, including increasing concern for natural or home birth (cf. Bewell 1988; Newton 1996; and Hanson 2004, esp. ch. 1). It is curious that during the era when women were defined primarily in terms of their capacity to give birth, public images of pregnant bodies were taboo, while now that women continue to break barriers in business and politics, images of pregnant women are regular staples of television, movies, and magazine covers at supermarket checkout stands, as if to remind us that women, no matter what else they do, can and should be mothers. Indeed, the conflict between having a career and having children remains a concern for middle-class women; and popular culture reflects and informs the meaning of that relationship. Several recent films take up the theme of career women wanting babies, and suffering from what Sylvia Ann Hewlett calls "baby hunger" (2002). More current representations of pregnancy are not coincidentally related to more liberal views of women, but rather promote a return to valuing women's reproductive capacity as their best asset and promoting the view that, for women, having a baby is necessary for a worthwhile life, regardless of what else they may have achieved.

Just as the meaning of *woman* has changed, so has the meaning of *pregnancy*. The history of pregnancy affects how we view, represent, and conceive of pregnancy, and moreover, how women experience it. In the words of sociologist Clare Hanson (whose book *A Cultural History of Pregnancy* examines the history of representations of pregnancy primarily in Britain), "the pregnant body . . . is doubly mutable. It is mutable in the obvious sense that it undergoes continuous physiological (and sometimes pathological) change, and mutable culturally, in that it is viewed through constantly shifting interpretative frameworks. These interpretive frameworks are constructed through the interrelation of medicine and culture" (Hanson 2004:3). Perhaps more than any other human experience, pregnancy signals transformation and possibility, with their concomitant fears and anxieties. The pregnant body is capable of significant physical changes in a relatively short period of time. Moreover, pregnancy is a means to new life and the continuation of the human species. In this regard, the pregnant body may be a screen for our fantasies and fears about ourselves as people and as *a people*.

At the movies, the screen metaphor becomes literal when cultural anxieties and hopes play themselves out on the bellies of pregnant characters. In Lasse Hallström's film *Once Around* (1991), there is an especially poignant scene in which the older husband Sam Sharpe (Richard Dreyfus) of the pregnant protagonist Renata (Holly Hunter) turns a 16mm projector playing home movies of her childhood toward her pregnant belly (see cover).

In this scene, Renata's pregnancy literally becomes a screen for images of family life, while metaphorically it becomes a complex trigger for nostalgia of lost childhood and innocence, hopes for future children that combine the best of their genetic possibilities, and a means of reconciling the tensions not only between the struggling couple but also between their ways of life and their cultural differences. In brief, this scene projects onto the pregnant belly all of the hopes and dreams of past and future that can bring people and peoples together. This moment of hope is short-lived when the imagined male dream child turns out to be a girl and the husband dies of heart failure soon after her birth. Certainly, the "realities" of pregnancy have not been as popular as our fantasies about it. And while recent films give us a bit more "blood and guts" than early Hollywood films, they continue to package pregnancy in particularly appealing, even glamorous, ways to promote a new type of family values with fantasies of women having it all, or at least realizing that having babies is more important than anything else.

## MODEST MATERNITY: PREGNANCY IN THE 1940s AND 1950s

> The culture's separation of pregnancy and sexuality can liberate [pregnant women] from the sexually objectifying gaze that alienates and instrumentalizes her when in her nonpregnant state. The leer of sexual objectification regards the woman in pieces, as the possible object of man's desire and touch. In pregnancy the woman may experience some release from this alienating gaze.
>
> —IRIS YOUNG (1990:166–67)

Just a few decades ago, it was not proper to use the word *pregnancy* in polite company. There were, and are, various euphemisms used instead, such as "expecting," "with child," "a bun in the oven," "in the family way," and cruder versions like "knocked-up." Pregnancy was not only a private affair but also somehow shameful. It signaled that a woman had sex and seemingly stimulated the public imagination in "unwholesome" ways. In the words of Robyn Longhurst, "Not only was the word 'pregnant' excluded from public discourse but so too were the bodies of pregnant women" (Longhurst 2000:457). Other scholars examining the history of pregnancy echo this sentiment; for example, Robbie Davis-Floyd says "pregnant women were . . . expected to remain secluded in their homes, as their presentation in public was somehow felt to be improper" (Davis-Floyd 1993:25). Early advertising campaigns for maternity clothes also indicate that a woman's pregnant body should be well-covered; and while she should be pretty, she also should be modest and pure, even childlike, which is reflected in maternity fashions from the 1940s and 1950s (cf. Matthews & Wexler 2000:31). Adrienne Rich recounts a telling tale of being invited and then uninvited to give a lecture when pregnant, which suggests that pregnancy was considered titillating, even pornographic, in its connection to sex: "When the [school]master responsible for inviting me realized that I was seven months pregnant he cancelled the invitation, saying that the fact of my pregnancy would make it impossible for the boys to listen to my poetry. This was in 1955" (quoted in Matthews & Wexler 2000:7). Showing the pregnant belly, even when fully clothed, was considered immodest and indecent.

During the 1940s and 1950s Hollywood mostly avoided the issue of pregnancy, preferring instead to skip from romance and marriage to instant family. Women characters had children, but they were never seen giving birth to them. For example, in two of the popular Doris Day–Rock Hudson trilogy films, Doris Day's character is pregnant at the end of the film: in *Pillow Talk* (1959), Jan (Day) remains offscreen by the end, while Brad (Rock Hudson) announces that *he* is having a baby, a running joke in the film; at the end of *Lover Come Back* (1961), Carole (Day) is seen being wheeled into a maternity ward covered in a white sheet, still not looking obviously pregnant. Given that Will H. Hays's Production Code did not allow pregnancy to be shown on film—and required that pregnancy take place within marriage—it is not surprising that so few films of the era dealt with the topic. There are, however, a few exceptions in which the depiction of pregnancy reveals cultural attitudes of the day.

In *Christopher Strong* (1933), *Leave Her to Heaven* (1946), and *A Place in the Sun* (1951), pregnancy is soon followed by death. And in *People Will Talk* (1951), Debra Higgins (Jeanne Crain) unsuccessfully tries to commit suicide by shooting herself after she learns that she is pregnant. In *Christopher Strong*, Katherine Hepburn's character kills herself in a fiery plane-crash while setting a flying record rather than make her pregnancy public and ruin the career of her lover. In *A Place in the Sun*, a supporting character played by Shelley Winters falls out of a boat manned by her ex-lover, who watches her drown rather than save her after making his angry and desperate feelings about her pregnancy perfectly clear. In *Leave Her to Heaven*, after her doctor has confined her to bed rest, Ellen (Gene Tierney) throws herself down a staircase to instigate a miscarriage so that her husband will find her attractive again; she is successful in terminating the pregnancy, but eventually dies herself. Embarrassed, she refuses to allow even her husband to see her in her pregnant state; and she is insanely jealous of her husband's attentions to her sister (Jeanne Crain) during her confinement. Throughout the film, although Tierney's wardrobe goes from tailored suits, and even a modestly cut swimming outfit at one point, to flowing robes and the sheer billowing negligee she dons for the staircase episode (after also applying lipstick and making sure her face is perfect), she never looks the least bit pregnant.

Perhaps the most extensive treatment of pregnancy in an early Hollywood film is Preston Sturges's *The Miracle of Morgan's Creek* (1944), which walks the line at the border of the Hays Production Code. Again, the protagonist's pregnancy is never shown and neither is the birth. Rather, Trudy (Betty Hutton) is shown wrapped in all white from head to toe, and referred to as "not well," which is easily interpreted by other characters to mean pregnant. The word *pregnancy* is avoided throughout the film, as is any depiction of the pregnancy itself, in spite of the fact that Trudy is pregnant from early in the film. The film deals more with other people's reactions to Trudy's pregnancy. Her father and family are so shamed by it that they move to another town where no one knows them and where their friends secretly visit them.

Although *The Miracle of Morgan's Creek* can be seen as a parable of teenage pregnancy outside of marriage, in order to meet Code standards, director Preston Sturges contrives to have Trudy drink spiked punch at a dance and marry a soldier who ships off to war the next morning, a soldier whom, in a sense, she—and the audience—has never met. This mystery husband is never found and, after many pratfalls, Trudy ends up marrying her longtime admirer Norvel (Eddie Bracken). She gives birth to sextuplets—all boys—and Norvel becomes a hero around the world for his virility. The birth scene is played for comedy as nurses run back and forth through the hallway where Trudy's family is waiting. Trudy's offscreen birthing is also unseen by her as she does not know that she has given birth to six babies until Norvel tells her well after the event has taken place. In *Miracle*, although she is married, Trudy's pregnancy is hidden and shameful. And even when she "miraculously" gives birth to sextuplets, the feat is credited to Norvel, who had nothing to do with it. The pregnant body is literally banned by the Production Code, and although the birth scene is slapstick and action-packed (with no screaming woman in labor or mucous-covered newborns, which come later in Hollywood), still woman's reproductive capacity threatens chaos and excess in the birth of not just one baby, but many. This is perhaps the first in a long line of birth scenes that represent the fecund body as out of control and outside of the law. Throughout the film, the primary anxiety over Trudy's pregnancy is one of circumscribing it legally. In the end, it takes the governor's pardon and decree to legally sanction the marriage of Norvel and Trudy, which also by implication establishes (or assumes) Norvel's paternity.

## ABJECT PREGNANCY AND ALIEN BIRTH: PREGNANCY IN THE 1960s AND 1970s

The 1960s and 1970s saw many changes in reproductive technologies and attitudes toward women's bodies. It was a time of the space race and the civil rights movement. In the 1960s, ultrasound technology used in the navy was introduced into prenatal medicine and, for the first time, images of the developing fetus could be seen. DNA testing for paternity became possible, which could eliminate questions about who fathered the baby. In 1971 the first printing of *Our Bodies, Ourselves* was published. In 1972 the first sperm bank opened. And in 1973, *Roe v. Wade* legalized abortion. Swedish photographer Lennart Nilsson's images of fetuses on the covers of *Look* (1962) and *Life* (1965) magazines purported to give us the first view onto the beginnings of life. Nilsson gave us an image of a "fetal spaceman" floating free-form without any maternal encumbrance—or protection (cf. Berlant 1994). These images have become icons around which right-to-life groups rally in the name of "unborn" babies. Yet, as we now know, most of the images are not of live fetuses, as Nilsson claims. Moreover, the startling effect of these floating bodies was created by adding skin tones, through lighting effects, and by enlarging fetuses (cf. Berlant 1994). Still, the confluence of these images with the space race, the introduction of ultrasound technology in prenatal medicine, and the fight to legalize abortions come together to create a focus on the fetus apart from what became known as its "maternal environment." More recently, the notion of "maternal environment" takes a new twist with the advent of Assisted Reproductive Technologies (ARTs), particularly when it involves another woman gestating donor eggs inseminated by her partner's sperm, as in the widely publicized case of celebrities Nicole Kidman and Keith Urban, who called their surrogate "our gestational carrier." In the 1960s, with the widespread use of prenatal ultrasound, the maternal body and the fetus were imagined at odds with each other in new and more dramatic ways. In the words of Rosalind Petchesky, "the fetus is not only 'already a baby,' but more—a 'baby man,' an autonomous, atomized minispace hero" (1987:64).

This image of fetus as space hero came to life on the big screen in Stanley Kubrick's 1968 masterpiece *2001: A Space Odyssey*. The film ends with a fetus floating into space, completely unmoored from the seemingly obsolete maternal body (for a discussion of this image, see Petchesky 1987 & Berlant 1994). Kubrick's film engages issues of evolution, progress, and human development; more specifically, it juxtaposes humans and apes, machines, and possibly intelligent aliens. It is noteworthy that other films from this period display similar anxieties about humanity in relation to gestation and birth. Released the same year, Roman Polanski's *Rosemary's Baby* turns pregnancy into a nightmarish pact with the devil to gestate his spawn. And Mia Farrow's Rosemary manifests paranoia on the verge of insanity, which we eventually find out is justified (cf. Fischer 1992; Hanson 2004, esp. ch. 2). Director Rand Ravich's homage to *Rosemary's Baby*, *The Astronaut's Wife* (1999) gives us another crazy pregnant woman, Jillian (Charlize Theron), this time impregnated by an extraterrestrial alien who came to Earth in the form of her husband (Johnny Depp). Both Jillian and Rosemary struggle with alien forces within themselves that threaten their sense of identity and their physical well-being. These films dramatize anxieties about the splitting of identity during pregnancy and women gestating the nonhuman species.

From *Rosemary's Baby* (1968), *Alien* (1979), and *Aliens* (1986) to *Species* (1995) and *Splice* (2009), women have been giving, and continue to give, birth to aliens that threaten human life as we know it. As we will see, this anxiety over women's role in the reproduction of the species has taken on new forms in infertility treatments that produce multiple offspring associated with animality in popular media that refer to them as "broods" or "litters." The playful humor in the names given by women to the ultrasound images of their fetuses—names such as thumper, cletus-the-fetus, shrimp, and squirrel—also suggest that women see something more animal-like than human in these images. For example, *Baby Mama* (2008) has a running joke that Angie (Amy Poehler) has passed off an ultrasound of a squirrel as one of a human fetus.

If earlier representations of pregnancy such as the Doris Day films and *The Miracle of Morgan's Creek* insist on a pure, nearly virgin birth, horror flicks separate female sexuality from reproduction in a different way. While the maternal is desexualized in the earlier films, to the point that we see neither sex nor the pregnant body, in horror films both the sex and the pregnant body are threatening. The sex is violent and the pregnancy abject. For example, in *Rosemary's Baby*, *The Astronaut's Wife*, and *Splice*, procreation is the result of a rape or violent sex. In these films, echoing earlier Hollywood images of female sexuality, women's role in reproduction is rendered passive, if not unwilling. Yet, as we will see, these women are blamed for their evil spawn nonetheless.

Unlike Kubrick's floating fetus that signals a possible future for humanity, with *Rosemary's Baby* Polanski imagines the horror of the fetus as a hostile otherworldly invader that threatens humanity from inside women's bodies. The fetus in Rosemary's (Mia Farrow) womb is making her ill. Rosemary's abject pregnancy and monstrous birth resonate with Simone de Beauvoir's description of pregnancy as possession, "as if she [the pregnant woman] were possessed by foreign forces" and "the species gnawing at [her] vitals" (1949:30). On one level, *Rosemary's Baby* can be read as a cautionary tale to liberated women of the 1960s to avoid pregnancy and domestic motherhood; for example, Lucy Fischer suggests that we interpret the film as a nightmarish tale of what every pregnant woman endures (Fischer 1992:3). Whether the fetus signals hope for, or destruction of, humanity, with the introduction of visual technologies it is represented as separate from its "maternal environment," or at least at odds with it. It doesn't need a mother or it makes her sick.

Whether the fetus is imagined as animal, as alien, as monster, as devil, as spaceman, or as nonhuman, it has become an icon that represents our fears of an abject Other within that threatens our identity as human, while at the same time it has become definitive of human life, the most innocent and pure citizen in need of legal protection, evidenced by the role of abortion debates in American politics and laws to protect so-called "unborn citizens" (cf. Berlant 1994). By the early 1990s hundreds of women, mostly women of color, were arrested for endangering their "unborn children" through drug use and alcohol. Planned Parenthood featured a series of advertisements called "Mommy Don't" that targeted women of color and warned against drugs, smoking, and drinking while pregnant. And in February 2011, a huge five-story billboard in New York City's SoHo neighborhood featured the photograph of an adorable little black girl with the headline "The most dangerous place for an African American is in the womb," again targeting African American women and making them the perpetrators of harm to adorable innocent children. While historically the pregnant body has been subject to various disciplinary standards and regimes, the ability to view and monitor fetal life apart from the mother's experiential reports of fetal activity (the quickening) brought with it legal restrictions on pregnant women's activities. Women can now be sued on behalf of their "unborn child" and criminal charges can be brought by the state against women considered threats to their fetuses. In 2001, Regina McKnight was sentenced to twelve years in prison in North Carolina for homicide by child abuse when her baby was stillborn.

Whether the fetus is imaged as an unborn citizen in need of protection, or a dangerous alien, with ultrasound technology it captured the popular imagination. And once the fetus could be seen apart from the maternal body, that body becomes merely its container and/or "the maternal environment." The split subjectivity (described by feminist philosophers as the model of human subjectivity that a phenomenology of pregnant embodiment provides) is imagined as abject and dangerous within popular culture. The pregnant body is the site of a splitting that evokes both fear and desire and renders that body an ambivalent cipher of our wildest dreams about the continuation of the species, of the nation and citizenship, and women's role in that reproduction.

A central question that drives Julia Kristeva's 1976 reflection on maternity in "Stabat Mater" (1983), namely whether or not the woman is the subject of her own pregnancy and the biological changes in her body, is the source of a deep-seated cultural anxiety about women's role in the reproduction of the species. As Kristeva puts it: "The unspoken doubtless weighs first on the maternal body; as no signifier can uplift it without leaving a remainder, for the signifier is always meaning, communication, or structure, whereas a woman as mother would be, instead, a strange fold that changes culture into nature, the speaking into biology. Although it concerns every woman's body, the heterogeneity that cannot be subsumed in the signifier nevertheless explodes violently with pregnancy (the threshold of culture and nature) and the child's arrival (which extracts woman out of her oneness and gives her the possibility—but not the certainty—of reaching out to the other, the ethical)" ("Stabat Mater," reprinted in 2002:329–30). In this same essay, she goes on to suggest that only an ethics that considers the experience of maternity, and the always ambiguous bonds it creates, can make life bearable (2002:332).

Addressing anxieties caused by the ambiguous status of the pregnant body, which is split between nature and culture, Kristeva's writings revolve around turning this ambiguity in to a creative life force. In some of her later work, Kristeva again attempts to revalue pregnancy and maternity by insisting that women's role in reproduction is a creative one, even one of genius, which, in her words, is our only hope against the "automation" of all of human experience. Because each mother-child relation is singular and unique, Kristeva says, mothers might represent "our only safeguard against the wholesale automation of human beings" (2002:402). Insofar as we still require women to gestate and give birth to babies, and insofar as childcare cannot be automated or performed by machines, women continue to carry the burden, or labor of love, of introducing children to language and sociality.

Yet this very special innovation, what Kristeva calls genius, has not been valued as such by our culture, a culture that reduces mothers to fetal containers. Only by valuing the genius of women and mothers in relation to future persons—or as Kristeva insists, in relation to the continuation of the species—can we talk about reproductive freedom that values women's experience and choices, with all of their ambiguities. As we will see, recent Hollywood films display and yet cover over, dissolve, or resolve these ambiguities and thereby fall back into conservative ideals of motherhood and family.

Contra Simone de Beauvoir, Kristeva argues that rather than give up or avoid motherhood, we should revalue it. Rather than accept that motherhood renders women docile or like animals merely reproducing the species (or other species), during the 1970s and '80s other theorists such as Adrienne Rich, Luce Irigaray, and Sara Ruddick in various ways argue that maternity is an activity of a desiring human-speaking subject. For example, in *Of Woman Born* (1976), Rich argues against idealized and pathologized ideals of motherhood and for valuing women's own experience as mothers and, moreover, women's singular role in the reproduction of the species. This is the same year that Kristeva published her ode to pregnancy, childbirth, and motherhood, "Stabat Mater," and went on to develop what she saw as the void of the maternal in Freud and orthodox psychoanalysis. Throughout the late 1970s and 1980s, in various works, Luce Irigaray described how the history of philosophy has covered over its maternal origins and indebtedness to the mother and her materiality and sensuousness. And Sara Ruddick published *Maternal Thinking* (1989), in which she argues that maternity requires creativity, insight, and rigor that form a discipline, not unlike others accepted as such.

Following these thinkers, Iris Marion Young created what is still considered one of the most developed phenomenologies of pregnant embodiment. Young not only suggests that the pregnant subject challenges traditional theories of subjectivity but also articulates the subjectivity of pregnancy as unique and purposeful

(Young 1990). She argues that pregnant embodiment enables a unique relationship to past and future, and to space and time. Pregnancy opens the body to otherness in ways that make the experience porous physically and mentally. This porosity, Young suggests, can be a model for more open relationships with others and a more porous notion of subjectivity than philosophers typically provide. Young proposes an active and resexualized conception of maternity that restores desire and subjectivity to the maternal body.

While Young suggests that the desexualization of the pregnant body can open a space for "self-love" through a release from the "sexually objectifying gaze that alienates her," she also insists that, "Patriarchy is founded on the border between motherhood and sexuality. . . . Freedom for women involves dissolving this separation" (Young 1990:166; 2005:87–88). She argues that while "[s]ome feminist discourse criticizes the sexual objectification of women and proposes that feminists dissociate women from the fetishized female body and promote instead an image of women as representing caring nurturing, soothing values . . . [a] more radical move would be to shatter the border between motherhood and sexuality. . . . Crashing the border means affirming that women, all women, can 'have it all' " (Young 2005:89–90). By having it all, Young didn't necessarily mean having family and career, although she may have meant that too. Rather, she meant that recognizing the pregnant body as not only a desirable body but also a desiring body would be liberating for women.

## PREGNANT CELEBRITY: HOLLYWOOD'S BABY BOOM!

From our vantage point, seeing nude and bikini-clad pregnant bodies on magazine covers at the grocery store, Young's proclamation seems prophetic. For, just one year after the publication of Young's influential book of essays, which includes "Pregnant Embodiment" and "Breasted Experience," Demi Moore made history posing nude and heavily pregnant for the cover of *Vanity Fair* magazine in 1991. Moore's glistening tanned body, an outrage to many, transformed the pregnant body from desexualized and shameful into something glamorous, even sexy. Annie Lebowitz's cover photograph of pregnant Demi Moore ("More Demi Moore"), with the magazine sold in plastic wrapper to conceal her belly, incensed the public. But it also changed our image of the pregnant body. Lauren Berlant describes the change: "Once a transgressive revelation of a woman's sacred and shameful carnality, the pictorial display of pregnancy is now an eroticized norm in American public culture" (1994:146). Imogen Tyler argues that the Demi Moore image was a counterbalance to the emphasis on the fetus: "Through its deployment of reflective surfaces, this skin-tight image of pregnancy displaces the cultural imaging of the maternal as open, porous and undifferentiated . . . the Moore photograph re-envelops the foetus within the pregnant body" (2001:76). At the same time, however, the skintight reflective surfaces make her pregnant belly appear as yet another celebrity accessory to be glamorized and objectified. It is as if Demi Moore is wearing her pregnant body as the latest fashion. This sentiment was made all the more poignant when Moore appears on another *Vanity Fair* cover a year later, with her thin post-pregnant body covered in body paint that looks like she is wearing a man's suit. In this later photo, in a strange sense echoing the first, she is literally wearing her skin (cf. Tyler 2001).

Iris Young and other feminists writing in the 1970s and '80s may not have been able to predict what would happen when maternity and sexuality came together to create a sexy pregnancy, or what one website calls "knocked-up knock-outs" (www.knocked-upknock-outs.com), but Young's insistence that women's own experience of themselves as sexual subjects should be primary has not yet been realized within popular images of pregnancy. Discussing a bikini contest for pregnant women in New Zealand, a phenomenon that is popular around the industrial world, Robyn Longhurst identifies a paradox in the way that pregnancy has "come out of the closet":

"The 'bikini babes' both subverted and affirmed hegemonic constructions of gender for pregnant women. They subverted the construction of pregnant women as modest and inwardly focused by exposing their stomachs and making a claim for being pregnant, public and proud. Paradoxically, this claim was made by way of a 'beauty' pageant" (2000:469). Pregnancy may have "come out of the closet," but has pregnant sexuality or maternal sexuality? In Hollywood and popular media, do we see representations of women's subjective experience of their pregnant embodiment? Or, rather, do we see representations of the pregnant body as sex objects for others, or objects of what film theorist Laura Mulvey called "the male gaze" (2009:19)?

"Momshells," "hot mamas," "MILFs" ("mothers I'd like to fuck"), "Yummy Mummys," "Knocked-up knock-outs," and in some way even "baby mamas," appeal to both men and women. Indeed, if the underlying values of making pregnancy sexy and desirable are family values, then they are effective only insofar as they make pregnancy look attractive to women and paternity look attractive to men. These labels and the media attention to pregnant celebrity constitute something like a new cult of motherhood. Hollywood bad-girl become earth-mother, Angelina Jolie tops most lists of hot mamas and yummy mummys; her celebrity motherhood helped spark the MILF movement. And the "Brangelina" clan has become the poster family for multicultural and therefore seemingly progressive American family values. Along with making a large family look easy, they make adoption, childbirth, and having it all as beautiful as a rainbow. But, like more traditional objectifications of the female body in art and film, recent sexy and cute images of the pregnant body are represented as "to be looked at" for visual consumption by both men and women. What is new in the representation of women's bodies as objects is that now it is not an idealized female form that is opposed to the maternal body but rather that the pregnant body itself has become desirable, if not entirely attractive. Still, it is important to consider the complicated ways in which representations of pregnancy as desirable both objectify women and promote conventional family values at the same time that they bring pregnant embodiment "out of the closet" and empower women.

A reality television show is searching for "momshells," another MTV program (*16 and Pregnant*) features pregnant teenagers, and another re-creates and simulates young women giving birth who didn't know they were pregnant. It is noteworthy that "momshell" is a play on the notion of sexy women as "bombshells," which suggests that female sexuality, like a bomb, is dangerous; maternity becomes associated with a deadly weapon. Moreover, mom*shell* also connotes the idea that the maternal body is a shell, a container. MILF is an obvious sexual reference used in popular parlance by men about mothers who are hot. Republican vice presidential candidate Sarah Palin was called both a MILF and a GILF ("governor I'd like to fuck"), ignoring whatever qualifications—such as they are—that she had for the job. There are even T-shirts and onesies that say "My Mother is a MILF"—what would Freud have to say about that? Insofar as the 2008 presidential election had women candidates on both sides, there were many references to these women's bodies and to their roles as mothers. Sarah Palin was not the only candidate reduced to her reproductive, if sexy, body. Michelle Obama was referred to as "Obama's baby mama," a term that is used in popular parlance to suggest an unmarried black woman whose only relationship with a man is as the mother of his children. This term not only reduces her function to bearing a man's children but also defines the woman herself as a baby as well as a mama. These examples from popular culture demonstrate not only our culture's obsession with the maternal body but also our culture's continued objectification of women's bodies and the reduction of those bodies to reproduction even when they have college degrees from prestigious universities and they are running for the highest offices in the country.

## TECHNOLOGICALLY ASSISTED REPRODUCTION (ART): PREGNANCY IN THE 1980s AND 1990s

> The new developments in reproductive technology have encour-
> aged the contemporary emergence of popular attitudes—at
> least among the middle classes—that bear a remarkable resem-
> blance to the nineteenth-century cult of motherhood, includ-
> ing the moral, legal, and political taboos it developed against
> abortion. . . . It is as if the recognition of infertility is now a
> catalyst—among some groups of women—for a motherhood
> quest that has become more compulsive and more openly ideo-
> logical than during the nineteenth century.
>
> —ANGELA DAVIS (ORIG. 1991, REPRINTED IN 2000:478)

New reproductive technologies exploded onto the market in the
1980s and 1990s. In 1978 the first "test-tube baby" was born. In
1981 the first baby was born as a result of in vitro fertilization
(IVF). So-called "Baby M" was born in 1986 and surrogacy started
making headlines. In 1997 Dolly the sheep was cloned, and that
same year the oldest known pregnant woman gave birth at age 63.
In 1998 sperm banks were taking in $164 billion a year and fertility
clinics were growing industries. In Hollywood, the possibility of
"test-tube babies" and viewing the fetus in utero gives rise to fantastic tales such as *Junior* (1994), in which muscle-bound Arnold
Schwarzenegger is impregnated and gives birth via C-section, and
*Look Who's Talking* (1989), in which another macho celebrity,
Bruce Willis, lends his voice to a talking fetus inhabiting Kirstie
Alley's womb. If the fetus is an autonomous person and the maternal body is merely a container, then we can imagine this "little
man" living inside a woman's body, waiting to be born. Or we can
imagine transplanting the fetus from its maternal container into
another container, say a bodybuilder-turned-actor's abdomen.
The late 1980s and 1990s also saw an increase in attention to pregnancy as an acceptable theme for film, particularly comedies where

reluctant men mature into proper fathers during the course of the movie. This domestication of men into paternal figures comes at the expense of the pregnant woman, who is used primarily as a backdrop against which the men "find" themselves and learn the true meaning of love and family.

For example, in *She's Having a Baby* (1988), Kevin Bacon's character imagines himself in a straitjacket crashing into a wall and bursting into flames when his wife, played by Elizabeth McGovern, tells him she stopped taking "the pill" because she wants to have a baby. Eventually, he comes to terms with his newly formed family, but only after he nearly loses both in childbirth. In *Nine Months* (1995), Hugh Grant's character crashes his sports car when his girlfriend, played by Julianne Moore, tells him she is pregnant. Thanks to warnings from his friend (Jeff Goldblum), he begins to suspect his girlfriend of deceiving him and getting pregnant "on the sly"; he even imagines her turning into a praying mantis and devouring him. Once he gets over his fantasies of being eaten alive, and prompted by the "little heart beat" he sees in the fetal ultrasound image, he trades in his sports car for a family car and embraces marriage and fatherhood. And *Father of the Bride II* (1995) is the story of how George Banks (Steve Martin) comes to terms with both his wife's and his daughter's simultaneous pregnancies.

In this era of pregnancy films about men, Lisa Krueger's *Manny & Lo* (1996) remains exceptional among Hollywood's pregnancy comedies in that Manny (Aleksa Palladino), a pregnant teenager, and her younger sister, Lo (Scarlett Johansson), who is narrating the film, develop an alternative all-female family unit with an eccentric spinster (Mary Kay Place), whom they have kidnapped to act as a midwife. *Manny & Lo* may have started the turn in Hollywood to viewing teenage pregnancy as cute and funny. Teenage pregnancy looks cool in films like *The Opposite of Sex* (1998), *Saved!* (2004), *Juno* (2007), and *Expecting Mary* (2010), and in headlines about Jamie Lynn Spears and Bristol Palin, who was featured on the cover of *People* magazine smiling, looking pretty, wearing her high school graduation gown, and holding her infant son (Westfall 2009). Media blamed celebrity and Hollywood glorification of teen pregnancy for the so-called "pregnancy pact" near Boston where teenage girls were trying to get pregnant, buying Early Home Pregnancy tests in bulk, and showing disappointment when tests were negative. An advertisement in the *New York Times* sponsored by the Candies Foundation (2008) sports photos of Jamie Lynn, Bristol Palin, and the girls in Massachusetts and announces in big bold letters "America, Wake-Up! We Have an Epidemic," playing on the long-standing association between pregnancy and disease (in spite of the fact that teenage pregnancies have been declining in recent years).

At the other end of the spectrum, tabloids are also full of actresses and career women who have put off having families and are now desperately racing against their "biological clocks" to have babies (what Sylvia Ann Hewlett called "baby hunger" [2002]). Turning the pro-choice rhetoric on its head, Hewlett argues that, for career women, not having babies becomes a "creeping nonchoice" and "unwanted choices," where they "accidentally" have given up their right to choose by ignoring their biological clocks, which leaves them desperate and unhappy (Hewlett 2002:21, 26, 84, 254, 262). The language of pro-choice is co-opted for seemingly feminist arguments in favor of renewed family values. But Hewlett also warns against what she sees as the trauma of IVF, which is increasing dramatically. In the United States in 2005, 135,000 IVF cycles were performed, yielding 52,000 births, more than double the number in 1996. And in 2006, a 67-year-old woman gave birth to twins.

As IVF makes motherhood possible for older women and increases the chances of twins and multiple births, popular culture reacts with both fascination and horror at these "abject" high-tech pregnancies. For example, in *Baby Mama*, Sigourney Weaver plays the powerful CEO of a surrogacy agency who, in her 50s, has an infant of her own and is pregnant again and gives birth to twins by the end of the film; her menopausal births are another running joke in the film, and Kate (Tina Fey) calls the birth of

the twins, "gross." The tabloids had a field day with Nadya Suleman's giving birth to eight babies. One internet magazine called
her "a new species" and another internet gossip column reads
"Octomom extends tentacles into reality television" (bangordaily-
news.com; accessed June 6, 2009). Certainly the nickname "Octomom" suggests a monstrous animal-like creature that gives birth
not to babies, but to litters or broods. As we will see, associations
between so-called "Octomoms" and hybridity suggest anxiety not
only over animality but also over racial mixing.

Like the animalesque and alien births of horror films, stories of
multiple births spark traditional associations between pregnancy
and animality. They bring to the surface anxieties over women's
central role in the continuation of the human species by invok-
ing images of women giving birth to nonhuman creatures or litters. These "unnatural" births seem to confirm long-standing
conceptions of pregnancy, the maternal body, and childbirth
as abject, which paradoxically put women closer to nature, not
in the romantic sense sometimes employed in discourses about
pregnancy but in an inhuman way. The fear is that new reproductive technologies will produce nonhuman cyber-babies or animal
litters that threaten humanity as we know it. The science fiction
film *Moon* (2009) is interesting in this regard in that the Lunar
company mining the moon for energy uses clones—who don't
know they are clones—rather than train new employees; in this
film, the clone protagonist stays on mission through the strength
he gets from prerecorded messages from what he takes to be his
pregnant wife and eventually his baby. In most of these science fiction films, it is not only the question of what a woman gives birth
to, but the rate at which she does so, that captures the popular
imagination and threatens with the accelerated time of new reproductive technologies.

As we might expect, infertility and "baby hunger" have become
subjects for recent Hollywood films, most of them comedies. Films
such as *Juno* (2007), *Baby Mama* (2008), *Miss Conception* (2008),
*Away We Go* (2009), *The Switch* (2010), *The Back-up Plan* (2010),

and others on the horizon, deal with career women who have put off finding partners or having babies until it may be "too late." Characters in these films realize that their sacrifices may not have been worth it and long for a baby more than anything else. Many of them go to desperate lengths to have one. For example, Heather Graham's character in *Miss Conception* stalks funerals, hoping to snag a potential father to inseminate what doctors tell her is her last egg. And after unsuccessful attempts at artificial insemination, Kate in *Baby Mama* hires a surrogate to carry her artificially inseminated egg. *The Switch* depicts independent woman Kassie (Jennifer Aniston) inseminating herself at home with what she thinks is the sperm of her preferred donor but turns out to be the sperm of her neurotic best friend, and of course, future partner. In *The Backup Plan*, Zoe (Jennifer Lopez) meets the man of her dreams the day after she is impregnated with sperm from a sperm bank; the original title of the film was "Plan B," presumably until studio executives realized that this is the name of the morning-after pill, which may suggest that she opts for "plan b" so that she can have a more romantic pregnancy; in the end she is pregnant by her new lover and expecting a "real" and more romantic baby.

These films reassure us that men have not become obsolete in reproduction and that the nuclear family is still the ideal family. In addition, romance trumps technology as babies are conceived from passion, even as accidents, rather than scheduled medical procedures. These films assuage fears about the possibility of reproduction without sex raised by new technologies. Once again, the issue of the separation of reproduction and sex or sexuality is at the center of our notions of gender and family. Unlike the era of just a couple of decades ago when Iris Young and others argued that dissociating pregnancy from sex made women into passive containers for reproduction, now the dissociation of pregnancy and sex threatens to make sex unnecessary for reproduction.

There are other new anxieties too. If a few decades ago we could be certain about maternity but paternity was always in question (until the advent of DNA testing), now anxieties over paternity extend to maternity. When a couple of decades ago Adrienne Rich described the differences between paternity and maternity in terms of visibility and the physical facts of reproduction and childbirth, she didn't anticipate forms of IVF that involve egg donation and change the physical facts of maternity. Rich maintained that, "Because the fact of physical motherhood is so visible and dramatic, men recognized only after some time that they, too, had a part in generation. The meaning of 'fatherhood' remains tangential, elusive. To 'father' a child suggests above all to beget, to provide the sperm which fertilizes the ovum. To 'mother' a child implies continuing presence, lasting at least nine months, more often years" (Rich 1976:12). But if one woman can carry the biological child of another, motherhood itself becomes a question. Hollywood's "who's your daddy?" becomes "who's your mommy," as evidenced by the end of the film *Bella* where a mother meets her daughter for the first time since her birth and asks, "Do you know who I am?" To which the daughter replies, "You are my momma"—and there is not a dry eye in the house (for a discussion of questions of maternity raised by ART, see Cussins 1998).

IVF and anonymous sperm donors also raise the question of paternity in new ways when the father of a child might be a "turkey baster," which is the center of a running joke in both *Look Who's Talking* and *The Switch*, with the latter originally titled "The Baster." If IVF brings with it anxieties over the separation between sex and reproduction and the obsolescence of both heterosexual sex and the nuclear family, it also makes it possible to imagine extending choice to issues of DNA and genetic makeup of offspring. So-called "designer babies" become a possibility. There is a funny scene in *Baby Mama* where Kate is choosing a sperm donor based on a computer simulation of the baby that would result from a combination of donor DNA and hers; in one case the result looks like Alfred E. Newman's famous cartoon face from the cover of *Mad* magazine.

In comedy, anxieties about new reproductive technologies are played for laughs, while in horror and science fiction they become the stuff of nightmares. One aspect of the fears and desires evoked by new technologies is the changing time of reproduction. What was once a lengthy process that involved "chemistry" or at least sex between a man and a woman now may involve appointments at fertility clinics and embryos inserted into wombs. Moreover, the results of this process may not be just one baby but several if doctors and patients do not opt for "selective reduction" of fetuses. The speed of reproduction is a common trope of horror films wherein aliens give birth to so many offspring that it threatens to overrun the planet. And as babies become products of technology, there is a fear that love and romance will disappear from human reproduction such that it becomes just another type of automated production of commodities for sale.

## THE TIME OF PREGNANCY: THEN AND NOW

As the pregnant body has gone from asexual, even abject, to sexual object, its commodification has produced changing rhetoric about time and desire. More middle-class women put off having babies until they have established their careers; IVF is increasing dramatically as women "race" against their so-called "biological clocks." Within the popular imaginary, IVF extends women's choice not only to postpone having babies but also to what babies they will have. As more women turn to IVF and sperm banks, and as genetic engineering becomes a real possibility, the language of choice becomes the fantasy of planning, controlling, and eliminating chance from reproduction. Women choose sperm based on the profiles of donors. And genetic engineering promises "designer babies." In addition, IVF seems to turn back the clock and give women more time to choose. Seemingly no longer limited by natural cycles of fertility, reproductive technologies appear to give women more choices and more control. Yet, as Angela Davis so poignantly argued more than twenty years ago, these new technologies also create new myths and ideals of maternity that oblige women to seek expensive, dangerous, and invasive medical interventions in order to fulfill their "biological destiny" and thereby their own desires by having a baby (for a discussion of the complexities of new fertility technologies, see Donchin 1996). A successful career is not enough in this new cult of motherhood that compels women to stop at nothing to have it all.

Unlike when Iris Young and others argued that dissociating pregnancy from sex made women into passive containers for reproduction, now the dissociation of pregnancy and sex threatens to make sex unnecessary for reproduction. While de Beauvoir argued that women need to be free from reproduction (perhaps she would embrace new technologies that eventually could make reproduction possible without pregnancy), and Young argued that women's liberation depends upon sexualizing pregnancy through an identification of reproduction with sex, recent Hollywood films manifest an anxiety over this separation, but for very different reasons. It is not that pregnancy can't be sexy or that women's role in reproduction is imagined as passive. To the contrary, in some of these films women are actively seeking reproduction as a means of fulfillment to compliment career success and other achievements. New technologies bring new anxieties about both men and women becoming irrelevant for reproduction, and more anxieties about the disassociation between heterosexual sex and reproduction.

For example, *Baby Mama* and *Miss Conception* resolve anxieties about new reproductive technologies by assuring us that, despite the odds against it, "good old-fashioned" heterosexual sex is at the origin of life. In *Baby Mama*, both Kate and Angie get pregnant through heterosexual sex—even though Kate is menopausal and Angie was supposed to have been artificially inseminated to act as Kate's surrogate. In *Miss Conception*, Mia (Heather Graham) is, unbeknownst to her, already pregnant from sex with her boyfriend. *The Switch* recuperates the biological nuclear family even though Jennifer Aniston's character believes she has used sperm from an anonymous donor. These films reassure us that men have not become obsolete in reproduction and that the nuclear family is still the ideal family. In addition, romance trumps technology as babies are conceived from passion, even as "accidents," rather than from scheduled medical procedures. These films assuage fears about the possibility of reproduction without sex raised by new technologies. They idealize heterosexual sex at the origins of life. Once again, the issue of the separation of reproduction and sex or sexuality is at the center of our notions of gender and family.

Whereas Young and others questioned the separation of sex and reproduction on the grounds of women's desire, these films implicitly challenge the separation of sex and reproduction out of anxieties over the possibility of reproduction without heterosexual sex or sexual desire. In other words, the desire for babies can be separated from sexual desire insofar as new reproductive technologies make it possible to conceive without sex. Yet these films reassure us that babies are not products of technology but rather of passion, and that sexual desire is necessary to fulfill the desire for babies. In films such as *Baby Mama* and *Miss Conception*, women work through their instrumental attitudes toward relationships with men and sex—that is to say, wanting sex with men in order to get pregnant. Their so-called "baby hunger" is satisfied only insofar as it coincides with sexual desire. Women's desire for babies and sexual desire are brought together to give us a more romantic ideal of both heterosexual relationships and the family.

In *Baby Hunger: The New Battle for Motherhood*, Sylvia Ann Hewlett argues against the "empty promise" of high-tech reproduction and in favor of nuclear families and younger mothers. Hewlett's book is a cautionary tale about women waiting until it is "too late" and their "biological clocks" have run out. She describes the "creeping nonchoice" that career women face when they don't have children "in time." Hewlett sets out a timeline for young women: find a man ("give urgent priority to finding a partner. This project is extremely time sensitive and deserves special attention in your twenties"), have babies ("Have your first child before 35, do not wait . . . even if you manage to get one child 'under the wire' you may fail to have a second"), then focus on your career ("Choose a career that will give you the 'gift of time' ") (2002:261). While indicative of the difficult choices women face when balancing careers and family, Hewlett's book also recuperates and updates long-standing notions of women's bodies as threatening. She figures women's "biological clocks" as "ticking time bombs" about to explode, leaving women childless and unhappy. She imagines women racing against time and an empty future that results from poor choices by young women and "false advertising" by the medical establishment. Her conclusion is even more retrograde in that she claims that young, middle-aged, college-educated women have a duty to themselves and to their "nation" to have children while they can rather than risk trying to have a family "under the wire" after focusing on a career (2002:266). This argument echoes nineteenth- and early-twentieth-century eugenics proposals that encouraged middle-class white women to reproduce because they supposedly would pass on the best genes and thereby ensure the evolution of the human race.

Hewlett's *Baby Hunger* stands in dramatic opposition to Iris Young's and Julia Kristeva's suggestions about women's time particularly in relation to pregnancy and childbirth. If Hewlett gives us a nightmare of time bombs, racing against time, and babies under the wire, Young and Kristeva imagine a radically different experience of the temporality of female embodment. If the time of pregnancy and childbirth figured by Hewlett is compressed into the urgency of *now*, Young and Kristeva describe an expansive sense of time that stretches into both the past and the future. While the time of "baby hunger" is driven by anxieties of modern technology and careers leading to an empty future, the time of pregnant embodment imagined by these feminist philosophers a couple of decades ago conjures a temporality at once subjective and natural. Hewlett's pragmatic, if frantic, outline of a linear timeline for the successful woman juts up against these feminist figurations of pregnant time in ways that both disturb and illuminate.

Returning to the seminal work of Iris Young, we can trace a radically different notion of the time of pregnancy, or what Kristeva calls "women's time," opposed to the "ticking time bomb" of a woman's "biological clock." In a series of essays in *Throwing Like a Girl*, Young developed a phenomenology of pregnant embodiment that not only challenged traditional theories of subjectivity but also articulated the subjectivity of pregnancy as unique and purposeful (Young 1990). She argued that pregnant embodiment enables a unique relationship to past and future, and to space and time: "The pregnant subject, I suggest, is decentered, split, or doubled in several ways. She experiences her body as herself and not herself. Its inner movements belong to another being, yet they are not other, because her body boundaries shift and because her bodily self-location is focused on her trunk in addition to her head. This split subject appears in the eroticism of pregnancy, in which the woman can experience an innocent narcissism fed by recollection of her repressed experience of her own mother's body. Pregnant existence entails, finally, a unique temporality of process and growth in which the woman can experience herself as split between past and future" (1990:160). Pregnancy opens the body to otherness in ways that make the experience porous physically and mentally. This porosity can be the basis for reconceiving ethical relations. Rather than threatening, Young imagines women's bodies as pregnant with the future. Of course, pregnant embodiment's futurity may just highlight the "empty promise" of a future that, for whatever reason—and there are many—does not lead to childbirth and thereby the openness to this Other within become another beloved person. Or, as Caroline Lundquist suggests, it may point to a dreaded future that the pregnant woman experiences as constricting if not outright oppressive; she argues that in some circumstances pregnancy may recall a traumatic past of rape and assault that does not provide the continuity or comfort that Young imagines (Lundquist 2008).

Young's discussion of the split between past and future as a temporality that arches between the pregnant woman's repressed bodily relation with her own mother and the anticipation of her relation to her future child is indebted to Kristeva's discussions of pregnancy in "Stabat Mater" and in perhaps Kristeva's most famous essay, "Women's Time" (1979) (see Kristeva 2002:349–68). In "Women's Time," Kristeva proposes that women's bodies give them a cyclical and monumental temporality that interrupts linear time. She maintains: "As for time, female subjectivity seems to offer it a specific concept of measurement that essentially retains repetition and eternity out of the many modalities that appear throughout history of civilization. On the one hand, this measure preserves cycles, gestation, and the eternal return of biological rhythm that is similar to the rhythm of nature. Its predictability can be shocking, but its simultaneity with which what is experienced as extra-subjective and cosmic time is a source of resplendent visions and unnamable *jouissance*. On the other hand, it preserves a solid temporality that is faultless and impenetrable, one that has so little to do with linear time that the very term 'temporality' seems inappropriate" (Kristeva 2002:354).

A stark counterpoint to Hewlett's invocation of clocks running out and racing toward a family, Kristeva figures women's time as other than clock time, as repetitive cycles, punctuated by monumental moments like the onset of menses, childbirth, and perhaps menopause. If Hewlett is right about the experience of many middle-class women in the United States, then Kristeva's account of women's time is either a thing of the past, a romantic idealization, or, as she often suggests, a reminder that the temporality of bodies is repetitive, cyclical, and monumental rather than linear and teleological. In other words, despite the dangers of essentializing the menstruating childbearing maternal body that Kristeva's theory evokes, her reminder that bodily time cannot be reduced to clock time may help to diagnose Hewlett's ticking time bomb as a symptom of anxieties or fears about the body that take us back to what Kristeva describes as the abjection of the female body, particularly insofar as it is (or is not, as the case may be) a maternal body (1980).

In "Stabat Mater," Kristeva maintains that the experience of pregnancy, birth, and motherhood puts a woman back in touch with her own relationship to her mother, not only in terms of an identification with her experience as mother but also in terms of her repressed or bodily memories of her own intimate relationship with her mother's body. In other words, there is an (unconscious) erotic, or at least sensuous, dimension to the bond between daughter and mother that is reawakened in pregnancy, birth, and motherhood. This sensuous relationship not only betokens maternal sexuality beyond traditional conceptions of it but also a different notion of time insofar as pregnancy and childbirth give the woman a singular relation to the past, her own past, and her relationship with her mother. Indeed, women's connection to sensuous experience in general becomes for Kristeva the promise of a future beyond technological mediation and mechanization that renders all of human experience automatic. Contra notions of speed associated with technology, Kristeva suggests that the time of pregnancy and motherhood might offer a counterbalance through the monumental and cyclical experiences of sensuous time. Kristeva argues that mothers might be our only hope against the automation of human life precisely because they are more attuned to the sensuous dimension of experience.

In a chapter of *Hatred and Forgiveness* entitled "The Passion According to Motherhood," Kristeva says, "allow me to take the mother's side" and proceeds to describe "the extraneousness of the pregnant woman" as the narcissistic withdrawal wherein "the future mother becomes an object of desire, pleasure and aversion for herself" (2010:85). In this state, which Kristeva claims is not unlike "possession," the pregnant woman is completely absorbed by emotions invested in her own body as the "hollow" habitation of a future love-object that she will have to allow to become a subject. Kristeva's description of the narcissism of pregnancy echoes Iris Young's description of the self-love that the pregnant woman can experience in relation to the belly that is both her own and not her own. Kristeva recounts a maternal progression toward what she calls the "miracle" of love. It is a progression that twists and returns, not a linear progression but rather one of repetitions of psychic attachments and detachments that allow the woman to love her child and yet to wean it and let it go. Kristeva describes this move from self-absorption, to love of the child, and then eventually release or weaning of the child, as the "miracle" of maternal passion; the mother embodies both passion and dispassion, or passion and working-through passion.

On Kristeva's account it is not primarily passion that is uniquely human but rather dispassion or the sublimation of passion, which is essential to maternal passion as successful mothering. Provocatively, she insists that insofar as it is sublimation, maternal passion is not only a model for all human passion but also "the furthest from its biological foundation" (2010:86). Maternity, then, cannot be reduced to biology, a biological clock, or merely the cyclical rhythms of the body. Clearly, this claim is antithetical to traditional views of women's role in reproduction, which, as we know, has been and continues to be seen as a matter of biology, even animality. In this way, Kristeva applies de Beauvoir's lesson, that one is not born but rather becomes a woman, to motherhood. While de Beauvoir suggests that in motherhood women are reduced to their biological reproductive function, Kristeva complicates any straightforward connection between maternity and biology. While Kristeva's insistence on the mother's passion as negativity is akin to de Beauvoir's suggestion in *The Second Sex* that human females are more pained by their relation to reproduction than female animals because they can reflect on the experience, Kristeva, unlike de Beauvoir, valorizes maternity.

Yet Kristeva claims that she is not "pro-birth" or endorsing a new cult of motherhood because she emphasizes what she calls "the structure" of motherhood, which she also sees in analysis, writing, and art. Like childbirth, analysis (and writing, art, and mysticism) can bring "a time of new beginnings and rebirths and a certain serenity" (2010:120). Yet this time of rebirth is possible only through the repetition of death, linear time, and language, through which the mother articulates the meaning of her sensuous experience in relation to her child. In this way, Kristeva argues that motherhood and psychoanalysis share the same goal, which is to turn passion into dispassion through sublimation (2010). Explicitly rejecting the cult of motherhood, Kristeva suggests that the structure of motherhood, like the structure of writing, art, and analysis, is not primarily about giving birth but about rebirth and the cyclical time of flowering and dying off necessary for life. What she finds compelling about motherhood, then, is not limited to the actuality of pregnancy and childbirth but rather takes these experiences as models for human existence as sensuous and thereby open to the cycles of life and death. Against the automation and speed of reproduction promised by new reproductive technologies, as long as babies are born from women's bodies, however that may be, and as long as human beings raise and care for their young, there will be material sensuous bonds that cannot be mechanized, no matter how much we try.

Kristeva's recent discussions of maternal passion as the psychic repetition of attachment and detachment, passion and dispassion, unique to, and definitive of, humanity, not only elevate the maternal body and motherhood to the transcendent status de Beauvoir denied it but also propose maternity as a model for an ethics of ambiguities and ambivalences that goes some distance to advance ongoing feminist discussions of motherhood, sexuality, and pregnant embodiment. In spite of her insistence that it is not, Kristeva's revaluation of maternity could be read as an endorsement for motherhood. But it can also be read as a corrective to the devaluation of maternity within patriarchal cultures and within Western intellectual history. Moreover, insofar as her recent revaluation of maternity turns on accepting, if not embracing, negativity and ambiguity, it addresses some of the most problematic aspects of motherhood and sexuality.

Beyond the myth of "having it all," (middle-class) women are trying to figure out how to have both/and. And in spite of their tendency to simplify and resolve the ambiguities and ambivalences of women's choices about issues of motherhood, sexuality, and pregnancy, recent Hollywood films also show us characters struggling with them. Recent pregnancy films show us women refusing the either/or of traditions that make them choose career or family and relationships. Even as they perpetuate the ideals of "having it all," they also display deep-seated anxieties about women's reproductive choices in an age of changing technologies. Although the pregnant body is still the butt of the joke, it is also the object of attraction and desire, and occasionally even a subject of its own desires. For, although the border between motherhood and sexuality is breaking down, and this may signal advances for women, it may also reinforce stereotypes of women and pregnancy that are restrictive for women. Feminists must continue to diagnose the ways in which changing popular images and figurations of motherhood, sexuality, and pregnant embodiment enhance freedoms for women even while at the same time they discipline, constrict, and limit women's freedom.

# 2

## MOMCOM AS ROMCOM

### PREGNANCY AS A VEHICLE FOR ROMANCE

**IF THE FIRST** romantic "screwball" comedies were named after the screwball pitch in baseball—a pitch that curves in ways that you don't expect—then the recent phenomenon of pregnant romantic comedies throws us another curve.[1] From the earliest romantic comedies in Hollywood through contemporary romcoms, the standard formula for the genre remains the same: boy meets girl (or now girl meets boy), tensions run high, opposites attract, and sparks fly, until through some type of transformation, the two individuals become properly coupled. The vehicle for such transformation is the basis for both the romance and the comedy in these films. With the recent subgenre of pregnant romcoms— momcoms—pregnant bodies have become the media for this transformation and also the source of romance and comedy. *Momcom* is defined by the prominence of pregnancy or the pregnant body in the narrative of the film. Although throughout the history of Hollywood there have been plenty of films—from melodramas to comedies—about motherhood, until relatively recently there have been few films about pregnancy itself. Recently, however, there has been an explosion of films about pregnancy. In this new sub-genre, both the female and male characters are transformed into suitable romantic partners through the process of pregnancy. The physical transformations in the woman's pregnant body represent emotional and character transformations in both male and female characters. In these recent films, rather than the end point of romance, pregnancy and impending parenthood is the beginning point from which romance, love, and coupling, if not marriage, ensue. Pregnancy has become a contemporary form of romance on the high seas, complete with seasickness-cum-morning-sickness and water breaking.

In this chapter, we explore how this new subgenre of roman-tic comedy both continues and transforms traditional forms of romantic comedy, by tracing changing notions of romance from screwball through recent undercurrents of romantic pregnancy or pregnancy as romance. Role reversals, mistaken identities, and masquerade so prevalent in this genre have their contempo-rary counterparts in pregnancy films. And the iconography of romance—flowers, candlelight, and slow dancing—have changed to incorporate big pregnant bellies and midnight cravings. How did the tensions of the early sex comedies (Rock Hudson's play-boys looking for sex and Doris Day's "professional virgins" saving themselves for marriage) morph into improbably fertile one-night stands that start the unsuspecting couple on the journey of preg-nancy that eventually leads to romance, love, and proper coupling? If the classic "sex comedies" of the 1950s and 1960s gave us sexual tension and romance leading to marriage and then sex and then pregnancy, contemporary momcoms start with sex and pregnancy as the medium for sexual tension, romance, and comedy. How can we explain this seeming reversal of marriage, sex, and pregnancy?

## SCREWBALL ROMANCE

The vehicle for romance in screwball comedy is often literally a vehicle! There is romance on the high seas, romance on buses, romance in military transports, and of course on trains, in automobiles, and even in a few planes. Movement is key to screwball, whether it is moving vehicles or moving bodies falling, kicking, swinging, dancing, and all the while enjoying various pratfalls that have become emblematic of screwball comedy. The thrill of the moving image itself is part of the romance in these early comedies, which inherited the exaggerated movements of silent films while exploiting the possibility of fast-paced dialogue with the inception of "talkies."

In these early romcoms, locomotion is romantic. Trains and buses are more than just means of transportation. They are the means of escape and of transport to other worlds. They also provide lessons in how "the other half" lives, whether it is the glamorous upper-class evening-gown-and-tux-wearing crowd or the lower-class "lost men" or hobos living on the streets in a tent city and hopping trains. Both the romance and comedy in these films often come from the movement between these realms. Crossing over and passing into another world is the essence of romance in that it affords the opportunity for opposites to attract, to overcome obstacles, and finally to come together as a couple. The tension between two worlds and the misfit trying to fit in, or the misfit being educated in the ways of the other world, provide the comedy.

For example, *Sullivan's Travels* (1941), *My Man Godfrey* (1936), and *It Happened One Night* (1934) turn on rich people posing as hobos or as poor people. In *Sullivan's Travels* and *My Man Godfrey* the protagonists set out to masquerade as hobos in order to make a point about social class. In *It Happened One Night*, Ellie (Claudette Colbert) learns lessons in street smarts and is taken down a notch by newspaperman Peter (Clark Gable) after she runs away from her wealthy father and flees on a bus without any money. Class passing is both romantic and funny. It leads to adventures and misadventures that characterize screwball and betoken what was considered "romantic" in 1940s Hollywood.

Sex passing or cross-dressing is another vehicle for romance, comedy, and transformation. For example, in *Some Like It Hot* (1959) and *I Was a Male War Bride* (1949), men disguised as women facilitate love and marriage. Even *Bringing Up Baby* (1938) has a scene with David (Cary Grant) wearing a woman's negligee that is played for laughs but also reverses traditional gender roles and leaves him at the mercy of Susan (Katherine Hepburn). Entering the world of the "opposite sex"—or as Jack Lemmon's character puts it in *Some Like It Hot*, "a whole other sex"—is an adventure full of pratfalls and lessons in how this other world operates. Through both class and sex mobility, these characters mature, become more sensitive (Jack Lemmon and Tony Curtis in *Some Like It Hot*, Irene in *My Man Godfrey*) or well-rounded (Gary Grant's David in *Bringing Up Baby*, Ellie in *It Happened One Night*), and thereby become more suitable mates as a result. Seeing how the "other half" lives is educational and transformative.

In these early films, romance conjures its traditional meaning as fantastical, extraordinary, adventurous, and even heroic rather than its more contemporary popular meaning related to love.[2] In the style of romantic literature, only with a comic twist, these films present a world of wealth, glamour, travel, and adventure that is far from the everyday reality of Depression-era filmgoers.[3] And although love and heterocoupling play important roles in these films, ideal romance is about adventure and fun rather than finding true love, unlike contemporary films about finding a soul mate, "the one," or the love of one's life. So, how do we get from screwball's conception of romance as adventure and travel to present notions of romance as candles, flowers . . . and pregnancy? Indeed, how do we get from finding "the one" to being pregnant with the other?

## SEX VERSUS ROMANCE: ROUND 1

In *Romantic Comedy: Boy Meets Girl Meets Genre*, Tamar Jeffers McDonald traces the evolution of the genre through four main periods: screwball comedies, the sex comedy, the radical romantic comedy, and the neo-traditional romantic comedy (2007). Using and extending McDonald's categories, we will focus on changing conceptions of romance in relation to masquerade, mistaken identity, and the use of alter ego as the motor of both coupling and comedy in order to follow the development of the genre through recent pregnancy films. McDonald defines the sex comedy: "The sex comedy pits woman against man in an elemental battle of wits, in which the goal of both is sex. Only the timing and legitimacy of this differs from gender to gender, with women wanting sex after, and men before or without, marriage" (2007:38). Masquerade is a standard ploy used by the man to bed the woman and/or to teach her a lesson. The untouchable good girl brings out both desire and resentment in the man, who is attracted to her but also annoyed by her attitude toward his playboy lifestyle. This is the story in the Doris Day and Rock Hudson films *Pillow Talk* (1959) and *Lover Come Back* (1961). In *Some Like It Hot,* Joe/Geraldine/Junior (Tony Curtis) uses masquerade to get close to Sugar (Marilyn Monroe) and gain her trust. Through the masquerade, the man, to his own surprise, becomes more sensitive to the woman's position and inevitably falls in love with her. His alter ego allows him to explore his more "feminine" side through which his wild ways are tamed and he becomes an acceptable mate for the good girl, or in the case of Sugar, the vulnerable girl who always falls for the wrong type of guy (the playboy type that Joe is at the beginning of the film). By the end of the film, Joe no longer simply wants to bed Sugar; he is in love with her and understands how men have taken advantage of her in her past relationships. He wants to change his ways so that he will be different, more sensitive and willing to commit to her.

In the Doris Day–Rock Hudson films, the successful single career women played by Day are likewise domesticated through the course of the films. Both the career girl and the playboy must be domesticated and brought into a proper heterocouple circumscribed by marriage that results in successful reproduction. By the end of both *Pillow Talk* and *Lover Come Back*, the pair is married and Day's character is pregnant (fig. 2.1). It is noteworthy that in these early films the playboy character is not portrayed as immature, as he is in contemporary films; it is not about growing up and accepting responsibility in early Hollywood, but about domesticating sexual desire. In contemporary films, the womanizing man is presented as immature and/or irresponsible (e.g., *Knocked Up*, *Wedding Crashers*, *Ghosts of Girlfriends Past*). Representations of both the playboy and the career girl characters have changed in recent films. And neither is as attractive as they were in the older films. If now playboys are seen as immature, career women (no longer girls and this is part of the problem) are seen as controlling ballbusters. Reminiscent of Hollywood's femme fatales, these strong women characters are threatening, yet unlike the femme fatales they are also neurotic and therefore capable of being domesticated.[4] Their aggression can be overcome by love; and pregnancy most especially renders them more passive and therefore less threatening.

Although screwball often relies on masquerade and mistaken identity, unlike in sex comedy the charade usually reveals something about class that prepares the pair to couple, but not necessarily to marry. And when the masquerade is exposed, the deceived party—usually the woman—doesn't necessarily feel betrayed, as in sex comedy. For example, Irene in *My Man Godfrey* doesn't care that Godfrey turns out to be an aristocrat posing as a "lost man"; furthermore, she gets him to marry her in the end through the same forceful high jinx she has employed throughout the film. In other words, their marriage is not the result of some fundamental change in character.

In the sex comedies, on the other hand, the tensions between protagonists is offset through the alter ego of the masquerading

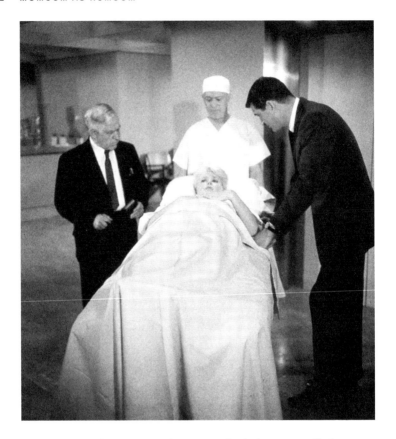

FIGURE 2.1 Carol (Doris Day) about to give birth, her supposedly "pregnant belly" hidden under a sheet (*Lover Come Back*, 1961). (Courtesy of Univeral Studios Licensing LLC, © 1961 Universal City Studios, Inc.)

man (in the case of Rock Hudson's character in *Pillow Talk* and *Lover Come Back* and Tony Curtis's character in *Some Like It Hot* and *Sex and the Single Girl*), who poses as nonthreatening and impotent, with a suggestion of homosexuality. The female lead has a relationship with two different men, one of whom she hates for his womanizing and one of whom she loves for his sensitivity; of course they turn out to be the same man, who is both sexy and sensitive—the best of both worlds. But by the end of the charade, the man's alter ego turns out to be his truer nature—or at least balances out his character—and he gives up his womanizing ways for his true love, the girl who didn't fall for his seductive playboy persona. For her, he becomes his alter ego: a sensitive, caring, loving partner ready to commit to a long-term relationship. Yet the sexiness and mischievousness of his playboy self remains. Now he is not only sexually desirable but also desirable as a life partner and father to a family. The good girl, of course, will also be a good mother to his children. In contemporary films, we see something similar when the "hot" but uptight career woman loses control and loosens up through pregnancy (*Knocked Up, Baby Mama*); she thereby becomes both sexy and a mother, a "MILF" in current parlance. In this regard, these films repeat screwball's tendency to leave us with the best of both worlds, namely, a humble or humbled character who knows what it is like to be poor, even if temporarily, but who is brought or brought back into an upper-class lifestyle. These characters learn the lessons of humility and the value of human relationships, but they are still rich at the end of the film (*My Man Godfrey*, *Sullivan's Travels*).[5]

Whereas in screwball the couple is warring from beginning to end even as they reconcile long enough to unite or reunite, in the sex comedies the revelation of masquerade makes the woman feel betrayed and boy meets girl becomes boy loses girl and has to win her back. This "fort-da" moment has becomes a standard of contemporary romantic comedy.[6] In fact, some recent films give us several such moments in which the couple appears to reconcile but doesn't and the boy loses the girl (or vice versa) over and over again until the end of the film (e.g., *How to Lose a Guy in 10 Days*, *Ghosts of Girlfriends Past*, *Fool's Gold*). Unlike screwball in which antagonism between characters is never fully resolved, sex comedy unites the best of both characters by transforming them through the course of the film; they both are domesticated and brought into "proper" roles as wife, husband, and prospective parents. The career girl presumably gives up her job to stay at home with the kids and the playboy gives up his womanizing to be faithful to his true love. She has tamed him but he also has tamed her. Her professional ambitions are exchanged for family values and heterosexual coupling; and in both characters, sexual desires are domesticated and "properly" circumscribed by marriage or, at least, a commitment to monogamy.

These films give us two models of romance: first, the antagonistic tensions of screwball between the male and female characters; and second, a tender but seemingly false relation between one character and the alter ego of the other. The tender courtship often involves candlelight dinners, dancing, or flowers and gifts that we have come to associate with modern romance. But the sexual tension in these films still comes from the sparks that fly between the "real" characters behind their masks. In a way, these relationships are a type of ménage à trois between the woman, the playboy, and his alter ego. The alter ego is a necessary transitional phase or character that enables both the man and the woman to have a more acceptable, "normal," and balanced relationship (which means a monogamous relationship circumscribed by the institution of marriage and traditional gender roles with the father as breadwinner and the mother as . . . mother). As we will see, in recent pregnancy films the pregnant belly and/or baby-fetus inside it take the place of the alter ego and provide the transitional phase that transforms the characters into suitable mates.

It is also interesting to note that in the Doris Day–Rock Hudson trilogy (the third being *Send Me No Flowers*, 1964), there is another alter-ego third character in each film, all played by Tony Randall. Randall's character presents an alternative sensitive man but perhaps too uptight and neurotic—or gay—to successfully heterocouple. This *gay cupid* plays an important role in bringing our protagonists together even while he may be trying to keep them apart. For example, in *Pillow Talk* he tries to convince Rock Hudson's character that marriage is desirable; in *Lover Come Back* he exposes Linus/Jerry Webster's (Rock Hudson) masquerade; and in *Send Me No Flowers*, he shares a bed and several homoerotic and suggestive scenes with Hudson's character. In this third installment of the trilogy, the couple is already married, which implies that their happiness at the end of the film may require these men working through or "properly" repressing their latent homosexual desires.

We have moved from romance as a sense of adventure and loco-motion or movement in screwball comedies to romance as love or tenderness and ultimately the suitability to marry and reproduce in sex comedies. This trend continues in contemporary films that end with a final scene of the female lead pregnant (*Fool's Gold*, *The Back-up Plan*, *Baby Mama*, *Labor Pains*), something suggested but never shown in early Hollywood. Indeed, the Hays Production Code prohibited showing a woman's pregnant body because it was considered "indecent." Certainly, if the frequency of its presence as a main character is any indication, a lot has changed since then, and now an entire subgenre of romantic comedy, along with pop-ular magazines and television, appear to celebrate the pregnant body. "We've come a long way baby" to get to baby bumps and heavily pregnant women as cover girls and film icons.

## SEX VERSUS ROMANCE: ROUND 2

As the sexual revolution of the 1960s and 1970s affected Holly-wood, the romantic comedy genre could no longer sustain its ten-sion through the question of if or when the couple would have sex. Sex became a given, desired by both men and women, with or without marriage. And with skyrocketing divorce rates, it was difficult to maintain the fantasy of happily-ever-after or true love. Simultaneously maintaining and parodying icons of romance such as rooftop dinners, flowers, and candles, along with the notion of soul mates or true love, Hollywood romances became more realis-tic and complicated. They didn't always have happy endings, and sex, marriage, and reproduction weren't necessarily any longer the goals of romance. More to the point, what McDonald calls "radi-cal" romantic comedies, or what Frank Krutnik calls "nervous romances," suggest that we are all masquerading and that we cannot distinguish our own true motives, let alone someone else's (see McDonald 2007; Krutnik 1990).

For example, in a scene emblematic of this period, and of Woody Allen's films in particular, *Annie Hall* (1977) shows an early conversation between the prospective lovers on a not-especially-romantic rooftop with flowers, trying to make conversation; in subtitles at the bottom of the screen, we see that each is thinking something very different from what they are saying, displaying not only their anxieties about love and sex but also their use of masquerade, only now in a less explicit way than earlier romantic comedies. Although radical romcoms retain some screwball elements, their "screwiness" usually comes from the characters' neuroses. And while these films may employ physical humor and sight gags, the resulting confusion and chaos can be read as the outward expression of the characters' inner ambivalence and conflict (e.g., Woody Allen's romantic comedies). Whereas earlier romcom gives us sexual tension as the conflict between "opposite" sexes and opposite character types, radical romcom gives us inner conflict that drives the narrative through the unpredictability of neurotic behavior.

In an era where sex and reproduction were uncoupled as a result of birth control, it is fascinating that sex and romance were also uncoupled (already suggesting a connection between reproduction and romance).[7] Radical romcoms may have lots of sex and not a lot of romance. Insofar as many of these films portray romance and love as a myth or a delusion, they leave us with sex. At the same time, however, so much sex is represented as meaningless since it can happen at any time with almost anyone. While in this period sexual liberation and sexual experimentation is embraced, in more contemporary romantic comedies sexual promiscuity, especially by men, is portrayed as immature, empty, and merely a prelude to true sexual fulfillment, which is possible only with the right woman, the one true love (and, like man's love object in sex comedy, usually a woman who is sexually unavailable to the man at the beginning of the film). Given the evolution of the relationship between romance, sex, and reproduction in Hollywood, romantic reproduction may be the logical next step in the romantic comedy genre's separation between sex and romance.

*My Best Friend's Wedding* (1997) is a prime example of the split between sex and romance.[8] There, Jules (Julia Roberts) is a successful career woman whose best friend Michael (Dermot Mulroney) is getting married to wealthy college student Kim (Cameron Diaz). Jules tries to stop the wedding because she loves Michael. But, in the end, Kim gets Michael and Jules is left with her gay best friend George, who ends the film with the line: "There may not be marriage. There may not be sex. But God knows there will be dancing!" While Jules will not get sex from her gay best friend, she will get romance. Jules also gets to keep her successful career while Kim gives up school and her potential career for Michael. Romance still requires that the woman give up her career for the sake of marriage and, presumably, eventually family. In addition, *My Best Friend's Wedding* is one of the first of many contemporary films about overly aggressive, manipulative, controlling career women, most of whom end up "tamed" or controlled in order to make them suitable partners because, in their original state, they are simply not very attractive characters. These films insist that even if she is sexy, there is nothing romantic about a controlling bossy woman; and she cannot be a proper love object until she loosens up and perhaps even gives up her career or at least gives in to male domination (*The Proposal*, *New in Town*, *The Ugly Truth*, *Knocked Up*, *Leap Year*). If she doesn't, she ends up alone (*My Best Friend's Wedding*; Holly Hunter's character in *Broadcast News*, 1987).

Judd Apatow's popular *Knocked Up* (2007) combines a controlling career woman and pregnancy to kick off another subgenre of romcom, what McDonald calls "hommecom," also known as "bromance."[9] In these romantic comedies that center on men, women are played for laughs, whereas nerdy slacker men bed beautiful successful women, clearly a male fantasy. Katherine Heigl, who stars in the film, took media heat for an interview in which she suggested that the women characters in *Knocked Up* were humorless control freaks while the men were sympathetic even though they were losers. Those slackers were big hits with audiences, who took pleasure in controlling women being taken down a peg. Like earlier films that enjoyed bringing high-class dames down a notch, these films enjoy bringing career women down, at least to within reach of plain-looking underachieving men. *Knocked Up* could be read as a commentary on social class since the women are upwardly mobile while the men are downwardly mobile. But like other recent films about uptight career girls, and like the sex comedies before them, they also display anxieties about successful women, who at least need to soften up if not give up careers in order to have successful relationships. Success in the workplace is at odds with success in relationships.

In films such as *Knocked Up*, *New in Town*, *The Proposal*, *Baby Mama*, and *The Switch*, women's strength and success is bought at the price of loneliness and isolation (literally, in *New in Town*). These women have an obsessive need to control everything, including what cannot be controlled. Their attempts at controlling what cannot be controlled, particularly men, is funny. And the men who win their hearts are the ones who stand up to them, who get them under control by breaking through their tough exteriors and reaching into their soft emotional cores. These men are not their economic or intellectual equals; that is to say, they are not traditional patriarchs. Even while they give up their role as breadwinners, they still retain their role as paternal figures, only now as more sensitive, more caring, and more maternal. These men take care of driven, ambitious career women who are too busy overachieving to take care of themselves. They also thaw these ice-queens and put them back in touch with their bodies, often the first step in preparing them to take up their maternal roles. This, however, is a familiar theme from early Hollywood romcom. The contemporary twist is, as the tagline for *The Back-up Plan* tells us, love, marriage, baby—not necessarily in that order! What the tagline doesn't mention is sex. Today, Hollywood need not bother with marriage. Rather, sex, baby, love—often in that order—are the contemporary triple threat. While we are used to seeing sex without love in contemporary Hollywood films, we are not used to seeing babies without sex. As we will see, uncoupling sex and reproduction causes so much anxiety that, often in the most contrived ways, these films manage to bring them back together. And the transformations that take place through pregnancy, particularly to the control-freak career woman, not only recouple sex and reproduction but also bring love and romance into the mix.

In *Knocked Up*, pregnancy is the softening agent that eventually makes the career girl more likable and tolerant and makes the slacker nerd grow up. Of course pregnancy also becomes the reason why our heroine worries about keeping her high-powered television job. Not quite Doris Day's characters before her (who gives up career for family), Alison (Heigl) wonders how she can balance her high-powered career and a baby. And like Doris Day's character in *Lover Come Back*, she is pregnant as a result of a one-night stand. Unlike Doris's characters, however, Alison is not in love with the father of her child. In fact, she doesn't even know him. Rather than pregnancy following from courtship, romance, and marriage, we get the reverse trajectory in recent pregnancy romcoms where pregnancy becomes the vehicle for courtship, romance, and heterocoupling, if not also marriage.

## ROMANTIC REPRODUCTION

Since the presumption has been that babies need fathers and pregnant women need husbands, Hollywood traditionally promoted families after marriage; but failing that, pregnancy can make claims on a man who otherwise wouldn't be a father or a husband; and it can domesticate a woman who otherwise might choose independence.[10] One of the earliest pregnancy comedies, ahead of its time, *The Miracle of Morgan's Creek* (1944) makes a father of unlikely hero Norvell (Eddie Bracken), who marries pregnant Trudy (Betty Hutton) and accepts her six baby boys (fathered by an unknown soldier after too much "punch" at a send-off party) as his own through a series of comic twists and turns around the Hays Production Code's prohibition against premarital sex and against showing pregnancy. In *People Will Talk* (1951), an unorthodox doctor (Cary Grant) not only tells an unwed pregnant patient (Jeanne Crain) that she is not pregnant (after she tries to kill herself) but also marries her in order to provide her with a husband and a father for her child. Although this film is not a comedy, it does make clear early attitudes toward unwed mothers insofar as the heroine would rather commit suicide than face public scorn. In these early exceptional films, reproduction is a means to romance for the heterosexual couple that is brought together through pregnancy as a problem that needs a solution, provided by the male protagonist.

It wasn't until the 1990s (after Demi Moore's controversial appearance, heavily pregnant and nude on the cover of *Vanity Fair*) that Hollywood warmed up to pregnancy, particularly in romantic comedies. Indeed, with films such as *Look Who's Talking* (1989) and *Look Who's Talking Too* (1990), *Junior* (1994), *Nine Months* (1995), *Fools Rush In* (1997), *Home Fries* (1998), and *Where the Heart Is* (2000), the subgenre of pregnant romance was born. In these films, pregnancy brings the couple together through a series of comic turns that revolve around a pregnant body and its various quirks. For example, in *Look Who's Talking*, the couple bonds over the birth and infancy of a baby who begins talking as a fetus. Here, an otherwise macho cab driver, James, played by sex symbol John Travolta, becomes tender and loving with the baby, who in some scenes acts as his alter ego, ogling women's breasts and making comments about Mollie's (Kirstie Alley) body. In addition, the baby acts as a bridge between social classes since his mother is a professional. In *Junior*, the couple bond through the pregnancy of a male scientist who has used the female scientist's egg to conceive; all is right in the end when the biological family is not only intact but the woman (the proper vessel for the baby) also becomes pregnant. *Nine Months* tells the story of a man's unwillingness to commit to marriage and children with his longtime girlfriend until he sees the beating heart of his future baby in a sonogram; only the baby makes the man commit to marriage and family life and overcomes the man's suspicions that his girlfriend got pregnant on purpose in order to trap him like a deadly praying mantis (an image repeated several times in the film).

*Fools Rush In*, like *Knocked Up* later, features a one-night stand between strangers that leads to pregnancy first and then romance, and in this case, true love and marriage; here the comedy is not only the effect of the pregnant body with its cravings and out-of-control hormones but also cultural differences between the uptight white businessman and the colorful Latina artist. In Hollywood, the uptight versus "screwy" was usually white man versus white woman and then woman of color or ethnic woman, where femaleness and ethnicity/race contribute to emotional, irrational, even crazy, out-of-control behavior. Now, with the trope of the controlling career woman, we have a combination of uptight and out-of-control (especially when pregnant) in the figure of a successful white woman, who needs to be counterbalanced, if not controlled, by a more laid-back and reasonable white man.

*Home Fries* and *Where the Heart Is*, like *Look Who's Talking* before them, start with a pregnant protagonist who is, or has been, ditched by her lover and eventually falls for a man who acts as a maternal figure by taking care of her and her baby. Again, we have a sensitive man as a counterbalance for an impulsive, sometimes clueless, woman, especially in *Where the Heart Is*, where the male protagonist takes care of the baby most of the time while the mother pursues various other interests. It is seeing him sleeping and holding the baby, seeing him as a potential father, that makes Novalee (Natalie Portman) first realize that she cares for him. From the moment he delivers her baby in a Wal-Mart store, they are destined to be together.

The runaway indie hit *Juno* (2007) is one of the first comedies about a pregnant teenager. Like Trudy in *The Miracle of Morgan's Creek* over fifty years earlier, Juno (Ellen Paige) is a spunky teen. Unlike Trudy, she is also a witty smart aleck who takes her pregnancy in stride. In contrast to *Miracle*, in *Juno* the girl's parents accept the news that she is pregnant calmly and her stepmother immediately takes over prenatal care. Although Juno gives up her son for adoption and does not marry the child's father, by the end of the film through the course of the pregnancy, birth, and adoption, the cute teen couple is united; the film ends with them singing an upbeat duet that declares their love for one another. Even the tough smart-mouthed Juno is softened up by her pregnancy and through it becomes a fitting partner for easygoing, laid-back, sensitive Pollie (Michael Cera).

Recall that in *Knocked Up*, successful career woman Alison (Katherine Heigl) has sex with slacker Ben (Seth Rogan) and gets pregnant. In some ways this is a classic opposites-attract film where ambition meets lazy and pregnancy is the means of bringing them together and balancing them out. Ambitious becomes more laid-back and less controlling, and lazy becomes more responsible and mature. In fact, pregnancy is the perfect counterbalance or alter ego for control-freak Alison (also epitomized by the character of her sister, who controls her husband to the point that he lies about meeting a bunch of guys to play games). Pregnant Alison is presented as out of control or controlled by her hormones. In one scene, Ben tells a raging Alison that her hormones are talking and not her, suggesting that she is possessed by an alien force that is making her do things against her will. Through her pregnancy, Alison's body becomes out of her control and she has to cede her will to her growing belly, overwhelming emotions, and the changes to her life and career that result. As her body becomes rounder and softer, so does her personality. She starts to watch videos with Ben and participate in his slacker activities with real interest. Through her pregnancy and Ben's reactions to it, she begins to care for him.

Ben likewise is transformed by the pregnancy, which creates a bond between him and his father in a scene where his father tells him how much his son means to him and that he too can be a good father. As Ben matures into a suitable father, he also becomes an appropriate mate for Alison. In the process, the film follows the classic boy-meets-girl, boy-loses-girl-and-eventually-gets-her-back pattern of the romantic comedy genre. Only, in this case, the losing and the getting her back is the result of his relationship to her pregnancy. When he doesn't show the proper involvement or interest, Alison tells him to get lost. But when he proves himself by reading all of the baby books and helping her through the birth, he wins her back. Because he becomes more responsible and she becomes less controlling, they can form a couple at the end. More importantly, they form a family. And in these romcoms as mom-coms it is because they are a family that they can be a couple. Like *Nine Months* where Sam (Hugh Grant) wins back his girlfriend by proving that he can be a good father—symbolized by trading in his sports car for a family-friendly SUV—Ben wins back Alison by becoming a responsible father. In both cases, through impending fatherhood the men mature into responsible partners: their acceptance of their role in the family is a sign that they can be proper mates.

More recently, in *Baby Mama* (2008), Angie (Amy Poehler) pretends to be pregnant to collect money from the surrogacy agency and remain close to Kate (Tina Fey). She fakes morning sickness and other "symptoms" of pregnancy and uses a prosthetic belly to maintain her charade (fig. 2.2). Several funny scenes are the result of her fake pregnancy—using pea soup to simulate barfing, the doorman witnessing her pounding on her prosthetic belly, the sonogram where she discovers she really is pregnant. As in traditional romantic comedies that use masquerade, the pretense leads to transformation, especially in the female leads and the development of their friendship. As in earlier romcoms, where the mask turns out to be a version of a truer self, here it turns out that Angie really is pregnant. Moreover, through the course

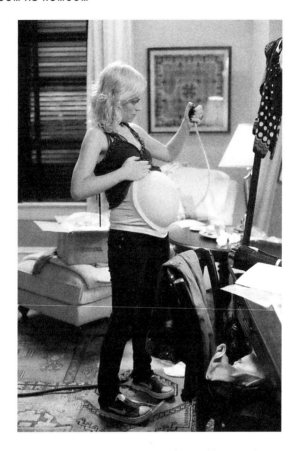

FIGURE 2.2 *Baby Mama*'s Angie (Amy Poehler) and her prosthetic pregnancy. (Courtesy of Universal Studios Licensing LLC, © 2008 Universal Pictures Company)

of her pregnancy and her relation with Kate, Angie matures into a responsible mother, which the film suggests she was not in the beginning. In addition, her pregnancy instigates the boy-loses-girl (or girl-loses-boy) moment when Kate's new boyfriend discovers she has not told him the truth about hiring a surrogate to carry her baby. The film ends happily with both women pregnant and seemingly part of one big happy family that celebrates the babies' first birthdays together.

*Labor Pains* (2009) also uses pregnancy as a masquerade worn by the female lead (fig. 2.3). In classic romcom fashion, the deception leads to character development, transformation, and coupling. The charade of pregnancy is the vehicle that carries both romance and comedy throughout the film. Whereas in earlier romantic comedies, characters dressed in disguises or impersonated other people, here the prosthetic belly and maternity clothes provide the mask. Of course, as in older romcom, the mask turns out to reveal a truer self, or at least a more balanced character. Thea's (Lindsay Lohan) pregnancy is her alter ego that allows her truer self to appear. As in earlier films, Thea's attempts to keep up her masquerade and the juxtaposition of her thin body (ego) and her pregnant body (alter ego) provide much of the humor in the film.

Yet while the pregnant belly transforms characters and reveals their truer natures, the fact that it can be removed also reassures us that there is a thin beautiful female body underneath. It is as if pregnant bellies can be worn over ultrathin bodies that can reappear at any time. The prosthetic pregnancies in these films signal our obsession with the "baby bump" and the post-baby bodies of celebrities who are expected to "get their bodies back" immediately after giving birth, as if their pregnant bellies were not their real bodies, which are lithe and sexy. This notion of the "real body" onto which the pregnancy is merely a temporary attachment is played for laughs in *The Back-up Plan* (2010) when Jennifer Lopez's character shows her boyfriend a picture of her "real ass" to reassure him that, underneath her baby fat, she is still sexy and desirable.

Echoing *Baby Mama*, in *Labor Pains* Thea pretends to be pregnant to keep her job. Through the process of faking it with prosthetic bellies increasing in size, she not only falls for a sensitive man but also discovers she is "better pregnant." It is noteworthy that although Thea is responsible for her younger sister whom she has raised, this is not what prepares her for motherhood. Rather, faking pregnancy is what prepares her for parenthood and makes

FIGURE 2.3 *Labor Pains*'s Thea (Lindsay Lohan) and her fake belly. (Reprinted by permission)

her more mature and self-assured enough to become a career woman. Her relationship with her younger sister is defined by nagging responsibility (and resentment) without the maternal softness that comes with pregnancy. It is her (fake) pregnancy that makes her a mother and not her role as caretaker for her sister.

Thea's faux pregnancy gives her life meaning. People begin to take her seriously in ways they hadn't before. It also gives her career opportunities—and, more important, ambition and self-confidence—that she never had before. She becomes an expert on pregnancy and women seek out her opinions. In a scene where her best friend and her younger sister are telling her to come clean and give up the pretense of being pregnant—since, as they remind her, she can't pretend to be pregnant forever—her answer suggests that pregnancy is her calling, that she is good at it, and that it gives her an authority and confidence that she never had before. In addition to her personal transformation through pregnancy, and because of it, her boss's brother Nick takes an interest in her. Like the sensitive male characters in earlier films, he takes a parental or protective role in relation to her pregnancy and by so doing proves himself a caring paternal figure. Through her "pregnancy" they fall in love. And the film ends with her really pregnant. As in *Baby Mama*, the fake pregnancy prepares the protagonists for real pregnancy and sets up the comedy, romance, and the possibility of mature, committed relationships.

As in earlier films like *Nine Months* and *Knocked Up*, in *The Back-up Plan* the male protagonist proves his worthiness to be a father by attending to the needs of the baby-to-be. In this case, he does so by buying a custom-made baby stroller for the twins that Zoe (Jennifer Lopez) is carrying as a result of artificial insemination with an anonymous donor's sperm. Their relationship turns on whether or not he accepts the twins as his own and whether he can prove he will not leave them. By the end of the film, after the birth of the twins, he is shown doing all of the childcare while Zoe is waiting in bed. He comes in to tell her about the babies' poop and she tells him that she doesn't want to talk about it because it ruins "the mood." Like *Baby Mama* and *Labor Pains*, the film ends with Zoe pregnant with a "real" baby as a result of sex with her new love—"the one"—that is stronger because it has already withstood pregnancy. This "real" pregnancy and "real" baby reassure us that finding "the one" and having it all are possible, although they may require patience and luck. Indeed, in this vein, both *Baby Mama* and *The Back-up Plan* can be interpreted as cautionary tales about moving to artificial insemination and technological babies too quickly when more romantic babies fathered by "the one" are right around the corner.

In addition, these films both display and assuage anxieties about boyfriends or husbands splitting when they find out their partners are pregnant. Whereas earlier films either flirt with a straying husband, as in *She's Having a Baby* (1988), or use the pregnancy as the boy-loses-girl moment as in *Nine Months* or *Baby Mama*, *The Back-up Plan* reassures us that all along the man is committed to both his beloved and her babies (even though he has just met her and the babies are not his). The boy-loses-girl moment in *The Back-up Plan* is the result of Zoe's familiar fear that the man doesn't want to commit to a family, especially when the children aren't biologically related to him. This is played in reverse in *Labor Pains* when Thea worries that Nick will leave her when he finds out that she isn't really pregnant. In all of these films, however, pregnancy brings the couple together and makes them closer than they would have been without it. Contrary to the worry that men can't commit to babies, these films reassure us that babies—or at least pregnancy—contribute to romance and long-term love relationships. Pregnancy becomes the means of finding romance and love, even one's soul mate or "the one," as in *The Back-up Plan*. The man's suitability as a loving partner is demonstrated through his ability to be a caring father. "The one" turns out to be the one who is willing to take on paternal responsibility and commit not only to the woman but also to the baby. The playboy or slacker must become the family man, who is the true romantic hero. In the pregnancy subgenre of romcom, both characters become fit mates and romantic partners through the transformations of the pregnant body. The future family that the pregnancy evokes or the fantasy of family has become the true romantic fantasy in an era of sexual liberation, affairs, single-parent households, and divorce as the norm. Pregnancy becomes the vehicle through which romance, love, and marriage are delivered.

Momcoms, in which pregnancy is a central theme, also often incorporate gross-out humor as part of the comedy. Like other recent gross-out comedies, here the body and its out-of-control emissions or cravings are funny because they cross the line of cultural taboos by exposing bodily boundaries.[11] Unlike some other gross-out comedies such as *There's Something About Mary* (1998), *American Pie* (1999), or *Along Came Polly* (2004), however, in momcom the pregnant body is both the object of the gaze and the butt of the joke. The semen spewing or explosive diarrhea in these other gross-out films are played for laughs, but these men's bodies are not also sex objects in any traditional sense; rather, they are the antisex object, the nerds and geeks awkwardly seeking sexual satisfaction. The pregnant protagonists in momcom, on the other hand, are beautiful sexy women whose changing bodies are funny precisely because their proportions, emissions, and bizarre cravings are at odds with their appeal as sex objects.[12] From Juno's blue slushy barfed into a vase to Angie's pea-soup puke, morning sickness is played for laughs. So is the urgent need to pee, which is what leads Novalee (Natalie Portman) to give birth in a Wal-Mart in *Where the Heart Is*. The pregnant body is a leaky body, even a gushing body, as water breaking becomes a joke in *Fools Rush In*, *Knocked Up*, and *Baby Mama*, among others. The gaseous emissions of the beautiful pregnant women Zoe (Jennifer Lopez) and Angela (Heather Graham) provide gross-out humor in *The Back-up Plan* and *Baby on Board* (2009). Of course, the size of the pregnant body as it moves through space—or gets stuck in it—is a source of comedy in most of these films. The pregnant body is the quintessential leaky body out of control, whose liquid and gaseous emissions—not to mention the "emission" of another body—conjure the uncanny predicament of human embodiment, not quite animal but not master of itself either. Throughout the history of comedy, the uncontrollable aspects of embodiment have been played for laughs. Funny pregnancies follow in this tradition, only now the "gross" pregnant body is the butt of the joke.

The changes in a woman's body during pregnancy have become the outward signs of deeper transformations in both male and female characters, changes that provoke humor and romance. The processes of pregnancy and childbirth are not only romanticized in all of their gross-out glory but also the vehicles for romance.[13] Pregnancy is a new form of adventure and masquerade that allows characters to assume a temporary alter ego that changes them into suitable romantic partners through the physical humor definitive of romantic comedies as they have evolved from screwball through nervous romcom to momcom. Moreover, this new subgenre of film complicates, and yet reassures us about, the connection between sex, romance, and reproduction. If the nervous comedies of the

1960s and 1970s uncoupled sex, romance, and reproduction, these recent films fuse them again but in the reverse order of their earlier predecessors in sex comedies. Now, rather than follow from romance, reproduction leads to romance; even sex with strangers can produce a happy ending if a romantic pregnancy brings the couple together. In sum, momcom is a new subgenre of romcom in which pregnancy provides the adventure, the transformation, the alter ego, the masquerade, the mistaken identity, the comedy, and the romance of earlier romcoms.

## ACCIDENT AND EXCESS

### THE "CHOICE" TO HAVE A BABY

Is it really so hard to grasp why so many young women would choose motherhood? Isn't this the path toward adulthood still thrust upon them by the old but persisting ideological constructions of femaleness? Doesn't motherhood still equal adult womanhood in the popular imagination? Don't the new reproductive technologies further develop this equation of womanhood and motherhood?

—ANGELA DAVIS (1991; IN 2000:482)

**TWENTY-FIVE YEARS AGO**, philosopher Margaret Simons described the complexity of women's reproductive choices: "few women in our society experience motherhood as a real choice" because so many women do not have other opportunities for personal development while others feel that by becoming a mother they must sacrifice other opportunities" (Simons 1984:357). In spite of changes since the 1990s, Simons' description still rings true as women's choices continue to be restricted by cultural and social expectations. Although many women are choosing not to have children, most women still feel some pressure to do so. And many women find themselves pregnant "by accident" and end up having families without planning to have them . . . or, at least, not yet. In addition, as Simons points out, most poor women do not have many options other than having babies. Many middle-class women still feel the tension between having a family and having a career. In some cases, the dream of "having it all" becomes an exhausting schedule of soccer and dance lessons, work, cooking, and cleaning, where the demands of juggling career and family require high levels of caffeine and prescription drugs like Prozac (an antidepressant) and Ambien (sleeping pills). More than twenty years ago, philosopher Iris Young described the experience of pregnancy as opening onto an expansive sense of time and space that gave the mother-to-be a new sense of herself in relation to others (Young 1990). But the pressures of contemporary mother-hood often leave women exhausted and frustrated by expectations of perfect children, well-kept houses, and "keeping up with the Joneses," along with having successful careers.

Critically engaging Young's description of chosen pregnancy, Caroline Lundquist develops a phenomenology of "rejected and denied" pregnancies, which further complicates the notion of reproductive choice. She concludes that "although the choice to carry an unintended pregnancy to term may always be socially conditioned, such conditioning doesn't necessarily imply a lack of freedom; a constrained choice may yet be a morally significant one. Even so, to assume the autonomy of such decisions would ignore the powerful social forces, many of them internalized, that condition reproductive choices" (Lundquist 2008:152). She argues that reproductive choice is not like other types of choice since there is always an element of passivity that cannot be controlled by sub-jective agency. In addition, she points out that even when unwanted pregnancies become "chosen," we should not underestimate "the socially overdetermined, potentially heart-wrenching process by which an unwanted pregnancy comes to be positively accepted" (151). Women's reproductive choices frequently involve vexed deci-sions in uncertain and complicated situations that are far from straightforward when it comes to freely choosing to have a baby.

In a strange and perhaps strained resonance with Lundquist's article, recent pregnancy films both reflect and transform changing social contexts, expectations, and norms for pregnant women and girls. They also show women struggling with unwanted or at least unplanned pregnancies; and while they may not explore in significant ways the social determination of such decisions, they do complicate choice. Many of these films show how women both do and do not choose pregnancy and childbirth. In this sense, although they all embrace women having babies and do not consider that they will not have them, they also complicate the notion of choice. Playing off of pro-choice rhetoric about "owning" one's body and having a right to decide for oneself, these films also take up the "accidental" and "unplanned" nature of many pregnancies. In this regard, they manifest an anxiety about the accidental and uncontrollable aspect of pregnancy.

As Anna's (Abigail Breslin) opening voice-over tells us in *My Sister's Keeper* (2009), most babies are accidents, the result of drinking and lack of birth control; the only people who plan to have babies are those who cannot. In this dramatic weeper, controlling pregnancy is not funny when "designer baby" Anna is 11 years old and suing her parents for medical emancipation. Like the funny women choosing to have their babies in momcoms, Anna too uses arguments familiar from pro-choice rhetoric ("my body, my choice"). Anna was genetically engineered specifically as a match for her older sister, who needs a kidney transplant. Unlike most babies, as she says, Anna is a "designer baby" and "not an accident." Yet, as the horrible cancer ravages her sister's life, and that of her whole family, Anna wonders about the accident that is life itself. Unlike the pregnancy comedies, however, in this tearjerker the accident cannot be redeemed through choice, in spite of desperate and forceful attempts by the girls' mother (Cameron Diaz); or the fact that Anna wins her lawsuit and the right to choose the medical fate of her own body. At the end of the film, Anna's voice-over tells us that she thought that she was brought into the world to save her sister, but that was not possible. She muses that she doesn't know why she lives and her sister dies; as much as we try, life cannot be controlled.

*My Sister's Keeper* teaches us that accidents happen even in the world of genetic engineering—it is noteworthy in this context that the Greek word *symptoma* means both symptom and accident. One lesson of this film is that even genetic engineering and medical manipulation cannot stop the symptom/accident from asserting itself. Still, as we will see, genetic counseling makes women not only responsible for the choice of whether or not to have the baby but also for what baby to have. This new form of eugenics caters to wealthy and middle-class white women; this is perhaps why anxieties over miscegenation drive many popular Hollywood pregnancy films in genres from comedy to horror.

Films such as *She's Having a Baby* (1988), *Juno* (2007), and *Baby Mama* (2008), in which characters are trying to get pregnant but can't, also show that pregnancy is not something that can be easily controlled. At one end of the spectrum, we have women who get pregnant by accident and then have to transform their accidental pregnancies into chosen babies. At the other end, we have career women racing against their "biological clocks" in order to get a baby in "under the wire," even if by "resorting" to ARTs. The anxiety over lack of control and "accidents" is resolved in these films through women's determination to have their babies and, in some cases, their transformation from reluctant to doting mothers. This anxiety over the accidental nature of pregnancy—and of life itself—runs deep in that no one wants to be an accident, which could amount to being unwanted. Everyone wants to be wanted, and these films reassure us that, in the end, everyone is wanted. As Juno's schoolmate says at the abortion clinic, "Every baby wants to be borned."

## "IT WAS AN ACCIDENT"

It is telling that in our culture we refer to unplanned pregnancy as an "accidental" pregnancy—especially when even planned pregnancies cannot be controlled (since, whether or not an embryo attaches to a uterus and a baby is born is, to a fundamental degree, out of anyone's control). If pregnancy is not chosen, if indeed it an accident, then, as abortion rights advocates argue, women should have the right to choose whether or not to carry fetuses to term and give birth to babies. Yet the idea that pregnancy is accidental suggests that, although women can decide to have babies or not, in a significant sense they do not *choose* to get pregnant. Pregnancy is something that just happens, by accident. In many of the recent pregnancy films this is the case. But what does it mean to think of pregnancy as an accident, especially when the sex that "caused" it is usually chosen, if not also planned (with the exception of rape, of course)?

In terms of an analysis of accidental pregnancy versus control over it, it is interesting that early advocates of birth control called for "voluntary motherhood" (Gordon 1973). These activists and suffragists were not arguing for artificial birth control, which they deemed "unnatural," but rather for controlled sexual relations and abstinence that would allow a woman to choose *when* to have children. They wanted to eliminate "involuntary motherhood," which they saw as the norm. It was not a question of whether or not women should have children, but when. Women were expected to have children, and pregnancy and birth were seen as natural parts of women's lives. But advocates for voluntary motherhood wanted women to have more control over the process. Obviously, we have made tremendous advances in the technologies of birth control and attitudes toward it since the nineteenth century, but even so, roughly half of American women get pregnant "by accident" before age 45 (Benfer 2009). Women are still expected to have children; those who choose not to are seen as somehow deficient or abnormal. Moreover, in spite of huge advances in birth control options and their availability in the United States, pregnancy is still something that just happens, something that ultimately cannot be controlled. The very association between pregnancy and accident points to the contingency of reproductive choices, choices that have become the subject of several recent Hollywood films. Hollywood's anxieties about reproductive choice and the often "accidental" nature of pregnancy are multifaceted. Seeing women turn "accidental" and unwanted pregnancies into chosen and cherished babies reassures us that we were not accidents because we were chosen by our mothers—a reassuring fantasy, to be sure.

One of the most conservative examples of turning an unwanted pregnancy into a wanted baby is the film *Bella* (2006), an anti-abortion tale written, directed, and acted by Catholic pro-life activists. It is the story of Nina (Tammy Blanchard) and her unplanned pregnancy, and from the beginning it is clear that she wants an abortion and is not ready to have a child. Her coworker José (played by Eduardo Verástegui—a real-life Catholic pro-life activist) convinces her to have the baby and give it to him to raise. On the back of the DVD, this act and José's compassion for both Nina and her unborn baby are described as "a simple gesture of kindness" that turns an "ordinary day into an unforgettable experience." This so-called "ordinary day" is the day that Nina discovers she is pregnant, certainly a monumental day in any woman's life. This touching film shows our gentle and caring protagonist José guiding, helping, and persuading Nina to have her baby. In the end, and through flashbacks throughout the film, we see Nina's beautiful daughter Bella, and another little girl like her, laughing and playing. We discover through the course of the film, as if to make the whole baby exchange more perverse, that on his way to sign a multimillion dollar soccer contract, José is in a car that kills a little girl and he uses this traumatic memory to convince Nina of the sanctity of life; he uses this story to convince her to have her daughter and let him raise her, in what seems to be a kind of penance for his earlier hubris and negligence that led to the death of an innocent girl. He doesn't want the "death of another innocent girl" on his conscience. By raising Nina's daughter, he redeems himself and her, while literally showing the audience the beauty of life in the person of Bella, the young, joyful girl playing on the beach. By the end of the film, no one—audience, mother, sensitive hero José—can imagine not allowing this gorgeous young girl to live and thrive.

*To Save a Life* (2009) has a similar theme. This Christian film deals with the problems of teenagers today and in so doing, like *Bella*, suggests that the protagonist of the film, Jake (Randy Wayne), might make up for not being there for his friend (who had committed suicide) by convincing his own pregnant girlfriend not to have an abortion. *Bella* and other recent films about accidental pregnancies that become chosen babies speak to an existential anxiety about the very notion of choice and being chosen, since pregnancy (like most things) is never something we can control. Furthermore, *Bella* is an explicit argument against abortion, and while other films may be subtler, most recent pregnancy films are implicitly against abortion as a viable option for "accidental" or "unwanted" pregnancies. Rather, in Hollywood films unwanted pregnancies become wanted and loved babies.


## CAUTIONARY TALES

Many films that do seriously raise the issue of abortion have a scary dimension that makes them feel more like cautionary warnings than pro-choice alternatives. For example, the HBO film *If These Walls Could Talk* (1996) begins with a montage of women's rights activists and pro-choice marches. But even as it is framed by these feminist images, it tells a tragic tale of three women who find themselves pregnant and must choose whether or not to have their babies. The first woman, Claire (Demi Moore), whose husband was killed in World War II, has an illegal abortion and apparently dies as a result; the second woman (Sissy Spacek) is married, already has children, and even though she didn't plan to have another, decides to have her baby; the third woman Christine (Anne Heche) doesn't want to give up her chance to finish college and have a career, so she has an abortion; but just after the doctor (Cher) finishes the procedure, an abortion protester bursts in and guns her down, leaving our protagonist traumatized and covered in blood. This supposedly feminist film explicitly connects abortion and death both visually and in terms of its narrative. Barbara (Sissy Spacek), the only woman who decides to have her baby, is safe, while the other two are traumatized or die. Although the quirky indie film *Citizen Ruth* (1996) does deal with abortion rights head-on, and makes fun of abortion protesters, in the end Ruth (Laura Dern) has a miscarriage and not an abortion.

In the Romanian film *4 Months, 3 Weeks, and 2 Days* (2007)—significant here, even though our focus is on Hollywood, because it was widely touted as a feminist film—the camera lingers on a close-up of the "face" of the aborted fetus lying on the bathroom floor, while it refuses to show the pregnant body (if anything, the woman's flat stomach, supposedly nearly five months pregnant, looks anorexic). Furthermore, the young woman protoganist's college roommate, whose later abortion sets the tone for the film, suggests that she may quit having sex with her boyfriend rather than face pregnancy or abortion (of course, in large part the story is about what happens when abortion is illegal). As the tagline tells us, "Two college roommates have 24 hours to make the ultimate choice as they finalize arrangements for a black market abortion." This line suggests that the ultimate choice is whether or not to have an abortion, but it also makes this choice ambiguous in that both women are faced with the "ultimate choice" but only one of them, the roommate, is pregnant. Although the narrative is a gripping tale of two women dealing with the trauma of pregnancy and illegal abortion, visually the film pits the woman's body against the fetus, which as we know from the title of the film is the true protagonist.

Although not a Hollywood film, *4 Months* is indicative of the separation, even opposition, between maternal body and fetus that seems to require that the camera, or gaze, focus on one or the other but not both. We only can see the pregnant body as a sexy body if we don't see the fetus growing inside it. In *4 Months*, we simply do not see a pregnant body, there is never one shown; but we see the fetus bigger than life, filling the entire screen. Compare this film to the Hollywood film that makes the fetus the protagonist of its story, *Look Who's Talking* (1989), which gives us a very unsexy pregnant Kirstie Alley, who at one point (wearing a black-and-white outfit) says she looks like a giant pilgrim and who is also seen in overalls or little girlish outfits with big bows. Certainly the unborn fetus voiced by Bruce Willis is the protagonist of this film. His complaints about his maternal environment and the birthing process make it clear that he is an autonomous individual at odds with his mother, if not in control of her.

The Hollywood hit *Revolutionary Road* (2008) ends with April Wheeler (Kate Winslet) bleeding and dying from an at-home abortion, after her husband (Leonardo DiCaprio) suggests that not only is she an unfit mother but also an abomination for even considering an abortion. Again, this film presents the story of a woman whose dreams are dashed by motherhood in the suburbs; the tragic ending can be interpreted as a warning against abortion both because it causes death and because it is selfish, the former perhaps resulting from the latter. The British film *Vera Drake* (2004) is a notable exception to the trend of connecting abortion to death, although the film's protagonist ends up in prison and one of her patients almost dies as a result of an infection caused by her abortion. Like *4 Months, 3 Weeks, and 2 Days*, *Vera Drake* is also a cautionary tale about the dangers of making abortion illegal. Still, the number of popular films that deal with the complexities of abortion are few, and most Hollywood films either avoid it altogether or implicitly warn against it. Even the quirky indie comedy *Expecting Mary* (2010) has an unsympathetic mother who advises her daughter Mary to have an abortion that they can hide by saying she has appendicitis, implying that although pregnancy is no longer something to be ashamed of, having an abortion is shameful and needs to be hidden. Rather than have the abortion, Mary runs away, and her pregnancy becomes a funny adventure through which she finds a more loving family and meets several oddball characters.

## FETAL PARADOX

In these films, it is as if the fetus is set up in opposition with the maternal body. This should not surprise us given that, as many feminists have discussed, since the development of ultrasound technologies that allow us to see the fetus, the fetus has been extended various legal rights figured as competing with its mother's rights.[1] In fact, lawsuits on behalf of fetuses have led to the conviction and imprisonment of many women. And abortion is still a hot-button issue in national politics. Some pro-life activists seem to value the life of the fetus over the life of the mother. In Hollywood and in the international films mentioned above, the focus is on either the fetus and potential abortion or the maternal body, but not both. There is something unsettling, it seems, about seeing the maternal body and the fetus as part of a dynamic symbiotic relationship. For example, in *4 Months, 3 Weeks, and 2 Days*, as aforementioned, there is a long lingering shot of a fetus, but we do not see a maternal body or any body that is visibly pregnant. The same is true in *Vera Drake*, *Citizen Ruth*, *If These Walls Could Talk*, *and Revolutionary Road*. In all of these so-called feminist films that tackle the issue of abortion, there seems to be a strict, if unspoken, code that abortions and fetuses cannot be shown in conjunction with the visibly pregnant bodies that they may inhabit. The women in these films remain slim, even anorexic-looking by everyday standards, showing no signs of even slightly expanding pregnant bellies or breasts.

It is notable that apparent exceptions are Amy Heckerling's *Look Who's Talking* and *Look Who's Talking Too* (1990).[2] In these films, the fetus as protagonist is represented with a distinctively unfetus-looking baby doll floating in a cloudlike womb that frequently threatens to become a storm unsettling our small hero/heroine. The fetus (voiced by Bruce Willis in the first film and

Roseanne Barr in the second) often complains about its maternal digs and makes snide comments about the actions of the body that sustains it. If ultrasound technology allows us to imagine the fetus as an individual apart from, and at odds with, the maternal body, these films bring that fantasy to life with talking fetuses and a clueless mother (Kirstie Alley) dressed in outfits that make her look like an overgrown child. It is as if, when showing the fetus, the maternal body must be infantilized and de-eroticized (as it is in *Look Who's Talking*). In most recent pregnant momcoms, where the fetus is never more than a blip on an ultrasound, the pregnant body is usually funny and gross, and occasionally cute and even sexy. In both *Look Who's Talking* films, on the other hand, the male fetus (and then baby boy) serves as an alter ego of sorts for the male lover and partner (John Travolta); for example, when the young Mikie sees a woman with large breasts, Travolta's character asks him, "Are you thinking what I'm thinking?" and Mikie responds "Lunch?"

With its "Other-within," the maternal body presents a conundrum for Hollywood. The fetal paradox is resolved in various ways in pregnancy films. In most comedies, the focus is on the woman and her relationship to her expanding body and the strange sensations of this Other-within. In *Look Who's Talking*, the film takes the unlikely perspective of the fetus by giving it voice and consciousness. In horror films, on the other hand, this Other-within becomes a threat, a dangerous alien or monster within that threatens not only the mother but also those around her. Whether they make this antagonism between fetus and mother funny or horrific, these films suggest that the fetus may be the one in charge rather than the mother; it is the will and choice of the fetus—or that of a higher power, usually evil in horror films—that directs the pregnancy and birth rather than the mother's will and choice. In the horror genre, as we will see, the opposition between the maternal body and the fetus becomes extreme to the point of a life-and-death struggle.

## "BABY HUNGER" AND EXCESSIVE "CHOICES"

> [M]otherhood among Black and Latina teens is constructed as a moral and social evil—but even so, they are denied accessible and affordable abortions. Moreover, teen mothers are ideologically assaulted because of their premature and impoverished entrance into the realm of motherhood while older, whiter, and wealthier women are coaxed to buy the technology to assist them in achieving an utterly commodified motherhood.
>
> —ANGELA DAVIS (1991; IN 2000:482)

Unlike the horror films that represent the fetus as a threat, the pregnant comedies reassure us that even if the maternal body may be funny, or even gross, the babies it produces are not only worth the labor but also complete a life that is otherwise lacking. In several momcoms, while the pregnancy is an accident, and the woman is not ready to have a baby, the birth of the baby gives new meaning to her life. For example, in *Waitress* (2007), although pie-chef Jenna (Keri Russell) is certain that she does not want a baby and even bakes "bad baby pie," when the baby is born we see her and her new baby girl in soft-focus as the center of the universe as everyone else in the room visually fades away. Minutes after her daughter is born, she dumps both her husband and her boyfriend, suggesting that her new love will take their place. In fact, given her reaction to the baby ("oh my god, OH . . . MY . . . GOD") and that the film ends with her and her small daughter dressed in identical yellow dresses walking into the sunset, the film implies that her daughter fulfills her life in ways that these men cannot. The film makes clear that Jenna's pregnancy with, and the birth of, her daughter puts her in touch with her own mother, who taught her to make pies; and likewise, she plans to teach her daughter to make pies. In *Saved!* (2004) teenager Mary (Jena Malone) gets pregnant after onetime sex with her gay boyfriend (her self-styled mission from God to "save him)." Like Jenna in *Waitress*, Mary does not want a baby—to the point that she is hoping that her period has stopped because she has cancer and not because she is pregnant (riding her bike home from "picking up" a pregnancy test, she says over and over "let it be cancer"). Her pregnancy causes her to question her Christian faith. Yet, once the baby is born, her faith is reaffirmed because, as her voice-over insists, there must be a God because her newborn daughter is so beautiful.

At the other end of the Hollywood spectrum from these women and girls who don't want babies, but find themselves in love with them when they appear, are the women who desperately want babies and will go to extremes to get them. In some recent momcoms, career women suffer from what Sylvia Ann Hewlett calls "baby hunger" and long for babies to fulfill them (Hewlett 2002). These films seem to suggest that Sigmund Freud is right when he maintains that having babies is the best way to cure women's neruoses. For example, in *Miss Conception* (2008) when Georgina (Heather Graham) finds out she is on her last egg, she haunts nightclubs and funerals trying to find "Mr. Right Now" to inseminate her before it is too late. Jennifer Garner's character in *Juno* has a successful career but wants a baby more than anything else. And successful businesswoman Kate (Tina Fey) tries artificial insemination and resorts to surrogacy to have a baby in *Baby Mama*. This is also the case with Zoe (Jennifer Lopez) in *The Back-up Plan* (2010), who wants a baby before it is too late even though she hasn't found "the one" (husband) and with Kassie (Jennifer Aniston) in *The Switch* (2010), who decides to have a baby as a single woman.

These films echo anxieties over reproductive choice, the accidental nature of conception, and the anxiety of waiting too long that fills the tabloids with stories of actresses (think of tabloid reports of Jennifer Aniston or Celine Dion longing for babies) who have put off having families and are now desperately racing against their "biological clocks" to have babies—women who suffer from "baby hunger." Turning the pro-choice rhetoric on its head, Hewlett argues that, for career women, not having babies becomes a "creeping nonchoice" and "unwanted choices," where they "accidentally" have given up their right to choose by ignoring their biological clocks, which leaves them desperate and unhappy (Hewlett 2002:21, 26, 84, 254, 262). Again, the language of pro-choice is co-opted for seemingly feminist arguments, only now in favor of renewed family values.

Within the rhetoric of either pro-choice or pro-life discourses, how can we account for what one of Hewlett's research subjects calls a "creeping nonchoice"? How can we even make sense of the phrase "unwanted choices"? In order to do so, we need to complicate our conception of choice—for the ways in which women choose or do not choose pregnancy and family are complex and contingent. It is rarely, if ever, the case that pregnancy is the result of a willful decision that can be controlled. Even when a woman decides she wants a baby, the route to getting one is often circuitous and always unpredictable, the difficulties of which are usually covered over in glossy spreads featuring 40-something celebrities giving birth or sporting baby bumps. The notion of "unwanted choices" and "creeping nonchoice" further complicates women's reproductive choice with the suggestion that women who do not have children have not necessarily chosen not to, even if they have not chosen to have families (Hewlett 2002:21, 26, 77, 254, 255). Interestingly, Hewlett also co-opts the language of choice, only now as a nonchoice; and her notion of "unwanted choice" echoes the phrase "unwanted pregnancy," only now *lack* of pregnancy is what is unwanted. In addition to the ways in which cultural and traditional expectations affect women's choices to have babies, women's reproductive choices are also imagined as further complicated by the unpredictability of human bodies and women's so-called "biological clocks."

As we have seen, Hewlett calls this biological clock a "ticking time bomb" and advises young women to start planning families early to make sure to get at least two babies in "under the wire" before they have to "snatch a child from the jaws of menopause" or, worse, before it is too late (2002:60, 64, 152). What she calls "baby hunger" suggests that women's yearning for babies is also not a choice but rather a craving or hunger that is beyond their control. Neither is the "biological clock" something that women choose; rather they are slaves to it. To avoid either "unwanted choices" or uncontrollable and unfulfillable hunger for babies, Hewlett advises young women to be more "intentional" about their life choices, particularly finding a husband and having a family. She argues that careers will wait, but families won't. She advises young women to heed their biological clocks and make decisions in light of their limited fertility as the guiding principle of their lives. In the end, she makes the eugenics argument that educated, middle-class women having babies is good for the country, suggesting that educated white women have a duty to have babies because they provide the "best" gene pool. Hewlett concludes that "having it all, it turns out, is a good idea—for individual women and for the nation" (2002:266). But she warns that feminism or other "hype and misinformation" lead women to believe that they can wait until they are older to have families. Her book advises women to make having babies their top priority while they are young, suggesting that adoption, like ARTs, is to be avoided or used only as a last resort.

Hewlett's manifesto has a tone of urgency and danger that suggests that pregnancy both is and is not a choice for women. This is to say, pregnancy is out of our control because of biological clocks and natural cravings for babies that are part of our genetic makeup. Not having babies becomes the unwanted nonchoice. And genetics itself becomes a reason for having babies. Yet Hewlett urges women to be more intentional about their life choices, to the point that her call to women to find partners and start having babies in their twenties is at odds with cultural notions of love and romance at the heart of traditional notions of family. As we have seen, however, these notions of love and romance are changing such that romantic love, at least in Hollywood, is the result of choosing to have babies now instead of waiting for planned pregnancy, Mr. Right, or a soul mate—"the one," as Jennifer Lopez's character Zoe says in *The Back-up Plan*. Even the title of this film—*The Back-up Plan*—implies that women are both in control but not in control of their reproductive lives: Zoe hasn't found "the one," which presumably was the original plan or plan A, so she has to move to plan B (recall that the film was originally titled "Plan B," until studio executives realized that this is also the name of the morning-after pill).

Although the issue of how to have both a family and career is an important one for women, Hewlett's conclusion, like the "conclusions" of Hollywood films, functions not only to reaffirm conservative family values but also the racist notion that educated white women have a duty to produce babies because they will produce better babies than uneducated nonwhite women. While education and financial security may produce "better" children in the sense of producing children who are healthier and might score better on tests, this is an argument for raising the standard of living for all rather than limiting the reproduction of poor nonwhite women while encouraging the reproduction of middle-class white women. Given that Hollywood shows us predominantly middle-class white women yearning for babies and getting them, it implicitly follows the eugenics message of Hewlett's controversial book—namely, that white women should have babies before it is too late and that babies are the answer to the problems these women face in their lives, including problems with faith or men (e.g., *Saved!* and *Waitress*). In addition, *Precious* (2009), one of the few filmic representations of black women having babies, is violent, abject, and horrifying. The same could be said of Todd Solonz's indie mindbender *Palindromes* (2004), in which the black version of Aviva is fat and unattractive while the white versions are thin and attractive. This juxtaposition of beautiful happy educated middle-class white girls and women having babies and abject violent uneducated black girls and women having babies works to reinforce latent racist eugenics notions that women of color need to stop having so many "bad" babies to "put on the welfare," as Precious's mother says, and white women need to start having more "good" babies to "uplift the nation" (cf. Ikemoto 1995–96; Ortiz & Briggs 2003; Robertson 2009; Morgan 2010).

## "FERTILE MYRTLE"

Even Jennifer Lopez's "big butt" again becomes the butt of a joke in *The Back-up Plan* when Zoe shows her lover a picture of her "ass" to prove that it used to be sexy before she got pregnant; of course, J-Lo's butt has been a controversial subject for years. Although it is unclear whether or not Jennifer Lopez is playing a Latina in *The Back-up Plan*, her character Zoe's fertility is played for laughs when she becomes pregnant with redheaded twins after artificial insemination. Something about a Latina mom giving birth to redheads is supposed to be funny—unless redheads themselves are funny. When right after their first sexual encounter Zoe's new lover learns that she is pregnant, he jokes, "I don't think it happens that fast," suggesting of course that in her it might. By the end of the film, having just given birth to twins, Zoe is pregnant with his child, which is her third. Zoe—one of the few possibly nonwhite protagonists of mainstream Hollywood mom-coms—gets pregnant very easily. And unlike most of the heroines of recent pregnancy films, she ends up with three babies instead of just one. Perhaps we should be suspicious that this fertile Latina sends the message that nonwhite women are hyperfertile and having too many babies.

*Quinceañera* (2006) also features a Latina protagonist in 14-year-old Magdalena (Emily Rios), who is still a virgin but gets pregnant after fooling around with her boyfriend (who we later find out ejaculated on her thigh and that is how she got pregnant). This Latina teen is so fertile that even the close proximity of semen gets her pregnant. Although her Catholic father expels her from the house when he discovers she is pregnant, the film ends with a happy family reunion and a coming-out party with the young protagonist heavily pregnant in her party dress. Like Zoe in *The Back-up Plan*, Magdalena appears hyperfertile to the point that just being near semen gets her pregnant. This image of the teenager as hyperfertile extends to the runaway indie hit *Juno*, which gives a new—positive—spin on teenage pregnancy. At the same time that Hollywood is cashing in on the anxieties of career women waiting too long to have babies, it is refiguring the pregnant teenager as heroine in films such as *Saved!*, *Juno*, and *Expecting Mary*. This "Fertile Myrtle," as she is called in *Juno*, is imagined as getting pregnant at the drop of a hat, or at least at the drop of semen.

The more recent *Precious* also shows a hyperfertile teen pregnant with her second child when the film begins. Rather than making teenage pregnancy funny and cute, this film shows the horrors of incest and abuse. Yet, in the end, it is her two babies that give Precious's life meaning in the midst of the trauma and despair that is the rest of her life. Precious is one of the only pregnant black teenagers in Hollywood film; and she is the only mainstream pregnant teen who is separated from her mother/family at the end of the film. Unlike *Riding in Cars with Boys*, *Saved!*, *Quinceañera*, *Juno*, and *Expecting Mary*, in which the pregnant teens are reunited with their families by the end of the film, *Precious* ends with our HIV-positive protagonist leaving with her infant and Down syndrome toddler, which, relatively speaking, is one of the most upbeat moments in this otherwise tragic film. Unbelievably, in *Juno* and *Saved!* the teens' parents have surprisingly understanding and accepting (and tellingly unrealistic) reactions to their daughter's pregnancy. Even Magdalena's mother in *Quinceañera* is sympathetic to her plight and tries to protect her from her father's rage. In *Precious*, on the other hand, the mother's rage is constant and even exacerbated by her teenage daughter's second pregnancy, which climaxes with her mother throwing Precious's newborn son on the floor. It is noteworthy that her mother's anger over Precious's pregnancy is a result of her jealousy of her daughter's pregnancy and not that she disapproves of it; to the contrary, she envies Precious and sees her babies as a way to get "the welfare."

Certainly the indie drama *Precious* is an anomaly amongst the other Hollywood comic charmers. This contrast contributes to the larger canvas of film in which middle-class white pregnant teens are represented as cute, funny, and end up warmly embraced by friends and family, while this black teen is doomed to a life of poverty and disease in spite of her own best efforts and those of her teacher. While the white babies born as a result of teen sex in *Manny & Lo*, *The Opposite of Sex*, *Riding in Cars with Boys*, *Juno*, and *Expecting Mary* are promised happy lives, and many of these films implicitly seem to endorse teen pregnancy, the babies born to Precious have very little hope of a better life. Unlike their white counterparts, they don't have a loving extended family, financial security, or the promise of higher education and/or success in their futures. *Precious* is a complex film that not only shows the conditions of poverty and illiteracy that many African American women face but also shows how babies, even those that are the result of incest and rape, can bring light into a young woman's life. Even as it forces its audience to confront the culture and poverty and violence that leave many African American women few choices, it also reinforces stereotypes.

The same is true of one of the few representations of African American pregnant teens before *Precious*—*Just Another Girl on the I.R.T.* (1992). While the protagonist of *Just Another Girl*, Chantel (Ariyan Johnson) is as plucky and smart-mouthed as Juno, she is not an entirely sympathetic character. In fact, in contrast to the character Juno, who was well liked by the critics, Chantel was defamed by critics, even those who acclaimed the actress and director (Leslie Harris) (see Thompson 2010:167). Although she is smart, ambitious, and wants to go to college to get out of the projects, Chantel won't play by the rules. In the film, her argument in history class for African American recognition seems ridiculous, especially when she says that the continents of people of color are represented on maps as smaller than they actually are. She gets pregnant and spends all of the money her boyfriend Ty (Kevin Thigpen) gives her to get an abortion, shopping instead; and then she begs his forgiveness, saying she was afraid. Yet she yells at him constantly. She also repeatedly yells at her best friend. Indeed, throughout the film she is yelling, giggling, or laughing, which makes it difficult to take her seriously when she gets into trouble. When she does have the baby, she wants her boyfriend Ty to throw it away in a garbage bag. He can't follow through with it. In the end she wants a social worker to help her find the baby. But Ty has already brought it home (he is a more sympathetic character than she is). The film ends with Ty and Chantel both doting on the baby, although they have split up. As Chantel tells us in voiceover, she is going to community college; living at home is difficult, but she still finds time to date; and she and Ty are getting their lives together. This story is very similar to some of those depicted on the teen reality show *16 and Pregnant*, which also end with the teenage mother committing herself to do right by her baby.

The fact that Chantel originally wants to commit infanticide but chooses to keep her baby rather than give it up for adoption—a choice that Precious also insists on even against the advice of her teacher—makes her less sympathetic than Juno. Indeed, very few Hollywood films consider either adoption or abortion as acceptable alternatives for pregnant women and girls. Mary Thompson analyzes the differences in presentation of black and white teen pregnancies in *Just Another Girl* and *Juno*, and concludes that Juno and the other white mothers in the film are presented as "good choice makers," while Chantel and other black mothers (think of Precious and her mother) are presented as "bad choice makers" in spite of the stark differences in their circumstances, which have everything to do with their race and class positions (Thompson 2010).

Precious's two children, who are likely to be orphaned and left to state care when their mother dies of AIDS because she cannot afford health care, and Chantel's baby, who will grow up with a single teen mother in the projects, have it much worse off than the babies of foul-mouthed, "bad" poor (white) teens like Dedee (Christina Ricci) in *The Opposite of Sex* (1998) and Lo (Aleska Palladino) in *Manny & Lo* (1996). In *Manny & Lo*, 16-year-old Lo (Aleksa Palladino) is pregnant after casual sex in a pickup truck at a wrecking yard; as her belly expands, so does her denial until her younger sister Manny (Scarlett Johansson) insists that Lo face the fact that she is pregnant and not just "fat." Perhaps not as smart as Juno, Lo, like Juno, is a smart-mouthed teen who is tough and independent. After Lo discovers that it is too late to get an abortion, the sisters kidnap a baby apparel store clerk (Mary Kay Place) to help them with the pregnancy and birth. In the end, the two girls and their surrogate mother, along with the new baby, form a close-knit family unit in this heartwarming alternative family values film. Although this all-female family is a welcome change from the heterocoupling prompted by pregnancy in most momcoms, still its happy ending covers over the difficulties of teen motherhood, especially for poor girls (who cannot kidnap a childless "old maid" who has always felt motherhood to be her true calling).

After watching Dedee in *The Opposite of Sex* smoking, drinking, lying, and stealing throughout her pregnancy, we see her healthy baby boy in a happy alternative family at the end; her baby is being lovingly raised by her gay half-brother Bill (Martin Donovan), a mild-mannered teacher, and his new boyfriend. The last scene shows her unable to leave the baby and her "family" behind as casually as she thought she could. In fact, the film suggests that this callous teen is growing up to realize that some relationships are worth keeping. As in other momcoms, her pregnancy is the vehicle through which she matures and is transformed into a kinder person. The reality television show *16 and Pregnant* is full of such coming-of-age stories in which a girl matures into womanhood through pregnancy.

*Saved!* also ends with an extended alternative "family" that includes Mary, the new teen mother, and her mother, her mother's boyfriend, her own boyfriend, and the father of her child and his gay lover, all of whom joyously come together around the new baby. Even as these films display anxieties about teenage fertility, some of them complicate notions of family in interesting ways. Even as the happy endings resolve all difficulties and thereby erase the complexities surrounding reproductive choice and motherhood for women and girls, these less mainstream notions of what counts as family present fresh alternatives to traditional family values. *The Kids Are All Right* (2010) is another example of an alternative family, with lesbian mothers and two children (although no teenage pregnancies).

Penny Marshall's *Riding in Cars with Boys* (2001) presents a more traditional story of 16-year-old Beverly (Drew Barrymore), who is forced to give up her dreams of college when she gets pregnant by her likable loser boyfriend (Steve Zahn). Beverly has decided to find a way to "go to Puerto Rico" to "take care of it," when the news of her pregnancy and decision not to marry the baby's father makes her own father cry in disappointment. Unable to go through with it and risk her father's disapproval, Beverly is forced to get married, have the baby, and give up her hopes of being a writer. Although Beverly is far from being a good mother, she is not only a sympathetic character but also her various failings as a mother are part of the comedy of this film. Like Juno, she is a feisty teen who, as the description on the back of the DVD tells us, "kicks life where it counts" (presumably in the balls as revenge for getting her pregnant). Like Juno, Lo (*Manny & Lo*), Dedee (*The Opposite of Sex*), and Mary (*Saved!*), Beverly is a no-nonsense teen who is even more driven and ambitious than her counterparts. These tough-as-nails teens are admirable in their strength even as they are threatening for their bad-girl ways and smart-mouthed backtalk to various authority figures, which is both part of their charm and the humor of the films and what makes them not your typical "sweet sixteen" stereotype. Although Magdalena in *Quinceañera* is one of the sweetest of the bunch, the tagline for the film is "Fifteen is not so sweet." These young, beautiful sweet-looking girls are not what they seem. They may be cute, but they are also sharp enough to cut through the hypocrisy and delusion of the adult world.

Recall how one of the first teenage pregnancy films, *The Miracle of Morgan's Creek* (1944), tested the Hays Production Code's censorship of pregnancy, teen pregnancy, and unwed pregnancy by giving us spunky Juno-predecessor, hyperfertile Trudy (Betty Hutton), who gets pregnant with sextuplets after drinking too much "punch" at a send-off party for the troops in World War II. Like her successors throughout the last several decades, Trudy is both tough and naïve, manipulative and charming, sexually promiscuous but cute.

It is this combination of innocence and sex appeal that seems to produce Hollywood's anxieties over teenage girls, who are called "fertile myrtles," and what is figured as the "epidemic" of teen pregnancy. In *Riding in Cars with Boys*, when Beverly's best friend announces that she too is pregnant, one of their parents pronounces it an "epidemic," suggesting that not only is teen fertility excessive and out of control but also might be contagious. In *Away We Go* (2009), one character, whose 30-something wife has had five miscarriages, laments that "every day a million 14-year-olds are getting pregnant without trying," while he feels "helpless" watching his "babies grow and then fade," suggesting that teenage girls are not only excessively fertile but also that it is unfair or somehow wrong that they get pregnant easily while his wife does not. Recall too the Candies Foundation ad: "AMERICA, WAKE-UP! WE HAVE AN EPIDEMIC, which, as we have seen, follows a long history of treating pregnancy as an illness, and now even as a contagious disease (see Hanson 2004).

At the extreme, teen pregnancy is figured as criminal. For example, in 1996 an Idaho prosecutor introduced legislation that would prosecute teenage mothers and fathers, particularly those receiving public assistance, for the public costs associated with their pregnancy, childbirth, and child care (Hardy 1996:A1). The prosecutor called teenage mothers "disgruntled" and "irresponsible," qualities he seemed to associate with being a teenager (Hardy 1996:A1). Teenage mothers, especially black and Latino teens, are imagined as criminals, carrying not only unwanted babies that cost society but also something like a disease that is spreading out of control. In the words of Angela Davis, "A poor teenage Black or Latina girl who is a single mother is suspected of criminality simply by virtue of the fact that she is poor and has had a child 'out of wedlock'" (1991; in 2000:483). If the few Hollywood films that feature teens of color are any indication, then some version of that opinion continues in films like *Just Another Girl on the I.R.T.* and *Precious*.

These images of teenage pregnancy as criminal or diseased seem at odds with other media and film representations of teenage pregnancy as glamorous or cool. Tabloid magazines featured photos of pregnant teen Jamie Lynn Spears as cover girl. And Bristol Palin was beautiful and smiling on the cover of *People* magazine in her high school graduation cap and gown and holding her adorable son Tripp (Westfall 2009). If a picture is worth a thousand words, then this one provides a stark contrast to the words printed below it: "Gov. Sarah Palin's daughter talks about her life with baby Tripp. 'If girls realized the consequences of sex, nobody would be having sex,' says Bristol. 'Trust me. *Nobody*'" (Westfall 2009, cover).

Yet, as we know, some media blame hit films like *Juno* and *Knocked Up* and teen celebrities like Spears and Palin for contributing to what they imagine as an increase in teenage pregnancy (despite the fact that teen pregnancy has been decreasing in recent years)[3] as well as anecdotes like the one about girls at a high school near Boston buying Early (Home) Pregnancy Tests (EPTs) in bulk and expressing disappointment when they were negative.[4] Echoing the "blue-line" or "pee-stick" scenes of Hollywood films (*The Astronaut's Wife, Waitress, Juno, Knocked Up*), women and girls are creating their own blue-line scenes and uploading "WombTube" videos to YouTube. The online magazine *Slate* calls these videos "addictive" because, like other aspects of pregnancy, they have captured the public imagination (Meltzer 2011). These young women are filming their early home pregnancy tests to catch the response live and post it online. Sometimes the same woman posts several as she attempts to get pregnant but is disappointed. Like their Hollywood counterparts, these blue-line scenes are full of suspense as the protagonists wait the minutes required for the test results.

The so-called "pregnancy pact" that reportedly had girls buying EPTs in bulk and sharing results also inspired a TV movie called

*The Pregnancy Pact* (2010) and a "reality" television show on MTV called *16 and Pregnant*. The show has proved so popular that teen mothers are invited back to check in about their lives a year after giving birth. And *US Weekly* magazine featured two of the teen moms posing together on the cover of an August 2010 issue. On one cover, the girls were dressed in matching white-and-pink out-fits, with bright white smiles, holding their babies (of course, the baby girl dresses in pink and the baby boy dresses in blue). This lead story gave details on the girls' feelings about motherhood, their own parents, and the fathers of their babies, along with their dreams of white weddings and careers. One of the teen mothers says, "I always wanted to be a cosmetologist, but now I'm leaning toward being a mixed martial arts fighter"; and another says, "I plan on moving to a bigger city like Chicago or San Jose Califor-nia and opening up my own Italian or Asian fusion restaurant" (Grossbart & Abrahamson 2010:40–41).

American popular culture just can't seem to get enough of these teen mothers. The article in *US Weekly* begins: "It started with a baby bump . . . on *16 and Pregnant*. By winter they [the four teens] were navigating motherhood . . . on their addictive spinoff *Teen Mom*. Now, with more than 3 million viewers follow-ing their stormy, satisfying lives on season 2, the girls tell *US* why giving birth was just the beginning" (Grossbart & Abramhamson 2010:38). Even as their rising birthrates are called "epidemic" and figured as criminal, there is an outbreak of pregnant teens in the media and a growing fascination with their lives, which *US* calls an "addiction."

Like the magazine article in which the teens talk about trying to put their babies first and be good mothers, most of the epi-sodes of *16 and Pregnant* end with the teen mothers committed to becoming more responsible, growing up fast, and raising their babies; many of them end with the mother and father united by their concern to make family their priority and to do right by their child. The few that consider adoption face resistance from other family members. And none of them seriously considers abortion.

Although the series shows some of the difficulties of pregnancies, childbirth, and parenthood, overall the show and most of its participants embrace conservative family values that lead young mothers and fathers to "mature" into the realization that family always comes first. The fantasy of the teenage girl with her criminal, dangerously pathological, and unbounded reproductive potential is domesticated into proper family life. In this way, what is imagined as teenage irresponsibility combined with dangerous fertility is brought back within the confines of acceptable societal norms.

Whatever their "struggles," as *US Weekly* calls them, the media focus on teenage girls having babies, shown smiling—or crying—for the camera, on television, and as magazine cover girls makes these young mothers desirable "stars." These images feed the fantasies of American audiences hungry for titillating stories of pubescent girls' particular combination of innocence and sexuality. These girls have become emblems for the valorization of a particular combination of innocent naïveté (the Forest Gump phenomenon) and captivation with female sexuality. At the same time that their bodies are figured as excessive, even diseased and criminal, their pretty smiles and stories of their artless inexperience in the face of pregnancy, childbirth, and motherhood make for fascinating entertainment. Audiences can both condemn these girls for their promiscuous and/or irresponsible sex, while sympathizing with their dreams, aspirations, and perseverance in the face of their abrupt transitions from childhood to motherhood.

Our interest in their guileless descriptions of pregnancy, childbirth, and fights with their boyfriends, like American culture's rapt interest in the idiot savant more generally, seems to indicate a nostalgia for lost innocence and a fascination with innocence lost. This is even more apparent in the reality television show *I Didn't Know I Was Pregnant*, which re-creates "true" stories of women and mostly girls who didn't know they were pregnant until they gave birth. In a strange sense, these girls, along with their fictional counterparts in films, reconcile the virgin-whore dichotomy, which still fuels popular imagination: they can be imagined as both virginal and whores at the same time. In addition, they present girls' coming-of-age stories in which maturity comes only with pregnancy and motherhood. The incongruity of figuring these girls, and teenage pregnancy in general, as part of an epidemic, even criminal, while exploiting their pretty smiles and innocence, is in keeping with age-old cultural stereotypes of female sexuality that split women into virgins and whores and our culture's fascination with that seeming contradiction.

The nubile sexy virgin or the virginal sex symbol is an attractive figure in popular culture. Even sex symbol Marilyn Monroe as Sugar in *Some Like It Hot* (1959) was called as harmless and "soft as a Persian kitten, warm and loving as everyone's fantasy of the perfect mother" (Bell-Metereau 1985:64); and her "dumb blonde" act in both *Hot* and *The Seven Year Itch* (1955) gives us another character that is both as sexy as they come and still innocent and naïve. In these complex representations of women and girls as both sexy and innocent, their innocence is part of what makes them sexy, and it is often represented as something they control in order to manipulate men. Bad-girl teen Dedee in *The Opposite of Sex* is a prime example of a girl who uses a combination of sexy flirtation and feigned innocence to get what she wants from men. It is noteworthy that she loses control of her situation and her strong manipulative ways during the birth scene when she cries and apologizes to her half-brother. In this scene, unlike any others in the film, she is shown without makeup, looking more like a scared teenage girl than a manipulative sexpot. Like the other teens and some of the women in these films, Dedee is afraid and not sure what is happening to her. Some of these girls even express a fear of death while in labor. Chantel in *Just Another Girl* is a bloody mess before she calls for help. When her water breaks, Beverly in *Riding in Cars* doesn't know what is wrong and is terrified. Lo of *Manny & Lo* is afraid she is dying and loses her tough-as-nails exterior altogether during the birth scene.

Most Hollywood birth scenes show girls and women completely out of control, screaming, crying, and swearing. Otherwise beautiful sweet women and girls become more like beasts snarling and snapping. Some, like Gail Dwyer (Joan Cusack) in *Nine Months* and Kristy Briggs (Elizabeth McGovern) in *She's Having a Baby*, even become violent and kick things. Many curse and yell at their partners and at the doctors (*She's Having a Baby, Junior, Fools Rush In, Knocked Up, Baby Mama*, among others). In all of these Hollywood representations of birth, women are out of control and birth is figured as excessive. The women are more like monsters or animals in these moments. And the excessive nature of birth is highlighted by the fact that, in some of these films, there is more than one woman giving birth or pregnant at the same time, as if pregnancy and birth are contagious diseases that threaten epidemics. *Junior* (1994), *Father of the Bride II* (1995), and *Nine Months* (1995) all show two chaotic deliveries at the same time. Both *The Opposite of Sex* and *Baby Mama* show one girl/woman giving birth while another finds out, or announces, that she is pregnant, again suggesting that pregnancy might be contagious.

In sum, even while recent Hollywood films hint at some of the complications of reproductive choices, they continue to display anxieties about girls' and women's fertility. In the end, they usually embrace conservative family values that endorse a woman's right to choose only if she chooses to have the baby. The "Hollywood Baby Boom" (as one tabloid calls celebrities having babies) prefers to resolve the complexities of women's reproductive choices with adorable babies. The language of pro-choice is recuperated into the conservative ideals of motherhood as a woman's calling and the fulfillment of her life. In a sardonic, but apt, run through recent pregnant romcoms, Eve Kushner concludes that there are eight lessons we learn from these films:

1. If you have an unplanned pregnancy, birth is the only option;
2. If circumstances make the pregnancy problematic, don't worry—everything will work out somehow; 3. You will glow

with pride and femininity as you proceed with the noble mission of carrying to term; 4. When you deliver the child, there will again be irrepressible joy and widespread celebration; 5. If you're a man, you may feel unready or unwilling to have a baby, in which case you are just a party pooper; 6. Babies only strengthen romances; 7. What this world needs is babies, babies, babies. Bring them on by the caseload; 8. A childless life is worthless, and anyone who doesn't want kids must be bitter and selfish and morally deficient. If you postpone or eschew parenthood, you'll face a future of unhappiness and regret. (Kushner 2000)

Hollywood has gone baby crazy, and if previews of coming attractions are any indication, we can expect the new cult of motherhood, or what Erica Jong calls the "orgy of motherphilia," to balloon.

# PREGNANT HORROR

## GESTATING THE OTHER(S) WITHIN

IT IS TELLING that mainstream comedies echo horror films in the violence and chaos of birth scenes. In *Look Who's Talking* (1989), Mollie (Kirstie Alley) growls in a monstrous voice while in labor, and in most of the other films women scream obscenities at their doctors and male partners. The birth scene in the comedy-drama *She's Having a Baby* (1988) closely parallels the dream sequence in *Aliens* (1986) where Ripley (Sigourney Weaver) imagines that an alien is tearing open her abdomen, down to the same medical apparatuses being kicked across the room and Kristi (Elizabeth McGovern) screaming "get it out . . . I have to have it out." In fact, watching the "birth" scene from *Aliens* along with the birth scenes from most of the pregnant comedies gives a new appreciation for how horrific popular images of birth really are. The blockbuster hit *Knocked Up* (2007) not only has Alison (Katherine Heigl) screaming obscenities at the top of her lungs but also shows her "crowning" as part of its gross-out humor when one of Ben's friends stumbles into the delivery room at this moment and returns traumatized, which leads to jokes about whether or not he can ever have sex again after seeing what her vagina can do. Best friend character Gail (Joan Cusack) in *Nine Months* (1995) curses at her husband and kicks his video camera with such force he falls backwards. While being wheeled into the delivery room, Angie (Amy Poehler) knocks over IV stands and accosts other patients in *Baby Mama* (2008). And in *Fools Rush In* (1997), Isabel (Selma Hayek) curses at her husband (Matthew Perry) in a torrent of Spanish. As we have seen, in films from *The Miracle of Morgan's Creek* (1944) with its sextuplets through recent Hollywood momcoms, pregnant women giving birth are imaged as excessive, out of control, and violent.

Of course, this is most explicit in the horror genre, where women's fertility is not only metaphorically threatening and excessive but also a danger that literally comes to life in the demon or alien seed that inhabits or possesses these (usually) unsuspecting, pregnant women. Some recent horror films present haunting and haunted pregnancies (*Pan's Labyrinth*, *Grace*, and *The Unborn*) that continue earlier tropes of pregnant excess as horror in older pregnant horror (*Rosemary's Baby*, *The Brood*, *Aliens*, and *The Astronaut's Wife*). These films not only signal anxieties over women's reproductive capacities but also over new reproductive technologies that replace "natural" sexual reproduction. In these films, as other critics have argued, the fetus is represented as a hostile Other-within who threatens not only the maternal body but also society at large (e.g., Petchesky 1987; Berlant 1994). In addition, women's relation to the continuation of the human species is made monstrous through their alien spawn. The challenge to personal identity posed by pregnancy causes anxiety not only to the individual through the "doubleness" of the pregnant body but also to humankind and the threat of *what* the woman's womb may harbor. On both the personal and social levels, women's reproductive function is imagined as excessive and dangerous. In some cases, the danger of excess shows up as the rate of reproduction that threatens the takeover of alien, monstrous, or animal-like broods that spawn faster than normal human reproduction. These instances manifest anxieties about the time of human reproduction. The time of new reproductive technologies that make it possible for women to give birth to multiple babies also often put women or doctors in the position of "selectively reducing" fetuses or multiple births. Real-life multiple births have triggered a horrific response from the popular media in which the so-called "Octomom" and reality-TV personality Kate Gosselin are both figured as monsters. These fears of new reproductive technologies and women's reproductive powers are echoed in Hollywood horror films, specifically the popular subgenre "pregnant horror."

## THE THREATENING OTHER-WITHIN

In the seventeenth and eighteenth centuries, as medicine was coming into its own as a separate science and business with practitioners, male midwives began to displace female midwives as pregnancy and childbirth became managed by medicine (see Bewell 1988; Hanson 2004). With the medicalization of pregnancy and childbirth came various instruction manuals on how to have a healthy pregnancy in order to have a healthy infant. In addition to emphasizing diet and exercise, these manuals also stressed the importance of the maternal imaginary and the pregnant woman's state of mind. In his survey of these manuals, Alan Bewell identifies "the striking emphasis placed on the power of a pregnant woman's imagination and desires to mark or deform a developing fetus," which accorded the female imagination with extraordinary powers (1988:109). He further analyzes various texts that suggest that "monsters are produced at the moment of conception when a mother's ardent gaze on an image overpowers the form-making power of the seed . . . *monsters are conceived when an image usurps the place of the biological father, if not in the bed, at least in the mind of his wife*" (Bewell 1988:111; emphasis added). This passage is significant when we analyze the figure or phantom of the displaced father in many horror films, as we will see.

This struggle between "maternal passion" versus "paternal seed" continued into the nineteenth and twentieth centuries, particularly with the expansion of psychiatric medicine and the inception of psychoanalysis. After all, Sigmund Freud maintained that the best cure for hysteria or excessive passions in women was pregnancy and childbirth. In a sense, we could see Freud's hypothesis as an endorsement for the male seed as an antidote to female passion. The association between women's desire, imagination, pregnancy, and monsters suggests that female sexuality itself is somehow monstrous and excessive. In addition, these associations betoken an anxiety that women's sexual fantasies are in excess of their male partner's not only in terms of the object of those desires (longings for something beyond him and therefore perverse) but also in terms of the agent of those desires (an imaginary that harbors almost magical powers to transform healthy fetuses into deformed monsters). Manuals advised pregnant women to avoid any strong or excessive emotion, suggesting that pregnancy itself is a state of excess that makes women easily excitable and therefore even more susceptible than usual to flights of fancy and perverse desires, a notion that continues today in filmic representations of pregnant women out of control of their emotions and of their own bodies.

The seventeenth- and eighteenth-century notions that women's monstrous desires give birth to monsters becomes the nineteenth-century idea that women's wombs and reproductive capacities cause excessive excitations and madness that can adversely and perversely affect their fetuses and infants. Excessive emotions in pregnant women are seen as leading to insanity, which in turn produces malformed infants. In *A Cultural History of Pregnancy*, Clare Hanson identifies two types of insanity associated with childbirth in the nineteenth century: moral insanity and hereditary insanity. Hereditary insanity is described as a mental precondition that is triggered by pregnancy, while moral insanity is a temporary state of madness caused by something external, which may be the pregnancy itself. One nineteenth-century doctor, George Man Burrows, explains hereditary insanity thus: "Gestation itself is a source of excitation in most women, and sometimes provokes mental derangement, and more especially in those with a hereditary predisposition. . . . Some are insane on every pregnancy or lying-in, others only occasionally" (quoted in Hanson 2004:62). In *Handbook of Midwifery* (1897), W. F. Dakin echoes the idea that hereditary madness may be brought on by pregnancy: " Childbearing is known to have a particularly marked influence in causing insanity in those women who have a hereditary taint of madness or of other marked neurosis" (quoted in Hanson 2004:90). Dakin goes on to describe the apprehension and dread these women feel about the possibility that something is wrong with their fetus, or a general "vague" sense of dread "of nothing in particular" (Hanson 2004:90). In the nineteenth century, this fear of incompleteness or malformation of the coming infant was figured as abnormal to the point of insanity. Hanson surveys an impressive body of nineteenth-century medical literature that describes these feelings in terms of an "anticipation of evil" and "morbid intensity of thought" that can lead to "melancholy" and even "a loathing of life" (Hanson 2004:61–64).

While the symptoms of moral insanity are the same as those of hereditary insanity, the causes are different. In hereditary insanity, the cause is internal to the woman's physical and mental makeup, while in moral insanity the cause is external to the woman and may include social factors around the pregnancy or even the pregnancy itself. In both cases, nineteenth-century doctors identify pregnancy as the trigger for either a latent condition or a temporary madness brought on by pregnancy or the social situation surrounding it. Furthermore, one of the central symptoms of both forms of insanity is anxiety or dread over the developing fetus and fear that something is wrong with it. Like earlier notions of maternal imagination and maternal passions, so-called moral insanity comes out of the theory that women's imaginations and thoughts during pregnancy affect the fetus. Hanson cites James Pritchard, who, in 1835, defined moral insanity as a "morbid perversion of the natural feelings" whose "symptoms of insanity occasionally display themselves during pregnancy, and under circumstances which indicate that they are dependent on that state" (Hanson 2004:62). With moral insanity, the woman is influenced by social and psychological factors that are independent of her physiology. In a sense, she has been corrupted by forces outside herself, which cause her to have morbidly perverse fantasies and episodes during pregnancy. Pritchard sees pregnancy itself as a state that can cause such moral insanity.

Pregnancy has been viewed as a condition that excites women into "sick" or "perverse" fantasies, many of which involve the fetus gestating within their bodies. Sigmund Freud notes that one possible cause of totemism in "primitive" peoples is the long period of gestation in human females, who therefore do not connect the causality of male fertilization and instead attribute their pregnancy to an animal or totem. One theory about the roots of totemism, says Freud, are in "the sick fancies of the pregnant women," maternal fancies so natural and seemingly so universal that they appear to be the root of totemism (Freud in *Totem and Taboo* [1913; in 1990:147] cites James Frazer's *Totemism and Exogamy* [1910], pp. 4 and 63). Clellan Stearns Ford also describes various rituals surrounding pregnancy and childbirth among "primitive" peoples who believe that maternal and paternal behaviors can lead to either healthy or malformed infants. Many believe that maternal fantasies or hallucinations can negatively affect the fetus (see Ford 1945; see also Bewell 1988; Newton 1996; and Hanson 2004).

The notion of maternal imagination continues in twentieth-century medical literature, where maternal fantasies are blamed for fetal deformation. The hypothesis that maternal emotions affect fetal development was popular throughout the twentieth century, perhaps culminating in the work of Niles Newton on the impact of a woman's emotions on everything from morning sickness and food cravings to miscarriage, fetal weight, infant irritability, and retardation (Newton 1996). Newton not only surveys the literature on the effects of maternal emotions on the infant and the rest of the family but also endorses the conclusion that women's moods greatly affect their pregnancies and fetal development and that the maternal personality also affects the infant through breast-feeding: "The emotions of pregnancy are not only of significance to the woman herself, but also appear to be very much involved with the health and welfare of the whole family unit. The emotions of the mother are experienced directly by the fetus, and indirectly by the infant after it is born and by the husband and other children" (Newton 1996:372). Newton suggests that women who have negative feelings during pregnancy not only have more somatic symptoms themselves but also pass on their anxieties to their fetuses and infants in the form of somatic symptoms. This notion is the contemporary form of the nineteenth-century idea that women's fears and fantasies during pregnancy, called "maternal impressions," negatively affect the fetus to the point of malformation. In fact, the fear of malformation is one of the most prominent recurring anxieties during pregnancy for many women (cf. Newton 1996). Women frequently have anxieties about their fetuses. It is usual to hear pregnant women saying "as long as it has ten fingers and ten toes." But when these worries become extreme, the medical establishment has deemed them a form of paranoia or insanity.

This fear of incompleteness—missing fingers or toes—resonates with Noël Carroll's theory of horror (1990:33). Carroll maintains that one facet of horror is the fear of monstrous incompleteness. Certainly a fetus developing in a woman's womb conjures anxieties over incompleteness. If, as Carroll maintains, we have deep-seated fears of incompleteness, which we find monstrous, then a developing fetus and the pregnant woman harboring it become primal ciphers for this fear. Pregnant horror films speak to this fear of incompleteness and malformation as an anticipation of evil in the form of the unborn fetus and often in the figure of the pregnant woman herself. As various feminist theorists have pointed out, monstrous birth and fear of women's reproductive capacities are a staple in the horror genre, from Hitchcock's *Psycho* (1960) and *The Birds* (1963), through Polanski's *Rosemary's Baby* (1968), to the *Alien* (1979) series and *The Brood* (1979), and more recently films like *Species* (1995), *Mimic* (1997), *The Astronaut's Wife* (1999), *Pan's Labyrinth* (2006), *The Unborn* (2009), *Grace* (2009), and *Splice* (2009) (for feminist analysis of some of these films, see Creed 1993; Grant 1996; Freeland 2000; and Oliver 2008). Common themes in these films include the madness of pregnancy, evil lurking inside the pregnant body, women's generative capacities out of control, anxieties about paternity and the paternal seed, general fears of pregnancy and birth as excessive and beyond human control, the proximity of pregnant women and animals, and women giving birth to nonhuman species—monsters, bugs, devils or aliens.

## ROSEMARY'S EXCESS: TOO INNOCENT OR DREAMING UP EVIL?

Roman Polanski's horror classic *Rosemary's Baby* (1968) exemplifies what Hanson calls moral insanity. In the film, Rosemary Woodhouse (Mia Farrow) is newly married to Guy (John Cassavetes), and all she wants to complete her happiness is a baby. Guy is a struggling actor who befriends their strange neighbors, the Castevets, an elderly couple (Sidney Blackmer and Ruth Gordon), and soon his acting career takes off. At first reluctant to talk about having a baby, after secretive meetings with the neighbors Guy becomes committed to the project and helps plan "baby night" when they will try to conceive. Aided by the spiked dessert provided by Mrs. Castevet, Guy succeeds in impregnating Rosemary with Satan's spawn. The sex scene is a nightmarish rape scene with a devilish creature mounting Rosemary against her protests while ghoulish onlookers chant Satanic verses. Rosemary's pregnancy makes her sick and weak, which is both the result of, and the justification for, Minnie Castevet giving her special herbs to help her along. Rosemary begins to suspect that something is wrong with her baby and threatens to go to a different doctor (someone other than the doctor selected by the coven of witches, her neighbors); but no sooner does she insist to Guy that she will see her own doctor, Dr. Hill (Charles Grodin), when she feels the baby move. In this moment of quickening, Rosemary exclaims, "It's alive," foreshadowing the birth of her devil baby. As the DVD description of the film puts it: "her normal life turns into a surreal nightmare. Slowly, she begins to realize that a seed of evil has been planted . . . and she is its host."

In classic Polanski style, it is unclear during the course of the film whether Rosemary is hallucinating or whether her strange fantasies are based on reality (for a discussion of the film in relation to Polanski's other films, see Chappetta 1969; on Polanski's ability to blur the boundaries between reality and fantasy, see Houston & Kinder 1968–69). Other characters in the film—her husband, both doctors, her neighbors—treat her as if she is mentally unstable, even insane. In a chilling scene when she realizes that her neighbors are witches and her husband is involved with them, she calls her former doctor, Dr. Hill, who is not part of the coven. Dr. Hill agrees to see her and reassures her that he will help, but betrays her by calling her husband and the coven's doctor, Dr. Sapirstein (Ralph Bellamy). As Houston and Kinder point out in their review of the film, this puts the audience in a strange position: "For the first time, the audience considers that Rosemary may be mad. After all, her explanation is fragmented and hysterical; in 'reality' Dr. Hill's reaction may be perfectly reasonable and appropriate. But, at this point the audience hopes urgently for Dr. Hill's belief. The audience thus urges belief in witchcraft" (1968–69:17).

Rosemary's husband and Dr. Sapirstein force her back into the apartment, where she goes into labor and gives birth in a scene reminiscent of the nightmarish rape scene, complete with the coven chanting around her. When Rosemary recovers from this hallucinatory scene, she asks for her baby but is eventually told that the baby died. Her maternal instinct tells her otherwise. Soon, she hears and follows the baby's cries into her neighbors' apartment where the coven is lovingly celebrating the birth of their Satanic offspring. Holding a large butcher knive to keep the coven at bay, Rosemary approaches the casket-like cradle, and even though she screams at the sight of the glowing demonic eyes looking up at her, in the end she embraces the baby with a mother's love, a love ultimately unshaken by the gruesome appearance of her baby. At his moment, her maternal care and mother's love appear as excessive when she embraces her Satanic infant. A more recent example of anxiety over the excesses of a mother's love is *Grace*, in which a mother (a vegan no less!) kills in order to feed blood to her "protein deprived" reanimated stillborn baby.

In his review of *Rosemary's Baby* in the *Village Voice* upon the film's release, Andrew Sarris summarizes what is horrific in Rosemary's plight: she is pregnant, helpless, and alone, with no one who takes seriously her concerns or pains. But what is truly frightening is related to shared anxieties over the state of pregnancy itself. Sarris says, "Thus two universal fears run through 'Rosemary's Baby,' the fear of pregnancy, particularly as it consumes personality, and the fear of a deformed offspring with all the attendant moral and emotional complications" (Sarris 1968). Sarris's description of the two fears resonates with the notion that Rosemary is the victim of moral insanity from external threats, including the people around her and her pregnancy itself. The evil in Rosemary's baby seems to come from outside herself. She is portrayed as an innocent, who, as Sarris points out, is used by those around her, including her husband. Although she eventually has doubts about the normalcy of her pregnancy, for the most part Rosemary is childlike and naïve. She jumps up and down cradling the phone like a baby doll when she finds out she is pregnant. With her short hair and lithe body, she looks almost prepubescent, a little girl playing house rather than a mature woman (cf. Waldman 1981; Wexman 1987; Fischer 1992). Rosemary as she is played by Mia Farrow seems to be innocence personified. It is the ambitions of her husband, who makes a bargain with the devil worshipers in order to further his career, and the evil practices of her neighbors, that unbeknownst to Rosemary taint her pregnancy and implant the demon seed inside her. Throughout her pregnancy she cedes control to those around her. By the time she asserts herself, it is too late (for a discussion of Rosemary's lack of suspicion versus her paranoia, see Valerius 2005). Like Rosemary, the audience eventually learns that her paranoia is justified and that she is not just a crazy pregnant lady; or at least she is not the one responsible for her insanity. As the DVD description tells us, she is the victim of an evil seed to which she must play host. She is seemingly surrounded by evil forces that corrupt her pregnancy and that lead to "moral insanity."

In her study of *Rosemary's Baby*, Lucy Fischer reads it as an allegory for various ways in which pregnant women have been figured as passive, crazy, infantile, pathological, and abject. She argues that the film represents the return of the repressed embodied experience of pregnant women as it has been erased from various discourses, from the religious and mystical, to the scientific and medical (1992). She maintains that Rosemary's experience of loss of control—to the point of being strapped down during the birth scene—is an allegory of the real experiences of pregnant women (1992:4). In addition, Rosemary's complaints are not taken seriously; she is rendered passive, to the point of restraints. But, Fischer points out, "even Rosemary's response to her demon-child suggests a mother's contradictory emotions," suggesting that Rosemary is an allegory for women's experience of ambivalence toward their infants, an emotion that appears threatening to both the mothers themselves and to a culture that promotes motherhood and unconditional mother love (1992:12). In Fischer's account, Rosemary both exemplifies the ways in which pregnant women are used and abused by those around them—what we might call "evil" outside—and the ambivalence of pregnant women toward pregnancy, childbirth, and their newborns—a type of "evil" within.

Other film critics have been more explicit in identifying an evil lurking within Rosemary herself, which is to say an evil imagined within all women, particularly pregnant women. In her treatment of the film, Virginia Wexman argues that Rosemary's pregnancy is the "triggering mechanism of her breakdown" (1987:38). Wexman claims that Rosemary resolves her own repressed and ambiguous sexual desires by "conjur[ing] up an image of power and violence that is both erotic and punitive: a diabolical rapist" (1987:38). This suggests that Rosemary's own perverse unconscious desires are the cause of her moral insanity; both the rape by the devil and the resulting demonic child, then, are her own abject fantasies. Wexman's interpretation of Rosemary's perverse imagination resonates with nineteenth-century ideas of maternal imagination and the link between the "sick" fantasies of pregnant women and malformation in their newborns. In this sense, the film signals that notions of the fearsome potency of maternal imagination continue into the mid-twentieth century.

Wexman also maintains that Rosemary's pregnancy causes her to find her body repulsive and abject; and her eating of raw meat is a sign of her own abjection. Rather than interpret these images as effects of the evil devil child lurking within or the evil all around her in the coven of devil-worshipping witches, Wexman sees abjection and ambiguity inherent within the character and body of Rosemary herself, abjection and ambiguity brought on by pregnancy. Specifically, Rosemary's abjection is connected to the ambiguity of her pregnant doubleness and her identification with her devil child. Wexman claims that "though we never see Rosemary's baby, the last image of Rosemary herself superimposes its unnatural eyes over her own; for the alien forces that terrorize her ultimately arise from within herself" (1987:41). She concludes that insofar as Rosemary becomes like a baby through her pregnancy, and she is identified with her demonic infant at the end of the film, the horror of the film is the result of "a horror of the helpless infancy we all once suffered" (1987:41). Like Fischer, Wexman sees

Rosemary as representative of all women, and all men, who begin life as helpless.

Rhonda Berenstein also discusses the identification between the monster and Rosemary, but rather than diagnose the ambiguous doubleness of pregnancy in terms of an anxiety over helplessness or powerlessness, to the contrary she sees it as a sign of an anxiety over women's reproductive power. She claims that in *Rosemary's Baby* and in *Aliens* the female protagonists are identified with monsters as a sign of a "pregnant anxiety" over women's reproductive powers, which are figured as both abject and fiercely forceful (1990:68). Berenstein concludes that "what both *Rosemary's Baby* and *Aliens* suggest is that . . . she [the mother] will always maintain some power in her reproductive capacity, even if that power scares the shit out of patriarchy!" (1990:69). Although Berenstein does discuss the nightmarish "birth" scenes in both films, she focuses on Rosemary as a mother rather than as pregnant (in spite of the fact that until the very end of the film she is not a mother). Certainly the pregnant woman is even "more doubled" than the mother insofar as she is neither one nor two; and insofar as she carries the Other within her. Moreover, women's reproductive powers are signaled most explicitly in the figure of the pregnant woman rather than in the figure of the mother whose children are physically separate from her. In these films (and others in the horror genre) there is a monstrousness associated with the doubling and ambiguity of pregnancy itself. Pregnant doubleness is represented as suspicious at best and monstrous at worst.

Although he doesn't discuss pregnancy, in *The Philosophy of Horror* Noël Carroll develops a theory of horror based on Mary Douglas's anthropological study of filth that speaks to our fear of ambiguity and doubleness. Carroll describes the object of horror: "objects can raise categorical misgivings by virtue of being incomplete representatives of their class, such as rotting and disintegrating things, as well as by virtue of being formless . . . an object or being is impure if it is categorically interstitial, categorically contradictory, incomplete, or formless (1990:32). Certainly, the developing fetus fits this bill: it is incomplete and in the beginning formless. But the maternal body also appears as categorically interstitial and contradictory in the sense that it is neither one nor two beings. Insofar as the maternal body is neither one nor two, its ambiguous state also threatens order and boundaries with what Julia Kristeva calls "abjection" (1980). Also following Douglas, Kristeva defines the abject as what cannot be categorized or confined; it does not respect borders or boundaries; rather it occupies a space of the in-between, what Carroll calls the categorically interstitial. Unlike Carroll, however, Kristeva identifies the maternal body as a prime exemplar of the abject in-between that defies categorization. In her now canonical *The Monstrous-Feminine*, Barbara Creed applies Kristeva's theory of abjection to horror films, arguing that the monstrous feminine poses an active threat to the patriarchal imaginary (rather than merely being a passive victim); Creed analyzes what she sees as five faces of the monstrous feminine in the horror genre: the archaic mother, the monstrous womb, the witch, the vampire, and the possessed woman (1993). Most of these faces are the face of the reproductive woman as monstrous and threatening.

In various essays on film in *Subjectivity Without Subjects* (1998), *Noir Anxiety* (2002), and a more recent essay on Hitchcock's 1960s trilogy *Psycho*, *The Birds*, and *Marnie* (1964), I use Kristeva's theory of abjection to develop an approach to uncanny subjects in film, particularly in relation to the maternal body (see Oliver 1998, 2002, 2008; see also Chanter 2008). Throughout this body of work, I argue that what is uncanny and/or horrifying in various films from Ingmar Bergman's *Persona* and Rainer Werner Fassbinder's *Despair* to various films noir and to Hitchcock's trilogy are the ways in which the maternal body threatens boundaries between one and two. For Kristeva, the abject is that which calls borders into question. And what could be more challenging to the borders of the self and of the human than a woman's pregnant body gestating a developing fetus? The abject is not horrifying because it is gross or slimy, but rather because it is ambiguous, neither one nor the other, neither solid nor liquid, which is why it is slimy. What is horrifying are the ways in which the monstrous is ambiguous—in-between one body (the mother's) and another (the fetus); in-between human and animal; even in-between female and male.

*Rosemary's Baby* exhibits anxiety over this ambiguity of the Other-within, the Other who both is and is not the maternal body, both is and is not yet human, both is and is not yet female or male. Given our earlier analysis of the moral insanity that threatens Rosemary's psychic and bodily integrity from the outside (or from the outside within), and given Berenstein's and Wexman's suggestion of an evil that is inherent in women's reproductive capacity, *Rosemary's Baby* also presents us with an ambiguity over the source of evil (for a discussion of the horror genre in terms of evil, see Freeland 2000). Does it come from outside the innocent and naïve Rosemary, who is corrupted by her husband's ambitions and the coven of witches? Or is it the effect of Rosemary's own ambiguous but repressed sexual desires or her ambivalent maternal emotions? In either case, it is triggered by her pregnancy. The question remains whether her moral corruption is the result of forces outside of herself or whether they originate within herself. Perhaps the inability to determine the boundaries between inside and outside is part of the categorical in-between of the pregnant woman's condition. Insofar as we cannot identify the source of the evil as clearly within Rosemary or outside of her, it is all the more threatening for the ambiguity of its source.

If, as Berenstein suggests, these films display an anxiety over women's power, they also manifest a fear of this power out of control and imagined as excessive. Whether, as Wexman suggests, we all suffer from anxiety over our own powerlessness as infants, or we all suffer more generally as vulnerable human beings subject to pain, disease, and death, the women in these films signal a monstrous power gone to the devil. This power has gone to the devil precisely because it is a power that we cannot control. Women's reproductive power is out of control. As much as we try, ultimately we cannot control procreation, pregnancy, and birth. In more philosophical terms, we cannot control life . . . or death. Rather, they happen to us.

As we have seen in previous chapters, our lack of control and choice is a great source of anxiety, particularly when it comes to women and reproduction. Perhaps because reproduction is the beginning of human life and essential to the continuation of the species, it triggers deep-seated anxieties about power, control, humanity, and the species. Indeed, in most pregnant horror films, the monstrous ambiguity of pregnancy leads to a literal monster that is not human and is not of our species. There is a sense of something sinister lurking in our midst or our past/future that threatens to extinguish humanity, something out of our control and in excess of human limitations. This threat that exceeds our knowledge and power is linked to birth and to death and brings death into proximity with birth/life.

The connection between birth and death is a recurring theme in psychoanalysis. For example, Freud claims that a woman's womb and reproductive organs are associated with death even as they are the bearers of life (2001a , 2001b:244–45). Kristeva suggests that women's life-giving capacities and fundamental role in the continuation of the species make them threatening to a patriarchal order that can never confine such power (1980). Moreover, the excesses of life and death, and particularly those creatures that somehow inhabit the liminal space between them, threaten the limits of humanity itself. These in-between beings challenge our sense of ourselves as definitively human and raise the specter that even human life may not be what it seems. Even a newborn baby or cute little children can be the embodiment of evil. In fact, they are perfect candidates for horror because abjection fascinates and horrifies insofar as it presents us with something that is not what it seems or something that cannot be categorized as simply good or evil. In other words, a beautiful woman or adorable child can be more terrifying, particularly in a pedestrian way, than a hideous monster because they are seemingly innocent and attractive; and they are more dangerous because they can pass themselves off as good when they are really evil.

## JUST ANOTHER CRAZY PREGNANT LADY: *THE ASTRONAUT'S WIFE*

*The Astronaut's Wife* ends with adorable twin boys riding the school bus, their mother waving to them from the curb. What could be more innocent and benevolent? Yet the audience knows the creepy truth that these cute little boys are evil aliens plotting to take over Earth and its inhabitants. The ambiguity over external versus internal evil evident in *Rosemary's Baby* is echoed in *The Astronaut's Wife*, where the protagonist Jillian (Charlize Theron) is impregnated with the alien seed of her possessed astronaut husband Spencer (Johnny Depp). If *Rosemary's Baby* is an example of moral insanity induced by pregnancy, then *The Astronaut's Wife* is an example of hereditary insanity triggered by pregnancy. Much is made of Jillian's history of mental instability, including attempted suicide and psychiatric problems that had resulted in her hospitalization in the past. Her history of mental illness is used by her husband and by her sister to discount Jillian's growing anxieties over her unborn babies (twins), her husband, and her pregnancy. At the end of the film the alien possessing her husband moves out of his body into hers, confirming that the evil is within her. Even before the alien moves into her body, Spencer—or the alien within him—tells her, "I live there. I live inside you."

Like Rosemary, Jillian sports a short haircut, almost like a little boy's cut. Unlike the clueless Rosemary, however, from the beginning of her pregnancy Jillian is actively trying to determine why strange things are going on around her. In addition, unlike Rosemary, Jillian is not ecstatic to learn that she is pregnant; nor is she pining away for a baby. Indeed, Jillian's ambivalence toward her pregnancy, evidenced by the fact that she tries to abort the fetuses by using the morning-after pill (after she suspects something is amiss), suggests that women's ambivalence about motherhood rather than ambivalence about their own sexual desires triggers evil (recall Wexman's problematic diagnosis that Rosemary's repressed sexual desires trigger her demonic fantasies).

A quick synopsis of the film is in order. Johnny Depp plays an astronaut, Spencer Armacost, whose mission mysteriously loses contact with Earth for two minutes. During that time, as we later discover, Spencer and his fellow astronaut have been inhabited by an alien intent on reproducing through their wives. Both wives get pregnant, but in the meantime Spencer's comrade dies violently and publicly. Jillian Armacost begins to suspect something strange when she finds out that the grieving widow, her friend Natalie (Donna Murphy), is pregnant with twins but then electrocutes herself with a radio in the shower. Like Ripley (Sigourney Weaver) in the *Alien* series (who tries to kill herself but does not succeed and who begs "Kill me!" in the opening nightmare "birth" scene in *Aliens*), she would rather commit suicide than unleash the evil inside her. This suicidal pregnancy is echoed throughout the film when Jillian's suicidal past is revealed and after a fall down the stairs fleeing her husband she is hospitalized to protect both herself and the babies. Jillian's pregnancy leads to suicidal thoughts, which is taken as another sign of her insanity.

When Jillian discovers that she is also pregnant with twins, her uneasiness is compounded. A former NASA scientist tries to warn her that they have been tracking strange radio transmissions since the mysterious blackout. And Jillian notices Spencer listening to strange sounds on the radio and generally acting peculiar. When Jillian is convinced that she is harboring evil within, she tries to end her pregnancy with pills. Spencer catches her in the act and violently tries to stop her. He threatens to harm her if she tries to harm his offspring again. At this point both Spencer and Jillian's sister become concerned that Jillian is showing signs of her previous mental instability. In the end, the possessed Spencer kills Jillian's sister. And in a showdown where Jillian is sitting with her toes in water, ready to electrocute herself, the plot twists and she electrocutes Spencer instead. The alien inhabiting Spencer repeats, "I live inside you" and the audience sees an image of the twins in utero. Then, in another twist the alien moves out of Spencer's body and into Jillian's. The film ends with Jillian sporting a new hairstyle and hair color and happily married to another military man, sending her adorable twin sons off to school. The last shot is of the twins on the school bus listening to the strange radio transmissions in their headphones while studying mathematics far too advanced for their age.

It is noteworthy that for Jillian, like Rosemary, the conception/sex scene becomes a violent rape. Both Jillian and Rosemary are violently inseminated by otherworldly creatures that take the form of their husbands. The trope of evil father surrogates who impregnate and then leave or die is common in pregnant horror. For example, other horror films that feature women raped by evil who go on to give birth to monstrous hybrids are *Demon Seed* (1977), where a woman is raped by a computer and gives birth to an AI-human hybrid; *X-tro* (1983), where a woman's husband is abducted and then returns and rapes her; and *The Incubus* (1982), where a woman space traveler is raped by an alien (see Creed 1993:43–44). These "fathers" provide the impure element that gestates in the wombs of unsuspecting women-containers, whose most active "evil" usually involves accepting their hybrid or monstrous babies and caring for them.

More recent examples of pregnant horror surrogate bad fathers occur in *Splice* and, to some extent, *Pan's Labyrinth*. In *Pan's Labyrinth*, the evil cruel stepfather not only threatens the mother of his unborn child but also her daughter Ofelia, who sacrifices herself in the end to fend off the forces of his evil. *Splice* ends with Elsa pregnant after being raped by her monstrous creation Dren. These surrogate fathers could be interpreted, as Wexman does, as the perverse fantasies of women whose imaginations are pregnant with horror. But to do so continues to blame women for evil; in fact, taken to the extreme, it blames women for their own rape. Alternatively, these surrogate fathers can be seen as symbols of age-old anxieties about paternity and questions of who is the father. For, traditionally, it has been assumed that while the identity of the mother is certain, the identity of the father is unknown to all but the mother. In fact, until the relatively recent invention of paternity tests to settle the uncertainty of paternity, women's word established paternity. If nothing else, pregnant horror makes us aware of how unreliable is women's word, particularly that of the crazy women of pregnant horror. Again, the woman is blamed even when she is the victim. With new reproductive technologies, particularly IVF (in vitro fertilization) through sperm donors, new fantasies of absent horrible fathers have emerged. The question of who is the father resurfaces with a vengeance in these films.

There is another subterranean hot-button issue haunting these films in which pregnant horror is the result of rape, namely abortion. Some critics interpret *Rosemary's Baby* as an argument for abortion, suggesting that the evil comes from outside Rosemary and that she should have the option to abort her devil seed rather than give birth to it (see Valerius 2005). Even Fischer acknowledges that the late 1960s context of the film places it in the middle of women's struggles for birth control and legal abortion. If these films in which women are raped by forces of evil trigger anxieties over abortion, it is because this is the one case where some—although certainly not all—so-called pro-life advocates draw the line. Many who otherwise oppose abortion do support it in cases of rape or incest. Even so, as Caroline Lundquist points out, rape-pregnancy is rarely part of the discourse over abortion rights. Obviously, the issue of rape-pregnancy is traumatic and troubling on many levels, one of which is the notion of "choice" associated with the victim's choice to abort or to have the baby (see Lundquist 2011). As in these pregnant horror films, as Lundquist argues, women pregnant as a result of rape often find themselves being coerced into carrying the babies to term; they still feel the social pressures to give birth and the social stigmas attached to abortion. Even as victims of rape, women are still held responsible for their reproductive "choices." Lundquist concludes:

> The tragic element of reproductive choice is especially prominent in rape-related pregnancy, and it is thus especially appropriate to think of this phenomenon in terms of the tragic. There may be something inherently tragic about women's reproductive lives more generally; pregnancy loss, explicitly or implicitly unwanted pregnancies, difficulties conceiving—all of these involve circumstances which are tragically beyond the agent's control, and all tend to involve feelings of loss, regret and personal responsibility. Moreover, public discourse on reproductive choice betrays the same ambivalence at work in rape-pregnancy; we seem to feel conflicted when it comes to morally assessing women's reproductive lives: on the one hand, we want to hold women responsible for their pregnancies, and on the other, we acknowledge an element of luck; thus discourse on unwanted pregnancy often reveals a pathological ambivalence. (Lundquist 2011)

Lundquist diagnoses a fundamental ambivalence at the heart of women's reproductive choices that haunts contemporary debates over reproductive choice; and, as we will see, it also haunts Hollywood films, including pregnant romcom and pregnant horror.

In *Rosemary's Baby* and *The Astronaut's Wife*, the women are both unsuspecting victims of surrogate fathers implanting their evil seeds and they are also just crazy enough to accept and even love the demonic/alien offspring produced through their impure unions. Indeed, we could argue that these films endorse the contradictory view that even women who are raped, even those raped by the devil or aliens, should not only carry their babies to term but also love them. The ambivalence evidenced by these films is that while these women are fulfilling their maternal duties, by doing so they also appear crazy. Both Rosemary and Jillian have paranoid fantasies that suggest that they might be mad. Jillian in particular is blamed for her mental instability and held responsible for her own victimization. The tagline for the film ("How well do you know the one you love?") suggests not only that Spencer is not who he seems but also that it is Jillian's fault for not knowing him well enough to recognize that he was possessed from the beginning. When she tries to explain to her sister that her husband may be an alien, she sounds crazy. Like Rosemary and other pregnant protagonists (including Alison in *Knocked Up*, who is mocked by Ben when he says that he is going to ignore her because her hormones are talking and not her), those around her—even those closest to her—don't take her complaints seriously. All are treated as insane or as rendered temporarily insane because of their pregnancies. Like Rosemary, in spite of her best efforts Jillian cannot stop the birth of something monstrous. Even after she kills Spencer, she cannot stop the alien who moves into her body. Although she is more forceful and has more agency than Rosemary, ultimately she is just as helpless. The monstrous alien/demon seed is unstoppable.

In *Rosemary's Baby* and *The Astronaut's Wife*, as we have seen, both the paternal and the maternal elements are in question. The paternal element is implicated in evil by violently implanting the devil/alien in the woman's womb—not incidentally through rape. The maternal element is implicated in these violent fantasies that take us back to the notion of maternal imagination and doctors speculating about women's "sick" fantasies that corrupt their babies. Or, more to the point, the fathers occupy an ambiguous place as both human and not human, both man and monster; their impurity is the agent of the woman's downfall. Yet the woman's—or her womb's—receptivity to this impurity is the result of her own ambivalence toward her male partner and toward her role in reproduction. Moreover, this ambivalence leads to her mental instability and questionable sanity, which makes her especially susceptible to evil. In both *Rosemary's Baby* and *The Astronaut's Wife*, the sanity of our pregnant protagonists comes into question; and clearly in the case of the second film, Jillian's mental instability precedes her pregnancy and becomes perhaps the dark reason why she can go through with it when her friend cannot. In other words, killing her husband and receiving not only the alien seed but also the alien himself may be possible because of her prior mental history. Like the alien displaced from Spencer's body into hers, her suicidal tendencies are displaced into homicide; and her own hidden destructive rage is displaced into the inner evil of the outwardly beautiful twins secretly listening to alien radio signals on the school bus. In the case of Rosemary and Jillian, women's mental instability, ambivalent emotions, and anxious fantasies give birth to monsters. From fantasies of evil paternal seeds violently implanted to the crazy women whose wombs not only accept but also secretly desire them, pregnancy is imagined as excessive. This excessiveness in the reproduction of the monstrous speaks to complex anxieties over reproduction, including an anxiety over absent or surrogate fathers who inseminate with something monstrous and then die or disappear, an anxiety over the generative mother as a breeding womb whose capaciousness is dangerous, and an anxiety over the continuation of the species—that is to say the human species.

## OMINOUS PREGNANCIES IN *STEPHANIE DALEY*

Although *Stephanie Daley* (2007) is not technically a horror film, it echoes the ominous tones of horrible pregnancies with emotionally unstable women fantasizing about absent fathers and giving birth to death. The title character, Stephanie (Amber Tamblyn), is a 16-year-old who faces murder charges for the death of her newborn. Lydie Crane (Tilda Swinton) is a pregnant forensic psychologist assigned to the case. The central question for Crane is whether or not Stephanie knew she was pregnant and intentionally killed her baby. The film's tagline is "the truth is what we believe." But in truth these characters neither know what they believe nor believe what they know. As their sessions evolve, stoic Stephanie elicits more confessions and more emotion from her pregnant therapist than she reveals about herself. Indeed, Stephanie acts as a blank screen onto which Crane projects her nightmarish fantasies involving her previously stillborn baby and her fears for her coming baby. The film begins with bloody footprints in the snow and a staggering teenager in a snowsuit being carried into an ambulance. The climax of the film is the bloody horror of Stephanie giving birth in the leg of her snowsuit in a bathroom stall at a ski resort, silently screaming in agony and terror. And, in between, Lydie Crane and Stephanie Daley dance around the girl's reticence about her pregnancy and childbirth and her impertinent questions about Crane's pregnancy and stillborn baby. Their sessions are interspersed with flashbacks to how Stephanie got pregnant and why no one knew about it, and to Lydie's troubled home life with her husband (Tim Robbins).

The film suggests a connection between the women's fantasies and superstitions and death, or more particularly, dead babies. As the stories of these women's pregnancies unfold, in one way or another they both associate pregnancy and dead babies with punishment for something they have done. In other words, in the worlds of their superstitious fantasies—which border on hallucinations and seem to signal mental instability (especially in the case of the psychologist)—they are to blame for the trauma that besets them. Like the nineteenth-century doctors who claimed that women's fantasies affect their unborn babies, these women "believe" that something about their mental states is not quite right and that therefore they have conjured their own worst nightmares. At the most basic level, they both "believe" that they deserve trauma as punishment and that they have brought on their misfortune themselves. In a world where "the truth is what we believe," as the stories unfold we see that they are both, in different ways, agents and victims of their circumstances. What we hear in their narratives, however, is that they believe that their superstitious fantasies signal that there is something deeply wrong with them at the very core of their psyches. In profoundly connected ways they believe that they are responsible not only for their dead babies but also for something far more sinister—their fantasies of dead babies. As their sessions progress, the forensic scientist starts to crack and begins to accept Stephanie's superstitions about her own pregnancy. There is transference from patient to therapist through which the central question of Stephanie's guilt becomes a question of the psychologist's guilt for her own stillborn baby. As the film progresses, both protagonists interpret the deeper meaning of their superstitions, dreams, and fantasies as evidence of their inadequate emotional coping mechanisms and as hieroglyphs for their subconscious evil intentions.

The "truth" that drives the narrative of the film and creates its suspense is the mystery of how a young girl becomes pregnant and does not know that she is pregnant; and more to the point, how she gives birth in the leg of her snowsuit without knowing she is giving birth. What kind of disavowal and denial must be taking place for this to happen? This question drives our fascination with the reality television show *I Didn't Know I Was Pregnant*. Is this the result of youthful innocence about such things, or is it a sign of something more perverse in the girlish psyche? Is this the same perversion that we witness in more mature form in the nightmarish fantasies of Stephanie's pregnant therapist? Does this evil lurk deep within the psyches of all girls and women, perhaps triggered by pregnancy? The film's fascination with these questions can be interpreted as an updated form of anxiety over the power of maternal imagination and pregnant insanity that echoes its pregnant horror sisters.

Women bordering on insanity and bloody footsteps are not all that *Stephanie Daley* shares with its full-on horror sisters. Like so many films in the horror genre, *Stephanie Daley* also plays on creepy associations between women and animals. Here, animals figure not only as ominous harbingers of danger but also as sacrificial lambs blindsided by death; so too with the women to whom they are intimately connected. Insofar as they represent the women's unconscious fantasies or desires, the animals in this film become complex symbols for the bloody trauma and leaky bodies of women's connection to the natural world. For example, Lydie Crane (note her last name is the name of a bird) dreams about hitting a deer with her car. At first, we don't know that it is a dream until we see her in bed with her cat—also looking dead—stretched over her head on her bed. In the dream, Lydie is in labor and driving herself to the hospital when she hits the deer. We see her trying to get help while the deer lays there bleeding to death. It is not a dream when she sees a dead cow alongside the road. These images of dead and bleeding animals, particularly the deer that Lydie hits and kills, represent her fear of having another stillborn baby and her guilt over her ambivalent feelings toward it. These bloody animals also echo Stephanie's bloody birth scene.

Women are not only associated with deer, but also the connection between felines and our female protagonists is repeated throughout the film. For example, Lydie is constantly rushing to pee, competing with her cat, Psycho, for access to the bathroom. Psycho's cat box also becomes an ominous presence in the film when Lydie finds a diamond earring in the box and begins to suspect her husband of infidelity. Moreover, she has been told to avoid the cat box because bacteria there might harm her fetus and jeopardize her pregnancy. She is irresistibly drawn to the cat box anyway, again possibly signaling her ambivalence toward her pregnancy. Like the feline's, Lydie's bodily functions indicate danger (their constant need to pee). This identification between Lydie and her cat named Psycho also suggests that she might not be mentally stable, that she too might be "psycho." In addition, Psycho becomes a cipher for marital tensions in Lydie's relationship with her husband, whom she repeatedly asks to clean the cat box.

Like Lydie, Stephanie is also explicitly associated with cats. For example, just before having sex with Corey, whom she has just met at a party and who impregnates her, she finds a white kitten. At that point, she is like the white kitten, an innocent virgin who just wants love and attention. Later, just before walking to Corey's house to confront him since he hasn't called her since their sexual encounter at the party, she pets a black cat, a familiar trope as evil omen, that here signals her loss of virginity. On her way through the woods to his house, a deer startles her. And when she is outside Corey's house, his dog barks at her as if she is a threat—or perhaps a feline prey—lurking in the forest; the barking dog scares her and she runs home without talking to Corey. The association between women and felines is a common trope in sci-fi horror films—think of *Cat People* and *Catwoman*. In *Stephanie Daley*, kittens represent innocence while cats represent something suspicious, even sinister, in these women's fantasies, whether they are fantasies of dead and bloody babies or fantasies of uncaring absent or unfaithful fathers.

In general, animals appear as omens—usually bad ones—that echo the female protagonists' bleeding, leaking bodies. Lydie's constant need to pee is mimicked by her cat, while Stephanie's bloody childbirth is echoed in scenes of bleeding deer. In a sense, Stephanie, and to some extent Lydie, appear as "deer in the head-lights," blindsided by social pressures to be a good girl or a good mother. In the eyes of their/our culture, this girl and woman are beasts—as the press about Stephanie's case makes clear—insofar as they admit to their ambivalence about pregnancy and childbirth that leads to infanticide or oblique fantasies of infanticide represented by the omens of dead animals.

## THE DEADLY DOUBLE AND MONSTROUS MULTIPLES

The proximity of birth and death in *Stephanie Daley* is another characteristic that the film shares with the subgenre of pregnant horror. In her book about the association between women and horror, *The Monstrous-Feminine: Film, Feminism, Psychoanalysis*, Barbara Creed discusses a slew of horror films in terms of their representations of abject wombs harboring broods of evil monsters that threaten not only death but also human extinction. As

Creed argues, in these films women's wombs take on a life of their own and become the object of horror in terms of what can inhabit them and in terms of their unstoppable and excessive generative powers that overrun filmic space with hideous spawn. In films like *The Brood* and the *Alien* series (1979, 1986, 1992, 1997), we see images of a generatrix out of control to the point that it threatens the human race by disgorging masses of inhuman offspring. In these films, women or motherly monsters are giving birth to broods and hordes that threaten not only with their slimy inhuman grotesqueness and their bloodthirsty killing but also with their sheer quantity. These images of reproduction as unstoppable signal fear of something excessive about birth itself. The anxiety of wombs gone wild, spewing (rather than birthing) countless offspring, generates nightmarish images of hordes of insect-like babies or monstrous aliens taking over the planet or the entire universe. Insects, even more than animals, are icons of horrible excess in their reproductive capacities.

Recent films continue to associate haunted pregnancy with insects. For example, in *Grace* baby Grace is surrounded by flies; *The Unborn*'s Casey cracks an egg from which a giant insect emerges; and Dren in *Splice* catches insects with her inhuman tongue. In these films, insects appear to represent a threat of the inhuman that may be harbored in women's wombs. Insects signal the excessiveness of pregnancy not only as beyond human but also as insect-like nonsexual or nonnatural reproduction. In these films, women's wombs are dangerous spaces and pregnancy is a foreboding of inhuman possibilities that threaten to overrun humanity with something terrible.

Although she doesn't specifically discuss pregnancy as such, Rosi Braidotti develops a Deleuzian account of science fiction films such as *The Fly* (1958), *The Brood*, *Aliens*, and *Tarantula* (1955) that revolve around this creepy connection between women and insects and spiders (Braidotti 2002). She argues that in various science fiction films insects represent "a generalized figure of liminality and in-between-ness which shares a number of structural features with the feminine" (2002:150). Braidotti identifies insects with "perfected hybridity" through their nonmammalian sexuality and reproduction, which involves laying eggs and a relatively short life-cycle (2002:158–59). "As such," she says, "they are likely to feed into the most insidious anxieties about unnatural copulations and births, especially in a 'post-humanist' culture obsessed with artificial reproduction" (2002:158). She suggests that the speed of their reproduction and of their transformations from eggs (and we might add larvae, cocoons, maggots, etc.) into reproducing adults produces anxieties related not only to the non- or post-human but also to the possibility of changes and transformations that take place quickly. To extend Braidotti's analysis, we could say that the speed of reproduction and the numbers of offspring produced suggest something inhuman, conjuring anxieties about the inhuman lurking in new reproductive technologies that move us away from sexual reproduction to embryo or zygote implantation. As we will see, Assisted Reproductive Technologies (ARTs), which remove and fertilize eggs and then implant lots of them in the hopes that one survives, produce science fiction fantasies of insects laying eggs and overrunning the planet.

In the *Alien* series, for example, the monstrous maternal alien lays thousands of eggs in the creepy egg chamber, which is abject not only because of its leaky slimy stickiness but also because of the sheer quantity of offspring. Discussing *Alien*, Creed says, "the central characteristic of the archaic mother is her total dedication to the generative, procreative principle. She is the mother who conceives all by herself, the original parent. . . . She is outside morality and the law" (1993:27). The threat posed by this archaic mother is multiple: she is an unstoppable generatrix; she is totally dedicated to reproduction; she produces offspring outside the norms of sexual reproduction; and her dedication to reproduction is so fierce that she operates outside of morality and the law, not to mention the realm of the human. *Grace* and *Splice* give us contemporary examples of unstoppable mothers who disregard norms and rules in order to reproduce, which of course leads to inhuman offspring.

In the 1979 film *The Brood* the female protagonist Nola's (Samantha Eggar) repressed rage manifests itself in undeveloped fetus-creatures that fill a sac hanging from her stomach. Again, the multitude of these creatures is creepy and represents the inhuman element of Nola's reproduction. Like other horror films, part of what is horrible about these creatures is their incompleteness; they are monstrous in their not-quite-humanness, or in their in-betweenness, which makes them uncanny reminders of our own formation out of unformed fetuses and brute genetic matter. Unlike most of its pregnant horror sisters where the connection is merely implicit, *The Brood* explicitly connects pregnancy's supposed borderline insanity with repressed rage; and it explicitly connects pregnant women's supposedly dangerous fantasies with their resulting horrible offspring. In *The Brood*, women's repressed emotions take on literal monstrous shape. Here, the nineteenth-century notion that women's imaginations and fantasies affect their unborn babies takes on its most dangerous form when Nola's anger gives birth to multiple, incomplete, not-quite-human offspring. And, as Creed points out, she does so outside of normal sexual reproduction and, like many horror heroines, at the expense of her male partner.

Although Jillian in *The Astronaut's Wife* does not present an image of what Creed calls the "all-devouring womb of the archaic mother," even she presents the uncanny figure of a self-generative mother when at the end of the film she becomes possessed by the alien. Like many of her horror sisters, she is widowed by the evil living inside her womb. Recent horrific single moms widowed, often by the evil they have spawned, include Madeline in *Grace*, Casey in *The Unborn*, and Elsa in *Splice*; at the end of the latter two, after their partners are brutally killed, the protagonists are pregnant with something ominous, possibly even evil, and certainly "not entirely human" (to quote the tagline from *Splice)*. Even creepier than Jillian's impregnation by her possessed husband, Spencer, is her own possession by the seemingly male alien who makes her more than just a receptive womb for his offspring. Now, she is truly not what she seems, which is all the more horrific in the final scene when she is kissing her new, presumably clueless, husband.

Moreover, *The Astronaut's Wife* suggests that there is something uncanny about twins. The doubleness not only of the maternal body but also of the fetuses within it is represented as sinister. The final scene of *The Astronaut's Wife* makes the binary relation between the twin boys into something creepy and threatening. That there are two instead of one suggests a doppelganger effect that, in the context of the horror film, makes twins and multiples uncanny. The uncanny fascination/horror of the doubleness of twins is taken to extremes in *The Unborn* (2009), in which Casey (Odette Yustman) is haunted by a young boy. The boy turns out to be the dead twin of her Holocaust survivor grandfather, who was killed by Nazis in genetic experiments on twins. As the film tells us, the infamous Dr. Joseph Mengele was convinced that twins could be used to unlock the genetic mysteries of the human body. Casey also discovers that she had a twin brother who died in utero. After a Jewish exorcism of the evil spirits, the film ends with Casey finding out that she is also pregnant with twins, a flashback to a line repeated throughout the film ("Jumby [the nickname of her dead twin brother] wants to be born now") and an ultrasound image of the twins in Casey's womb (fig. 4.1). Throughout this film, twins represent both the uncanniness of the double and the haunting of the unborn. From the title of the film, *The Unborn*, to the final scene of the ominous ultrasound image of twins, the unborn or dead twin haunts the living.

Other creepy films about twins and multiples make clear a fantastic connection between doubles and freakiness. For example, *Basket Case* (1982) and *Basket Case 2* (1990) feature surgically removed Siamese twins, one of whom is so badly deformed that he is carried by the other in a basket, until he escapes to seek bloody vengeance on all who have not treated him as human. *Head of Family* (1996) is about the Stackpools, a family of quadruplets who each possess a characteristic of one superhuman individual: the first is strong, but stupid; the second has super senses; the third

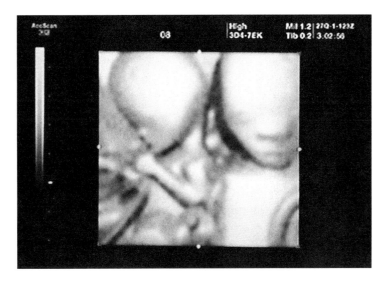

FIGURE 4.1 Casey (Odette Yustman) finds herself pregnant with twins after being haunted by the twin brother she didn't know she had, who died at birth, and by her grandfather, also a twin killed by the Nazis. (Courtesy of Universal Studios Licensing LLC, © 2009 Focus Features)

is beautiful; and the fourth has superior intelligence, but is all head and no body. This "head" of the family, Myron, controls his three siblings in his search for a normal body in which to transfer his superior mind. These quadruplets are not individuals but all parts of a horribly mutant family whose weirdness turns deadly. Here, multiples indicate a lack of individuality and a threat to "normal" singletons. Finally, in *Lebensborn* (1997), as in *The Unborn*, the connection between twins and genetic engineering is again explicit when evil geneticist Dr. Martin Speer tries to create a superior human being by experimenting on beautiful white Midwestern twins at the university where he works.

The association between twins and multiples and genetic engineering directly speaks to anxieties about new reproductive technologies that give rise to increased twins and multiple births. The use of twins in these pregnant horror films—and others such as *Deadly*

*Twins* (1985)—signals both the uncanniness of the doppelganger effect and the anxiety over the generative womb that gives birth to multiple offspring. These fears come together with new assisted reproductive technologies, for ARTs have dramatically increased the incidence of twins and other multiple births. Some real-life cases of octuplets and sextuplets (Nadya Suleman, Kate Gosselin) have become tabloid obsessions. With IVF, multiple implantations in a woman's womb lead to either some of the zygotes dying or being surgically removed, or the woman giving birth to multiples. Typically, women undergoing zygote implantation have several implanted at once because so many of them do not "take." One consequence is that doctors and women are often in a situation where they must decide whether or not to remove one or more of the fetuses and which one(s) to remove. This procedure is called "selective reduction," which is performed to enable one or two fetuses to develop fully for a healthier pregnancy and healthier babies; and, usually, women do not want three or more babies at once.

While *The Unborn* and other films whose images of unborn children certainly suggest that we are haunted by anxieties over abortion, they also signal more subterranean anxieties over new reproductive technologies that require selective reduction of embryos and fetuses in cases of multiple implantations. While abortion is visible in public debates, especially during elections, selective reduction is not. It remains hidden in a world of new fertility treatments, which is evidence of the social stigma still attached to infertility and the inability to conceive "naturally." In her book on new reproductive technologies, *Everything Conceivable*, in a chapter entitled "Deleting Fetuses: Selective Reduction, ART's Best-Kept Secret," Liza Mundy critically (and in a problematic moralizing tone) discusses how new reproductive technologies, especially in IVF, make it necessary or desirable to abort some fetuses for the sake of others. As Mundy says, "This, then, is another 'choice' facing today's woman and her partner: a termination situation in which the emotions are somewhat different from those surrounding abortion. These are wanted pregnancies, avidly sought" (2008:253). The combination of what has been called "baby hunger" and new technologies that give more fertility options leads to many middle- and upper-class women spending thousands of dollars on treatments so that they might have a child biologically related to either themselves or their partner. With these new options come new pressures and expectations such that some women opt for the implantation of donor eggs that have been fertilized with their partner's sperm so that they can carry and give birth to a child related to him even if not biologically related to them. While sperm donation is widespread and becoming more openly discussed, egg donation remains relatively hidden. Many women who use egg donation choose not to tell their children.

Given the growing demand for ARTs and IVF, we can interpret *The Unborn* and its pregnant horror sisters that feature threatening and bloodthirsty twins or multiples as the return of repressed anxieties over both abortion and the even more culturally taboo subject, selective reduction. IVF usually requires that one or more of the multiples will "die," while only one or two will live. Who decides which ones? How many will be removed? These questions haunt new technologies and our imaginations. Like the hushed tones of these "choices" in many women's lives, which are not discussed in popular media, *The Unborn* deals with these issues obliquely. *The Unborn* presents the haunting of unborn embryos, fetuses, or babies, signaling anxieties over abortion, selective reduction (chosen or otherwise), and even miscarriage, which also has reached record numbers, perhaps as a result of Early (Home) Pregnancy Tests (EPTs) that allow women to know they are pregnant earlier than ever before.

As we have seen, films like *The Unborn* display general anxieties about abortion and new reproductive technologies, and in general about incomplete and unformed (human) beings. *The Unborn*, *Stephanie Daley*, and *Grace* are haunted by dead or unborn babies. *Rosemary's Baby* and *The Astronaut's Wife* raise questions about what evil a woman's womb might be harboring. And their horror sisters such as *Aliens*, *Species*, and *The Brood* threaten with horrible wombs or womblike chambers spewing spawn and reproducing at inhuman rates. Many of these films suggest that women are capable of giving birth to evil, which is represented by the unformed, incomplete, and definitely inhuman offspring that threaten to overrun humanity. In sum, these films signal a complex of anxieties over reproduction, including fantasies of wombs as generatrix out of control, multiple births as inhuman and threatening, evil associated with women's role in reproduction, fantasies of demonic or inhuman surrogate fathers, pregnant women's insanity, fantasies of haunting unborn babies, and monstrous inhuman or hybrid creatures threatening the extinction of the human race.

## *SPLICE:* "NOT ENTIRELY HUMAN"

The 2009 horror thriller *Splice* presents a perverse Oedipal tale of a monstrous inhuman hybrid that turns deadly by the end of the film, at least in part as a result of abuse by its "mother." This film brings together many anxieties over reproduction previously discussed, only now in a potent brew that is part family drama and part science fiction horror with a pinch of graphic sex and a large dash of special-effects violence thrown in to satisfy contemporary audiences' expectations. But the secret ingredient that makes this film unique amongst its pregnant horror sisters is its explicit (rather than implicit) use of child abuse and incest to create its emotional pull. In the film, Elsa (Sarah Polley) and Clive (Adrian Brody) create a human-animal hybrid from Elsa's own DNA (unbeknownst to Clive). The result is Dren, a genetically engineered humanoid creature that exceeds all of its "parents" expectations, not only understanding human signifying systems including language but also morphing into an amphibian when necessary to breathe under water and sprouting wings to avoid falling off a roof. Indeed, Dren is full of surprises, particularly in terms of her sexual development. In a science fiction version of Oedipus, she eventually seduces her "father," then kills him and rapes her/his "mother" (after conveniently changing sexes from female to male). The film ends with a pregnant Elsa waiting to give birth to another presumably monstrous hybrid fathered by Dren.

On one level, *Splice* can be read as a post-human, post-sex/gender parable about the dangers of the hybrid or in-betweeness. Dren is neither fully human nor fully animal. She/he is neither female nor male. She is not purely mammal, nor purely amphibian, nor purely avian. She is, literally, neither fish nor fowl. Or, more precisely, she/he is both. Dren embodies the return of the repressed processes through which we all become human, female or male, and take up our sexualities—which is to say, precisely through the repression of difference and the abjection of that which we reject in ourselves, most especially our own animality. Dren is the return of repressed otherness within, an animal monstrousness that also wants love and affection.

In Deleuzian terms, we might think of Dren as becoming human, becoming animal, becoming female, becoming male, becoming amphibian, becoming avian; and her becoming, her in-betweenness, her neither-nor, is what makes her monstrous. Dren's hybridity and in-between status make her both threatening and powerful. Applying Rosi Braidotti's analysis of monstrous hybridity as both abject and reassuring, we could interpret Dren as the "ultimate survivor." When necessary to avoid drowning, Dren opens up gills, and when necessary to avoid falling off a roof, Dren opens her wings, and in order to seduce/rape both her father and her mother, Dren changes sexes. Although Braidotti's *Metamorphoses* was published years before *Splice* hit theaters, this film is a prime example of what she describes as the reassuring function of monsters insofar as "if not quite survivors, they are at least resilient in their capacity to metamorphose and thus survive and cope. . . . [M]onsters are 'metamorphic' creatures who fulfill a kaleidoscopic mirror-function and make us aware of the mutation that we are living through in these post-nuclear, post-industrial, post-modern, post-human days" (Braidotti 2002:201). Dren embodies the fantasy of Darwinian evolution on steroids, in which adaptations and transformations happen so quickly that humans are left behind even as they are the creators of the post-human, the ultimate survivor, the future of the "not entirely human" race.

Extending Noël Carroll's theory of horror as monstrous incompleteness, and following Barbara Creed's feminist analysis, Rosi Braidotti further develops the connection between the feminine and this incompleteness. She argues that as psychoanalytic feminists have shown, within the imaginary of Western culture the feminine is associated with lack, excess, and displacement, which she maintains is evidenced in science fiction films that "superimpose features from different species, displaying alternatively effects of excess or staggering omissions"; these excesses or omissions include various detachable bodily organs that can be reattached in new ways, which Braidotti reads as both monstrous and reassuring (2002:202). In her Deleuzian terminology, Braidotti describes this double effect as threatening to the dominant majority and inspiring to the oppressed minority; these detachable organs and reconfigured post-human, post-sexual creatures threaten the return of the repressed otherness within, which is horrifying for the self or the majority and liberating for the Other or the minority.

In psychoanalytic terms, detachable organs, particularly the phallus/penis, signal the mobility of power. If the phallus is the ultimate representative of patriarchal power, and if it can be grown and wielded by the feminine, as in the case of Dren, then power does not just belong to patriarchs. Rather, even cute critters cooing and wearing dresses like Dren can have it. When it suits her, Dren changes sexes and becomes male so that she can rape her mother and kill her father. In a sense, she is avenging her "childhood," which was full of abuse, particularly from her mother. Elsa and Clive experiment on Dren, put in her a cage, a box, lock her in a barn, restrict her food, and take away her cat companion. When Elsa decides to return Dren's beloved cat, in defiance Dren kills it with her deadly tail. This incites an enraged Elsa to brutally cut off Dren's tail, leaving a naked vulnerable Dren crying strapped to a table. Clive, like the audience, is horrified when he walks in on this scene.

*Splice* calls out for a psychoanalytic interpretation insofar as it is a twisted version of the already twisted Oedipus tale, in which the plot climaxes in having or not having "a tail." Dren's tail is not only one of her most salient differences from her human "parents" but also an obvious phallic weapon that she eventually wields against them. Her tail is a deadly stinger that becomes her penis when she changes sexes. She uses her phallic animal tail both to kill her father and to impregnate her mother. While her gills and wings give her extra human abilities, it is her stinger-tail phallus that gives her the power to kill; more than her other animal attributes, her tail threatens humanity. While she is female, she kills only smaller animals, but when she becomes male, she starts to kill humans. While she is female, she can be contained, restrained, and coaxed into submission. But Dren's superior animal-male size, strength, and abilities, combined with his newly acquired violent male urges, make him a threat that cannot be contained. Dren's rage at the end of the film, however, seems to be driven by the abuses she suffered as female, most especially her tail-cutting castration at the hands of her mother. The big bad male Dren avenges the helpless little girl Dren.

In terms of Freud's account of the little girl's Oedipal drama, in which she supposedly changes her love object from mother to father, she resents her mother for "castrating" her (according to Freud, once the little girl notices sexual difference, she feels castrated and cheated and blames her mother, who also has suffered the same fate). In Freud's story, the little girl wants to kill her mother, of whom she is also jealous, and marry her father. *Splice* gives a new spin to this classic fantasy. Dren avenges her castration at her mother's hands and satisfies her first loving longings in one act, namely the rape of her mother, but only after seducing her father. In fact, it is while Clive is comforting Dren because of her amputated tail that they have sex. Clive is portrayed as unable to resist the beguiling Dren and engages in this incestuous act with his teenage daughter surrogate for reasons seemingly beyond his control, one of which is Dren's resemblance to Elsa.

If Freud has a complicated way of explaining female sexuality with its turn away from the mother as love object toward the father, Dren solves this problem by simply changing sexes. That way, she can have both her father and her mother as sex/love objects and avenge them at the same time. As a further bonus, in terms of the classical Oedipal tale, Dren not only regrows her/his tail but also impregnates her/his own mother, in a sense reproducing her/himself as the future of the human race. *Splice* ends with a heavily pregnant Elsa looking out the window at a dark and dreary world, responding to advice that she consider terminating her pregnancy with an ominous "what's the worst that can happen," as if the worst has already happened.

Like her pregnant horror sisters Rosemary and Jillian, Elsa's mental health is presented as questionable. Through the course of the film, we learn that she was an abused and neglected child; and we see firsthand that she is capable of abusing Dren. Her husband Clive suggests that while she is unable to commit to having children because of her own messed-up childhood, she creates Dren as a child substitute. The fact that she won't have children the "normal" way through sexual reproduction, but chooses instead to genetically engineer her offspring, is seen by Clive as a sign of her mental instability. When we witness Elsa's hysterical and enraged reactions to Dren throughout the film, we are haunted by the idea that Elsa might be another crazy woman whose ambivalence about childbirth and motherhood are evidence of her mental instability and also the products of it. Like her pregnant horror sisters Rosemary and Jillian before her, and as if confirming her mental instability, a traumatized but resolute Elsa embraces her pregnancy and her unborn "child," even if it is the product of an unholy, alien, or in this case inhuman, father who raped her. Like Rosemary, Jillian, and more recently Grace's mother Madeline, Elsa becomes an outlaw mother harboring and protecting her evil inhuman baby even as it represents a murderous threat to the point of extinguishing or enslaving the human race. These crazy mothers of pregnant horror stop at nothing to have their babies. And they love them even if they are little monsters.

Perhaps more than any other genre, pregnant horror manifests anxieties over women's reproductive powers. Here, reproduction is figured as excessive, violent, and threatening in terms of the evil that may be harbored in women's wombs (and in their imaginations). Moreover, recent films that feature multiple births as spawn threatening the extinction of the human race can be interpreted as expressing latent fears over new reproductive technologies that make it possible for women to give birth to multiples, unless they engage in selective reduction. As we will see, these narratives also display anxieties over the technological production of humans that threatens the humanity of our species, as well as fears of hybridity and species-mixing that recall anxieties over racial-mixing so prevalent in the nineteenth century. Again, we see how changing images of pregnancy and changing technologies of reproduction bring with them new fears and desires even while they continue old ones.

# 5

## "WHAT'S THE WORST THAT CAN HAPPEN?"

### TECHNO-PREGNANCIES VERSUS *REAL* PREGNANCIES

IF *SPLICE* (2009) is a new twist on the classic Oedipal story, it is also a cautionary tale about new reproductive technologies, particularly genetic engineering. It is a science fiction nightmare that imagines moving from natural reproduction to technological replication through cloning and genetic manipulation. In one sense, this film is the familiar story of a mad scientist whose hubris in the face of his—or in this case, her—creation gives him a God complex that requires his comeuppance. Like many Frankenstein tales before it, *Splice* presents clever scientists, both of whom overestimate their own mastery and underestimate the autonomy of their creations. It is a familiar story, then, of scientists who treat—or mistreat—their subjects as objects in the name of science, but always complicated by their own subconscious personal investments, which are the true forces behind their drive to create a perfect or superhuman being.

In terms of pregnancy films, *Splice* presents a strange twist on another trope that is becoming a cliché in recent films, namely the *real* pregnancy and *real* baby versus the techno-pregnancy and techno-baby. A leitmotif in *Splice* is Elsa's reluctance to get pregnant and have children; instead she prefers to genetically engineer a child surrogate, Dren. At the end of the film, however, Elsa is pregnant and expecting to give birth. Of course, unlike her pregnant romcom sisters, Elsa's pregnancy is not merely an accident but the result of rape by an inhuman hybrid. Still, by the end, Elsa is pregnant through sexual reproduction and about to give birth—the old-fashioned way—rather than create her child in a lab. Perhaps because she chooses to carry the hybrid baby to term and thereby resorts to the "tried and true" means to a child, she says, "What's the worst that can happen?" After all, women have given birth as the result of sexual reproduction, even rape, since the beginning of the human race.

So, what is the worst that can happen? Of course, when that question is asked at the end of a horror thriller it suggests a sequel that takes place after Elsa's hybrid baby is born and perhaps grows up and becomes pregnant herself. In the horror genre, this is a naïve and ominous question. But in a romantic comedy, its meaning is very different. For example, *Due Date* (2010) suggests that the worst that can happen is that your white wife might have a black baby, whereas *The Back-up Plan* (2010) suggests that the worst that can happen is that a businesswoman gets artificially inseminated and that very day on her way out of the fertility clinic meets "the one," the man of her dreams. Other romcom films such as *Look Who's Talking* (1989), *Junior* (1994), *The Brothers Solomon* (2007), *Baby Mama* (2008), *Miss Conception* (2008), and *The Switch* (2010), in one way or another make fun of artificial insemination, as if it may be, or lead to, the worst that can happen, whatever that may be, whether it is reproduction without sex, miscegenation, children as products, or technology replacing love. In these films, IVF becomes the stuff of comedy and, even more unlikely, of romance. Whether or not our protagonists "resort" to

ARTs or IVF, the worst that can happen is that they don't get pregnant and/or don't get a baby by the end of the film.

In their lighthearted way, these films suggest that techno-pregnancy and techno-babies, if not the worst that can happen, are not as desirable as the "real" thing. Techno-pregnancy and techno-babies are the result of technologically assisted or "artificial" reproduction after all. If the means of their production is "artificial," then maybe they are too. For example, we can read *Labor Pains* (2009) as a parable about artificial versus real pregnancy. Although Thea (Lindsay Lohan) fakes pregnancy to keep her job, which requires wearing a prosthetic belly, by the end of the film her fake pregnancy leads to romance and a real pregnancy. Thea's prosthetic pregnancy—especially worn on the anorexic body of actress Lohan—also signals the way in which pregnancy has become an accessory that can be removed after use, and the imagined oscillation between lack (anorexic body) and excess (pregnant body). High-tech pregnancies and childbirth, including IVF and other ARTs, planned C-sections and so-called "mommy-tucks" (tummy tucks done along with C-sections), offer women more options but also put more pressure on women to fit families into busy career schedules and look good while doing so. These new technologies also produce new expectations, desires, and fears, some of which are manifest in recent Hollywood pregnancy films.

With an eye to representations of new reproductive technologies in these films, in this chapter we revisit themes of shame and stigma associated with pregnancy and childbirth, only now attached to ART pregnancies, ideals of romantic pregnancies and childbirth over technological ones, images of choice and excess as they play out in discussions of new technologies and so-called "designer babies," uncanny fantasies raised by these new technologies including monstrous births, multiple births, various forms of hybrids and miscegenation, and uncertainties over paternity and maternity. Even more than ARTs, cloning engenders fantasies of womanless births and the commoditization of human life. Hollywood representations of clones are almost entirely dystopian fantasies of the future of reproduction without wombs and without love. While cloning films may seem at the opposite pole from pregnancy films insofar as pregnancy is seemingly rendered obsolete in these science fiction tales, as we will see, these films share the same anxieties as pregnancy films, most especially the fear of separating sex from reproduction. This anxiety, as we have seen, is driven not only by the fear that heterosexual sex, and men, are irrelevant to reproduction but also and moreover that love has become irrelevant. For example, the documentary *The Business of Being Born* (2008) can be seen as a manifesto for choosing love over technology, and thereby choosing love babies over techno-babies.

## ROMANTIC PREGNANCIES ARE THE REAL THING

If not so long ago pregnancy was something to be hidden, a private matter that required modesty in dress and behavior, now with sexy pregnant bodies and protruding baby bumps on the covers of tabloids every week, a new stigma is attached to Artificial Reproductive Technologies and what goes on at fertility clinics. If a few decades ago a woman's pregnant body was obscene insofar as it was associated with sex—it was proof that she had sex—today the disconnect between sex and pregnancy made possible by new reproductive technologies appears as the new obscenity. Medical intervention into "natural" reproduction through "good old-fashioned" sex is represented as suspect, even gross or "unnatural." And women who use these new technologies to satisfy their "baby hunger" are pictured as monstrous—when they are seen at all. Even while they celebrate celebrity pregnancies and put on display pregnant teens, tabloids also vilify women such as Nadya Suleman ("Octomom") and Kate Gosselin, who use ARTs to have multiple infants; these publications present a shrewd but complex marketing strategy by, on the one hand, sensationalizing these births and turning these women into celebrities, and on the other hand, chastising them for using their babies for financial gain. Women who have multiple babies, and sometimes even women like Madonna or Angelina Jolie who adopt multiple babies, are pictured as excessive, even monstrous, and yet we can't get enough of them. Our own desire for what has become a spectacle of excess is itself excessive, if not obsessive, as we revel in tabloid pregnancies or a spate of television reality shows about pregnant women and teens. We are especially fascinated by pretty young girls having sex and getting pregnant, particularly if, like Stephanie Daley, they don't realize that they are pregnant and give birth into toilets and on bathroom floors (as in the reality show *I Didn't Know I Was Pregnant*). As we have seen throughout this book, our craving for pregnancy is manifest in Hollywood films that increasingly present pregnant women as entertainment. In this way, we all suffer from "baby hunger" or, we could say, "pregnant hunger." Pregnancy, which was once shameful because of its association with sex, has become titillating for the same reason. Without sex, however, pregnancy appears in these films as grotesque and excessive.

Recent ART films (artificial reproductive technology films) such as *The Brothers Solomon*, *Baby Mama*, *The Back-up Plan*, and *The Switch* present artificial reproductive technologies as both gross and funny. In these films, ART is an obstacle to overcome for the sake of romance and love. If in earlier romantic comedies class and sexual difference were obstacles to romance that created tensions to be resolved by the end of the film, here chemistry—literally—is the obstacle that has to be resolved by the natural chemistry between characters. In these films, the couple is united in the end through the adventures and mishaps of ARTs and "fake" pregnancy, which are overcome by natural sexual reproduction. *Real* reproduction and *real* babies replace *artificial* reproduction. More often, the techno-pregnancy is a fake that doesn't take, and by the end of the film the couple celebrates the unlikely event of real pregnancy.

In *Baby Mama* and *Labor Pains* fake pregnant women make scenes to imitate and parody stereotypes about pregnancy, from

food cravings to morning sickness, to great comic effect. Recall
that Angie (Amy Poehler) pours organic pea soup into the toilet
while making barfing sounds to keep up her charade. And both
*Baby Mama*'s Angie and *Labor Pain*'s Thea stuff, shift, and grab
their prosthetic bellies with abandon in funny scenes that make
pregnancy detachable. Like Dren's tail in *Splice*, these pregnancy
bellies are detachable, but also grow back. In the end, both Angie
and Thea really are pregnant. Fake pregnancies give way to real
ones. Stranger yet, menopausal and perimenopausal women in
*Miss Conception* and *Baby Mama* end up pregnant through sex
with their boyfriends when they least expect it. Similarly, Sigourney Weaver makes a comic appearance in *Baby Mama* as Chaffee
Bicknell, a sixtyish surrogacy broker who has a newborn already
(the old-fashioned way, as she says) and gives birth to twins, which
Kate (Tina Fey) and Angie find gross and disgusting. The idea
of this older woman giving birth is played for laughs, but behind
the jokes is the film's comment on ARTs enabling older and older
women to give birth, which the film finds gross. In these films, the
worst that can happen is that a woman will end up with a successful career but without a baby. Or she will wait until she is old
and does not conform to the norm of 20- or 30-somethings having
babies. Why is the image of older women giving birth uncanny?
Is it "gross" because Kate does not want to think of older women
having sex? Or because older women having babies brings birth
into close proximity with death? In any case, *Baby Mama*, along
with its more recent sisters *The Back-up Plan* and *The Switch*, can
be seen as warnings to young women to have babies while they
still can, with or without male life-partners. Of course, since these
films are romantic comedies, they always end up with male partners, and their babies are the products of romance. Even in *The
Back-up Plan*, although Zoe (Jennifer Lopez) has twins as a result
of artificial insemination, the film ends with her pregnant by her
new lover Stan (Alex O'Loughlin) with a more romantic "real"
baby. The film seems to warn that if she had only waited one more
day before resorting to IVF, she could have had a *real* family with

all her babies biologically related to their new dad. Interestingly, the way that Stan finally proves his love to Zoe is by accepting her redheaded IVF babies as his own.

## WHAT'S DAD GOT TO DO WITH IT?

In all of these films, paternity slips back in. IVF using donor sperm raises questions about paternity. "Who's your daddy now?" takes on new meaning in an age when sperm banks are big business and donors' identities are usually confidential. The anonymity of it troubles these films that act as "correctives" for women conceiving, giving birth, and raising children on their own, which is to say without dad. First and foremost, these films insist on sex for reproduction. As we have seen, they reassert the connection between sex and reproduction, even in the most unlikely circumstances. *Baby Mama*'s Kate is told that she has a better chance of getting hit by a bus than getting pregnant. *Miss Conception*'s Mia (Heather Graham) is told that she has one egg left, and rather than resort to IVF to make sure she gets her biologically related baby in time, she stalks funerals and bars looking for "Mr. Right Now" to impregnate her; of course, we find out she is already pregnant by her (recently but not for long) estranged boyfriend. And while Zoe in *The Back-up Plan* and Kassie (Jennifer Aniston) in *The Switch* decide to take matters into their own hands because their biological clocks are ticking and they don't have male partners, they still end up with romantic pregnancies and old-fashioned nuclear families. In all of these cases, the women end up having sex with the fathers of their babies, even if, as in *The Switch*, the baby is the product of IVF.

The conceit of *The Switch* is that Kassie Larson (Jennifer Aniston) decides she wants a baby and resorts to finding her own sperm donor because the anonymity of sperm banks is too creepy for her. Moreover, since she is a control freak—like most successful

30-something career women in Hollywood romcoms—she wants to make sure that she can control the process since she doesn't trust sperm banks; after all, anyone can say they are a Harvard graduate student on a semiprofessional soccer team who models in his spare time. Of course, her donor is the perfect specimen—tall, blond, good-looking, athletic, smart, and seemingly a sensitive, self-proclaimed feminist, guy, Roland (Patrick Wilson). Unbeknownst to Kassie, her best friend Wally (Jason Bateman), a neurotic nerdy guy—another familiar trope from recent romcoms—who has been in love with her for years, gets drunk at her insemination party and switches his semen for the donor's. Yes, she has a party with sperm-shaped party favors and much IVF humor about basters and such (the original title of the film was "The Baster," based on a short story called "Baster" by Jeffrey Eugenides).

Wally is so drunk that he doesn't remember masturbating using a magazine featuring Diane Sawyer as cover girl and accidently dumping his rival's semen before spilling his own seed to replace it. Of course, in some of these films men masturbating for sperm donation is played for laughs and fits right in with the "gross" humor of many recent romantic comedies of the raunchier "bromance" or "hommecom" variety. Wally isn't the only one who uses unlikely material as porn in order to produce a specimen for IVF. In *The Brothers Solomon*, when they are at the sperm bank giving their specimens, rather than select a pornographic magazine, both brothers choose (on the sly) a *National Geographic* magazine for its cover photo of a topless African woman. A comparable scene in the offbeat action-comedy *Kick-Ass* (2010) has the teen protagonist sexually aroused by a similar *National Geographic* image of a bare-breasted African woman. Wally eventually remembers that he switched his seed for the "hunk's junk" (as movie reviewer Katherine Monk [2010] calls it). His memory is jogged by the uncanny resemblance between Sebastian, Kassie's now 5-year-old son, and himself. Like Wally, Sebastian is a bit of a hypochondriac and even at five already suffers from the existential pain of life (associated in this film with Wally's neurosis). Of course, Wally and Kassie end up coupling, and with the adorable Sebastian they form a family-next-door, white middle-class nuclear family, celebrating Sebastian's birthday in the final scene. More important, there are no anonymous sperm donors, thus reassuring us that dad is still part of the family. Sex and reproduction are reunited at the end of the film—Kassie even sleeps with Roland just for good measure in case he really is the biological father of her son, as she believes.

Even the critically acclaimed indie film *The Kids Are All Right* (2010) insists on bringing sex and reproduction back together after the fact. In this unlikely story, the teenage children of two lesbians, both inseminated with the sperm of the same donor, go looking for their biological dad and find him. Nic (Annette Bening) and Jules (Julianne Moore) are a typical—or should I say stereotypical—suburban couple with Nic as breadwinner and conservative family anchor and Jules as a new-age hippie sort who can't seem to settle on a career. The twist is that both of them are women. The film goes out of its way to show that this lesbian marriage is just like any other marriage, including bickering, dull sex life, child-raising issues, impending empty-nest, and ultimately the threat of infidelity. Indeed, the title of the film reassures us that the kids are all right, even though two lesbian mothers have raised them without a man in the house (for, in the world of Hollywood films, this does not go without saying). Indeed the film's insistence on plugging Nic, Jules, and their son and daughter into the mold of the traditional nuclear family is evidence of the need for this message—namely, that an alternative family can be a "normal" family even without a dad. But if the film intends to show us that alternative families can produce kids who are all right without a dad, then the introduction of the sperm donor Paul (Mark Ruffalo) undermines its goal. Although Paul's insertion into the family disrupts it to the point of threatening its unity, he also "solves" the central problems that the kids are having when the film opens.

In an awkward moment at dinner with the family, Paul admits that he dropped out of college, a fact that the mothers, especially the uptight Nic, find appalling since they chose him as a sperm donor because of his education as evidence of his intelligence. This scene points to anxieties about knowing, let alone controlling, the sperm a woman receives from a sperm bank. How reliable are sperm banks? How do we know that the donor is really what he says he is? What if he says he is an architect when really he is a womanizing owner of a small restaurant? Later in the film, his son asks him why he donated his sperm and Paul answers that he doesn't know, that he needed the cash. The son wants to know the going rate for semen, indicating that he feels reduced to a dollar value by his father's actions.

When Paul admits that he didn't finish college, he responds to Nic's surprise by saying "I'm a doer." While this line may make him seem flaky, he proves true to his word. He is a doer. He gives 18-year-old daughter Joni (Mia Waikowska) the confidence she needs to stand up for herself, which apparently her mothers cannot give her. And he helps teenage son Laser (Josh Hutcherson) drop an undesirable friend, which the mothers tried to do but couldn't. He gives jobless Jules an important landscaping job to jump-start her career and in the process manages to jump her. Eventually he even wins over the hard-hearted Nic. Although he is literally locked out of the family at the end, his fatherly influence has changed its dynamics. He gets things done that the women cannot do, and it is these things that both threaten the family unit but also give his biological children the father that they apparently do need in order to be all right. Moreover, he successfully reunites sex and reproduction, reassuring us that men are not obsolete to reproduction. Seeing the biological father and biological mother having sex reassures us that even if the order has been reversed so that reproduction comes before sex, heterosexual sex and reproduction are still connected. Again, Hollywood reassures us that fathers are not just anonymous test tubes or vials from sperm banks, and that "good old-fashioned" heterosexual sex and reproduction are still on intimate terms, even in the most unlikely circumstances.

The demon seeds of horror where bad dads inseminate with evil have become anonymous seeds filling vials at sperm banks. Both signal anxieties about paternity. While horror threatens with evil paternity and the bad seed, recent ART films transform the threat of unknown origins and anonymous seed into sensitive guys happily taking up their paternal roles. In both cases, the father's seed is separated from his proper paternal duties and, we might say, takes on a life of its own apart from him. Whether dad makes a deal with the devil as in *Rosemary's Baby*, becomes possessed by an alien as in *The Astronaut's Wife*, or merely comes in a canister or cup as in *Baby Mama*, *The Switch*, and *The Kids Are All Right*, paternity is put into question. Who has inseminated this pregnant woman? Who is the father of this little monster, hypochondriac preschooler, or angst-filled teen? While Hollywood gives us plenty of examples of men separated from their seed, by the same token it emphasizes their role in reproduction and thereby, for better or worse, reestablishes paternity.

Given that absent fathers are the norm in American families, Hollywood's anxious attempts to reestablish some sort of paternal figure are reassuring fantasies that dad is still relevant. Vivian Sobchack argues that contemporary horror, science fiction, and melodrama in various ways address a paternal figure in decline (1996). She analyzes a tension between modern paternity and modern patriarchy that revolves around the father's relationship with his child: "If the child is figured as powerful at the expense of the father, then patriarchy is threatened; if father is figured as powerful at the expense of his child, then paternity is threatened. . . . Once conceived of as identical in bourgeois capitalist culture, patriarchy and paternity have been recently articulated as different—one powerful effect of white, middle-class feminist discourse" (Sobchack 1996:156). With both patriarchy and paternity in decline, if not in crisis, "patriarchy as a political and economic power structure and paternity as a personal and subjective relation" cannot occupy the same place (Sobchack 1996:156). Modern patriarchy still requires a strong father, while modern paternity requires a loving sensitive father, and the strong but loving, sensitive and playful father is hard to imagine (without resorting to a pregnant Arnold Schwarzenegger in *Junior*).

Sobchack claims that horror "plays out the rage of paternal responsibility denied the economic and political benefits of patriarchal power," and melodrama "plays out an uneasy acceptance of patriarchy's decline" by presenting a "sweetly problematic paternity in ascendance" (1996:152, 154). If horror displays repressed paternal rage at being unseated as patriarch but still held morally responsible for the family, melodrama lets dad off the economic hook but only insofar as he takes over some or all of maternal caring. The alternative to either is that dad becomes a child himself, which, as Sobchack points out, is often the case in science fiction. This is also the case in recent hommecom or bromance, where the male protagonists starts out boyish and immature and must be transformed into a mature man; in pregnant romcom this transformation process is often initiated by the anticipation of paternity. In contemporary romantic comedy both the patriarch in decline and the boyish or sensitive paternal figure are played for laughs. Sensitive slackers and directionless dads, from *Knocked Up*'s Ben through *The Back-up Plan*'s Stan, are a staple of recent romcoms.

When it comes to anxieties about the fall of the patriarch, *Children of Men* (2006) is exemplary, for it gives us pregnancy without sex or love, but not without men. As the title suggests, even in this gritty science fiction future, children are still "of men." Anxieties over paternity in decline loom large in this nightmarish thriller where the female lead Julian (Julianne Moore) is killed off in short order early in the film in the middle of a mission (and a conversation) with her former lover Theo (Clive Owen), who is left holding the bag, so to speak, the miraculously pregnant woman Kee (Clare-Hope Ashitey). As the DVD cover shouts: "The Year 2027: The Last Days Of The Human Race, No Child Has Been Born For 18 Years, He Must Protect Our Only Hope." He, of course, is Theo; and he does. After fighting off bad guys on all sides, and traversing a dangerous world populated by gangs and thugs, Theo delivers Kee presumably to safety, after delivering the baby (literally), and puts them both in a rowboat and sends them out to sea. What is unclear is what awaits the vulnerable young mother

and her newborn once the ominous fog parts and—hopefully—
her new protectors arrive. The surrogate white father, a reluctant
and burned-out Theo, shepherds the young black single mother to
safety—maybe.

*Children of Men* gives us a post-feminist, post-apocalyptic,
post-paternity, if not also post-patriarchal figure, jaded by disappointment, not the least of which comes from the strong woman
who cares more about her cause than about him. Confused and
reluctant, he pulls himself together and steps up to fulfill his paternal duties, not only to mother and child but also to the "human
race." His paternal responsibility for the family is no longer just
individual, or national, or even transnational, but universal—the
baby represents the universal hope for the survival of humankind.
The moral of the film seems to be that dad has to quit sulking
about his loss of political and economic power or personal cachet
in the family and get out there and kick some ass, whether he likes
it or not. The woman he loves is dead. She has left him with a
pregnant teenage girl and a kid that isn't his. Although there is talk
of it, there is no sex in this world without children. So, unlike his
comedy counterparts, this action antihero, this everyman, doesn't
have sex, which would not only be incestuous insofar as he is also
the pregnant teen's surrogate father and protector but also interracial, which Hollywood usually shuns (and then throw in the heavily pregnant body, and even an R-rated 2027 isn't ready for that).
But he does have responsibility, responsibility for the entire human
race. Talk about responsibility with none of the perks of patriarchy or paternity!

The scene in which Theo meets Kee stands out because the
young, heavily pregnant black teen is in a barn amongst the cows,
suggesting an association between her and these animals. This
association goes further insofar as she has very little dialogue and
gives birth screaming like an animal on a dirty floor. Moreover, she
is apparently the only fertile woman on the planet, which plays
into the notion of women of color's hyperfertility and the fantasy of the black primitive. The film leaves us wondering about the

significance of the fact that the future of the human race is a pregnant black teenager. On the one hand, we could interpret this as
a revaluation of unwed poor black mothers, who are usually stig-
matized as naïve at best and welfare queens or worse (think of Precious and her welfare queen mother, or the flippant yet naïve Chantel in *Just Another Girl on the I.R.T*). On the other hand, given the
connection between this young pregnant black woman and cattle,
given that she comes from an underclass, and given that a white
man protects her, we could interpret the film as an apology of sorts
for slavery and the rape of African women by their white masters.
There is no question that this film is haunted by the history of
slavery and race relations. This fertile black Madonna, who gives
birth to the savior of the human race, is "our only hope," suggesting that the future of the human race may depend on a new relation between white and black races. The black woman becomes
the symbol of hope and the white man her protector. *Children of
Men* not only reinstates paternity (even in its title) but also raises
the specter of interracial babies without interracial sex. The film
suggests that perhaps interracial mixing or at least cooperation is
the last hope for the future of the human race.

## FEAR OF MISCEGENATION AND HYBRID BABIES

Anxieties about the continuation of the human race (or species)
or of the white race, fears of race mixing, and hybrid babies drive
many pregnancy films. In horror and science fiction genres hybrids
appear threatening or fantastic and could be interpreted as alle-
gories for racial mixing. Whereas in horror, hybrids (particularly
human-alien or human-animal hybrids as in *Rosemary's Baby*,
*The Astronaut's Wife*, or *Splice*) threaten the extinction of the
human race as we know it, in romantic comedies hybrid babies are
funny insofar as they mess with racial categories. (It is noteworthy
that *Rosemary's Baby* was released in 1968 at the height of the civil

rights movement in the United States). In some recent romantic comedies, hybrid babies are explicitly about race, where anxieties over race mixing are defused through humor. In both genres, however, hybridization or mixing is, to quote *Splice*'s Elsa, "the worst that can happen." Whether it is the human race or the white race, hybridity and miscegenation threaten the very categories of race upon which our perceptions of embodiment have heretofore relied. In this way, these films may be both conservative cautionary tales about the dangers of racial mixing and fantasies that begin to imagine a postracial future. In either case, mixing produces uncanny results that unsettle our conceptions of racial identity.

As many race theorists and feminist theorists have argued, the category of whiteness operates as the invisible norm against which other races are made other (e.g., Chambers 1997; Hartouni 1997; Seshadri-Crooks 2000; Sullivan 2006; McWhorter 2009; Roberts 2009). In the words of feminist race theorist Seline Szkupinski Quiroga, "race is defined by and against whiteness, an unmarked, invisible, and unexamined category . . . so that all members of marked categories possess race in ways that whites do not (2007:144). Within the imaginary of Western intellectual history, the white race has been the human race and visa versa. In the seventeenth and eighteenth centuries, explorers captured people they deemed exotic and brought them back to Europe to put on display as animals or subhuman species (Sharpley-Whiting & Denean 1999). Within the history of philosophy, when philosophers (predominately white men) discussed the concept or category of *human* or *humanity*, they assumed whiteness, as evidenced by associations of non-Europeans and animals in their writings (e.g., Kant's remarks on South Sea islanders; 1785, in 1993:31).

Given the invisibility of whiteness as a racial category or racial marker, and the imaginary slippage between white race and human race, the threat posed by hybridity in science fiction and horror genres appears all the more an allegory for a threat to the assumed racial purity of whiteness. Couple this with recent representations of Africans and African Americans in romantic comedies, and Hollywood's anxieties over racial mixing emerge in Technicolor. From the masturbating scenes of *The Brothers Solomon* and *Kick-Ass* to the specter of racially mixed babies in *The Brothers Solomon*, *The Back-up Plan*, and *Due Date*, these comedies play with fears of racial mixing. And although *Baby Mama* does not feature a racially mixed baby, it gives and takes away the possibility of class-mixing; and also it takes its title from African American slang for an unmarried woman who is the mother of an estranged lover's babies ("baby mama"), which is how the black doorman Oscar (Romany Malco) refers to Angie, as Kate's "baby mama." Angie is a baby mama because she takes money from Kate to have her baby; as a black man knows, Oscar explains, a baby mama wants money. Because Angie is working class and is using surrogacy to make money, she is compared to a baby mama. As we learn, Angie is also scamming Kate, even though she is doing so at the behest of her loser boyfriend, who, like Angie, is portrayed as lovable, if laughable, "white trash." It is interesting to note that whiteness is visible in this insult, but only in order to distinguish different types of trash and to suggest that "white trash" is a white version of black.

*The Brothers Solomon* also features surrogacy, but here the scheming man behind the "white trash" woman's attempts to make money by having someone else's baby is himself a black man, James (Chi McBride), who is played for stereotypical laughs throughout the film. Just as Angie turns out to be pregnant by her boyfriend instead of with Kate's baby, Janine (Kristen Wiig) in *The Brothers Solomon* turns out to be pregnant by her boyfriend. The comic climax of the film is that she gives birth to a black baby and the stupidly innocent Solomon brothers still believe it is theirs. The main conceit of the film is that they are "making a baby for dad," to fulfill their dying father's desire for a grandchild and heir. When their father regains consciousness long enough to meet his new "grandson," he assumes what the audience does (and what his innocent sons do not), looks aghast at the black baby, and says, "Holy shit!"

The father's gasp at the sight of "his" mixed-race grandson, supposedly the result of IVF, signals an anxiety at the heart of IVF and other forms of ARTs, namely the fear of miscegenation. White women have sued when they have been wrongly inseminated with semen from a black donor, whereas women of color are expected by the medical profession to choose black donors. In other words, assisted reproductive technologies are put in the service of maintaining and policing racial boundaries and racial purity to avoid any race mixing. Several feminists have addressed the explicit and implicit racism in ART practices in the United States. For example, one of the first to analyze new reproductive technologies in terms of racism, Dorothy Roberts has argued that laws and conventions governing genetics and ARTs serve both the purity and invisibility of whiteness as a racial category (1997). More recently, Roberts maintains that the popularity of ARTs leads to "a new reproductive dystopia," in which white women are privileged consumers whose fertility is promoted while black women's access to technology and their reproduction in general are discouraged (2009). Seline Szkupinski Quiroga concludes that ART is "a cultural practice that promotes race-based hierarchies" (2007). And Jennifer Morgan goes further by suggesting that conventions and policies (or the lack thereof) regulating ARTs are not only inherited from an economics and taxonomics of slavery but also continue that legacy into the modern moment (2010; cf. Davis 2000). With ARTs, the genetic material necessary to make a baby is bought and sold. As the popular phrase "designer baby" makes clear, the resulting babies are like products or commodities of expensive reproductive technologies. It is not just that human life is being bought and sold in ART as big business that continues the legacy of slavery. Even more problematic is the fact that the sellers and consumers of this technology are segregated by race, which means that ART is, as Morgan concludes, "rooted in the economies of inheritance found in the New World hereditary racial slavery" (2010).

Race is the most fundamental category for separating sperm donors at most sperm banks. Donors are carefully catalogued

according to various characteristics, especially physical characteristics, most of which are implicit racial markers. And one sperm
bank in California offers a "Quality Assurance Program" that
separates specimens into color-coded vials: yellow caps for Asians,
black and brown caps for African Americans, white caps for Cau-
casians, and red caps for "unique ancestry" or mixed-race donors
(see Quiroga 2007:150; see also Hartouni 1997, and Bender 2006).
This color coding according to traditional color stereotypes associated with different races is supposed to ensure "quality," particularly insofar as mixed races are flagged with red caps, indicating possible danger. As Morgan points out, however, sperm banks
become aware of "mistakes" only when racial boundaries are
crossed (2010). In their studies of fertility clinics, Quiroga, Roberts, Bender, and others have concluded that policies and practices
serve to preserve the myth of white racial purity. The danger of
racial mixing is the greatest legal threat to the sperm bank business, which is why enforcing racial segregation at sperm banks is
of utmost concern. Race is the primary marker of donor sperm
precisely because sperm itself is not racially marked in any visible or genetic way. Without racial policing on the part of sperm
banks, all sperm looks alike, so to speak, which is why artificial
techniques such as color-coded vial caps are used. The anxiety over
the raceless nature of sperm is met with careful segregation policies in most sperm banks.

   In her interviews with women of color receiving IVF from sperm
banks, Quiroga found that they were discouraged from using the
semen of white men. All of the women of color she interviewed
described being coerced in various ways to choose "sperm of
color," or doctors chose for them (Quiroga 2007). In some cases,
they simply were not allowed to use "white semen." Law professor
Lisa Ikemoto analyzes the ways in which race, class, and sexuality play into women's and men's access to fertility treatment. She
argues that within the medical establishment white middle-class
women are the legitimate recipients of fertility treatment because
they are the only people deemed infertile (Ikemoto 1995–96). "The

too fertile include unwed adult women, teens, welfare recipients, and/or women of color. In fact, within the in/fertility discourses, all of these women are too fertile" (1995–96:1008). Ikemoto identifies a third category that she names "dysfertile"—lesbians and gay men, who have "been made invisible or irrelevant" and who are also discouraged from receiving infertility treatment and access to new reproductive technologies (1009).

Quiroga also found that in terms of heterosexual married women receiving treatment, both doctors and patients were usually primarily concerned to match the donor's physical characteristics with the physical characteristics of the "social father," the woman's male partner (2007:150). Quiroga identifies three goals in matching donor sperm to the male partner, all of which are aimed at ensuring that the child looks enough like the "social father" to pass as his genetic child, which perpetuates ideals of biological family even while subverting them through technology. The presumption is that since the mother contributes genetic material, and since she carries the fetus and gives birth to the infant, maternity is not in question. But paternity might be if the child does not resemble its social father. Racial segregation not only maintains ideals of racial purity but also of paternity. The fact that the father did not contribute genetically to the child can be kept a secret and his paternity can remain intact. Racial mixing, then, poses a threat not only to whiteness but also to paternity. When a white woman gives birth to a black baby, she is suspected of sexual and racial infidelity. And the white social father is imagined as somehow duped. *The Brothers Solomon* is a case in point where the fantasy of a white woman giving birth to a black baby not only challenges white paternity but also makes her suspicious, a liar and a cheat who dupes the white dads into taking responsibility for someone else's child.

Like *The Brothers Solomon, Due Date* (2010) has a running gag about the protagonist Peter's (Robert Downey Jr.) wife, Sarah (Michelle Monaghan) having an affair with a black football player, an old flame named Darryl (Jamie Foxx), and producing a racially

mixed baby. Peter's sidekick on his misadventure across the country to make his wife's due date (she has a C-section planned for
Friday) suggests that Sarah might be pregnant by Darryl and inno-
cently muses that the resulting baby will be like a "zebra." Like the
Solomon brothers, Ethan (Zach Galifianakis) is stupidly naïve but
likable as his moronic antics both horrify and endear him to Peter
and to the audience. The uptight Peter starts to doubt his wife's
fidelity and his friendship with Darryl, and his cross-country dash
is now fueled as much by his curiosity about whether the baby is
really his as his desire to be with his wife for the birth of their first
child. Again, it is assumed that if his wife is pregnant by Darryl,
it will be obvious when the baby is born. Sarah goes into labor on
Thursday, a day early, and although Peter arrives just in the nick of
time, bursting into the hospital to find his wife, he rushes into the
wrong room and, seeing a black baby boy, assumes the worst, that
his wife is guilty of racial infidelity. Of course, reassuring us that
the miscegenation scare was a false alarm and that white racial
integrity has been maintained, Sarah gives birth to a white baby
girl in the next room.

   Although Peter is relieved that his baby is white, he is surprised
that it is a girl. Based on ultrasound images, doctors had told him
it was a boy. But, as his wacky sidekick tells him, ultrasounds are
not always reliable at predicting the sex of the baby. In the context
of anxieties about miscegenation central to the plot of this film,
the fact that ultrasound images do not show the race of the fetus—
indeed on ultrasound images all fetuses are blackened—is significant. The conflation of sex and race is telling as the "wrong" race
becomes the "wrong" sex; and while Peter could not accept the
wrong race, which would be evidence that his wife was unfaithful
and his child mixed race, a bit disappointed he nonetheless accepts
the wrong sex, which at least is not ambiguous or mixed. In other
words, although he was expecting—and desiring—a white boy, he
can accept a girl because she is not racially mixed or a hybrid. On
a deeper level, perhaps, this raises questions of sex mixing or inter-
sex infants who are still seen as problems to be corrected because

they are outside the seemingly clear-cut binary categories of male and female. One lesson we can draw from this film is that it is not blackness itself that is "wrong"; for when Peter realizes that the black baby belongs to a black couple, then all is well. Rather, it is racial mixing or hybridity that is "wrong," insofar as it raises the specter of racial ambiguity that not only threatens the invisibility of whiteness but also and moreover challenges the very existence of a pure white race. The zebra, neither completely black nor completely white, appears as uncanny. As we have seen, this uncanny ambiguity is the motor for laughs in comedies and the motor for terror or fantasy in horror and science fiction films.

The elasticity of the pregnant body is also made suspect in *Due Date*. Although we don't know much about Peter's wife, Sarah, her former lover Darryl tells her husband that it is a shame that her "perfect" body will be ruined by pregnancy; perhaps she planned a mommy-tuck to go along with her C-section to maintain her sleek figure? The film also suggests that the attempt to control pregnancy and birth by planning a C-section is futile. The premise of the film is that the father/husband must be present at the birth of his child and will go to the ends of the earth to get there in time. Perhaps his wife planned the C-section to work around her husband's busy travel schedule. But, as in other pregnancy films, in *Due Date* pregnancy is out of control, excessive, and unpredictable—or predictable in its unpredictability. Whereas in horror this unpredictability is the stuff of nightmares, in comedy it is played for laughs. Given the star power and acting skills of Robert Downey Jr., *Due Date* might be an adventure-comedy and a buddy film that aims at high comedy; if this is the case, it misses by a mile. While anxieties over the unpredictability of pregnancy, marital infidelity, paternal absence, and racial mixing explicitly drive its plot, in the end, in typical Hollywood fashion, it reassures us that the business-class, white nuclear family is still intact and all of these threats to it have been quelled.

In this regard, *The Brothers Solomon*, which clearly aims at lowbrow comedy along the lines of *Dumb and Dumber*, is more complicated in its stupidity. It ends with an alternative family made up of two naïve middle-class white men, a working-class white woman, her black boyfriend, and their (meaning all four of them) mixed-race baby. In addition, unlike *Due Date*, *The Brothers Solomon* seems to confirm rather than deny interracial sex, which, as Robyn Wiegman notes, is absent in highly visible interracial families like Madonna's and Angelina Jolie's that result from international and domestic adoptions that allow white women to embrace interracial intimacy and collect racially different children without interracial sex (see Wiegman 2002). Even while it plays on racial stereotypes, *The Brothers Solomon* gives us a naïve version of color blindness that points to the ways in which race is a social marker rather than a natural one (if there is such a thing). The brothers have been raised in the Arctic wilderness, and this is why they are socially naïve and innocent. They do not see racial differences until others point them out. They are like children, learning about sex, race, class, and reproductive technologies. Their childlike innocence is silly and stupid in adults and therefore funny. Their supposed naiveté allows the film to exploit racial and sexual stereotypes in ways that may go beyond its lowbrow humor insofar as those stereotypes are deployed at the same time that they are called into question by this fraternal pair who don't know any better. For this reason, they can make racist and sexist remarks. And because this is a comedy and we are not meant to take those remarks seriously, we can laugh at them. The undercurrent, however, is that, like children, they tell it like they see it; they call a spade a spade; and we are as much laughing with them as at them. The climatic joke is that we "know" what they don't, namely, that white people don't make black babies. The narrative of the film does not have to say anything about the brothers' stupidity since it is assumed to be visually obvious in this racial sight gag.

The brothers' literal colorblindness, then, both denies racial difference and its social significance and suggests that racial difference is a cultural construction—or at least one that doesn't exist at the North Pole. On the other hand, the brothers get away with racial slurs disguised as innocence, particularly in a scene where James (Chi McBride) is portrayed as an "oversensitive" paranoid black man who reads racism into everything. And their acceptance of the mixed-race baby is presented as evidence of their stupidity. The poor white woman and oversensitive black man pull the wool over their eyes so that they don't see what is right in front of them, what the audience (and their father) does see, namely, that they have been had. Yet the film ends with the four of them happily together with *their* new baby, which may be a way of pulling the wool over the eyes of the audience insofar as the Hollywood happy ending requires us to accept this alternative racially mixed family as legitimate, if also uncanny. We don't find this racial mixing or the suggestion that race is a cultural construct unsettling because we can laugh at it; it is comedy.

Todd Solondz's *Palindromes* (2004) is another matter. While it has its funny moments and it is categorized as a comedy, its colorblindness is unsettling, even disturbing. In this strange indie film, teenage Aviva Victor intentionally gets pregnant because she wants desperately to have a baby. When her parents find out and try to convince her to have an abortion, she runs away from home and meets a lot of strange characters along the way. In the end, she returns home changed—or not, this is the question—by her experiences; in the final scene at a backyard barbecue hosted by her father, a family friend tells Aviva, "Whether you're 13 or 50, you'll always be the same. There's no free will," to which a morose Aviva (now Jennifer Jason Leigh) stares back blankly. For the audience, Aviva's physical changes are startling throughout the film. Solondz uses seven different actresses to play Aviva, changing them with changing scenes, and bringing them back again—maybe—later. Even more jarring is the switch from a lithe teenage white girl (Hannah Freiman) to a very large black adult woman (Sharon Wilkins). In *Palindromes,* like an art house version of *The Brothers Solomon*, no one notices these changes in Aviva, even as she changes from white to black or a size two to a plus size sixteen and back again. Everyone in the film treats her as if she is the same throughout; and she gives no clues as to her changing appearance. The film ends with a touching and sweet kiss between a small white adolescent boy and the large, black, young woman version of Aviva, made uncanny by the contrast in size, color, and age. Aviva's physical appearance makes no difference in the film, but it makes all the difference to the audience watching the film.

*Palindromes*—which means a word spelled the same forwards and backwards, for example, Aviva—suggests that physical differences don't make a difference. It also suggests that Aviva (life) embodies the universal need to have a baby. Is Solondz suggesting that the desire for pregnancy and babies is universal amongst all girls and young women whether they are black or white, plus size or anorexic? To be sure, the film isn't exactly pro-life since it has questionable and strange characters arguing on both sides of the question. But it does universalize Aviva's experiences by denying the difference that various physical differences make. We have to wonder whether this is a tongue-in-cheek maneuver, however, when we meet the Sunshine family headed by Mama Sunshine and peopled by children with various disabilities; Mama Sunshine is a laughable character who bakes "Jesus Tears" cookies and cheerfully reminds her children that God loves everyone no matter what their abilities. Given the contrast between the physical appearance of the actresses playing Aviva and the effect this has on the viewer, it is questionable whether or not Solondz succeeds in creating a universal character; certainly, he doesn't create a sympathetic character, not a single one. Furthermore, the fact that the black version of Aviva is fat and unattractive while the white versions of Aviva are thin and attractive, especially when played by the lovely Jennifer Jason Leigh, is problematic, particularly when coupled with the more critically acclaimed *Precious* (2009). Is Solondz trying to show how blackness itself is seen as unattractive, to make audiences squirm in their own racism? Or is he presenting blackness as abject by giving us cute and beautiful white girls in contrast to an overweight black woman, made even more awkward by her hairstyle (tight ponytail) and clothes (e.g., pink frock with baby doll white collar)? Is he showing us the mold into which we expect all girls to fit? Or is he showing us how blackness is seen as abject only insofar as it doesn't fit into it?

*Palindromes*, as its title suggests, is a difficult film to read, in large part because of the race-switching of the lead character and the colorblindness of the others. Kalpana Seshadri-Crooks's substantive interpretation of another indie film, *Suture* (1993), which challenges audiences with a similar sort of uncanny colorblindness, is helpful in thinking about *Palindromes*. In *Suture*, directors Scott McGhee and David Siegel pull a similar racial sleight of hand when Clay (Dennis Haysbert) takes the place of his brother Vincent (Michael Harris) after suffering amnesia in a car accident rigged by Vincent. In the narrative of the film, the two brothers are identical, but to the viewer of the film they couldn't look more different, especially since Clay is black and Vincent is white. As in *Palindromes*, the audience uncomfortably wonders why none of the other characters in the film notice the difference. Seshadri-Crooks argues that "by requiring us to suspend our *belief*, the film . . . forces a purchase of our visual pleasure at the price of our own raced subjectivities" (2000:104). Using a psychoanalytic framework, she maintains that the film "actualizes the discourse of race as a particular structure of anxiety," which can also be said of *Palindromes* (2000:107). Seeing others not seeing race causes anxiety and wonder in the viewer—we can't believe it and yet we have to in order to make sense of the film.

Seshadri-Crooks discusses the difference between the ways in which drama and comedy approach this excessiveness of race. To this end, she juxtaposes *Secrets and Lies* (1996), and its joke that a black daughter takes after her white mother, with the black and white identical twins in *Suture*. In the former, the excess of race is discharged through laughter; in the latter, no such discharge is possible within the narrative of the film. The same is true of stock Hollywood comedies like *The Brothers Solomon* and *Due Date*, which deal with the excesses of race through laughter. But the humor of *Palindromes* does not allow for such discharge. While the film is funny, even quaint and wacky in terms of some of its characters, it does not admit that the fluidity between white and black versions of Aviva is comic. This is not to say that either *Suture* or *Palindromes* takes itself too seriously. Rather, it speaks to the strange excess of race in these films; excess that is experienced as anxiety by the viewer. Seshadri-Crooks argues that "by refusing our demand that black and white be recognized, the film radically subverts our suture as subject of race" (2000:125). These films put into question the way in which race is sutured to our identities. "For us as spectators, our suturing to the film narrative is purchased at the price of our desuturing as subjects of race" (Seshadri-Crooks 2000:131). The film requires that we either "learn to see differently" or leave the theater disappointed and confused. As Seshadri-Crooks concludes, "*Suture* inaugurates an adversarial aesthetics in relation to the scopic regime of race. It literally utilizes the visual medium against the visual regime of race" (2000:131). Like *Suture*, *Palindromes* continues this adversarial relation to race by challenging the viewer to fess up to her own anxieties about race. As Seshadri-Crooks points out, it is not so much that we are unsettled by the film's assertion that there is identity where there is difference; rather, we are unsettled, undone, anxious, confused by the refusal of race as a fundamental mark of identity.

In the context of this project it is funny, if accidental, that in her analysis of the film, Seshadri-Crooks quotes French psychoanalyst Jacques Lacan describing a dream that displays the uncertainty of our own identity formation, which comes from a rupture between our perception and our consciousness of that perception. In Lacan's example the perception in question (or should I say that calls him into question) is auditory and not visual like the perception of race in these films. Lacan tells the story of being awakened from a dream by a knocking sound that becomes the very dream from which he is awakened: "When the knocking occurs, not in my perception, but in my consciousness, it is because my consciousness reconstitutes itself around this representation, that I know that I am waking up, that I am *knocked up*" (emphasis in original; XI:56, quoted in Seshadri-Crooks 2000). Lacan wakes up to the knocking because it is represented in his dream; and in that uncanny moment he knows both that he is dreaming and that he is waking up. Lacan goes on to "question" himself as to what he is at that moment, the moment of both dreaming and waking up, of both hearing the knocking and becoming aware of it as a figure in his dream. The moment that calls his identity into question is that of being knocked awake, or as he says, being "knocked up."

Certainly being knocked up, in the sense of being pregnant, is the most visible, perceptible state of being called into question by another, of being split in two, of experiencing the disconnect between perception and consciousness (pregnant women often describe feeling disoriented in their own bodies, imagining them to be smaller than they are and bumping into things, etc.). As we have seen, the pregnant subject, even more visibly than others, is reconstituted around representations of pregnancy. Seshadri-Crooks's analysis of race revolves around this rupture between perception and representation or consciousness of perception, which appears before us as a challenge to our personal identity. We could say, then, that the moment of being knocked up is the moment of conception, insofar as it is the relationship between perception and our conception of it that "fucks" us and leads to the bewildering state of being "knocked up." There is, however, something excessive about this passage, the passage from dreaming to waking, the passage from perception to consciousness, the passage from being knocked awake to being "knocked up," the passage from being knocked up to desuturing us as racial subjects (the passage from Lacan's seminar). What is fascinating in terms of our project is the way that Seshadri-Crooks's analysis of race revolves around this excessive passage when our identities are put into question by being *knocked up*. Is the desuturing of race dependent upon being knocked up? In other words, is the relationship between race and pregnancy really an accident? Or, rather, is it essential to both?

What we learn from the feminist literature on ARTs is that, like their predecessors, they are designed, implemented, managed, and policed to protect against racial miscegenation. Racial mixing is imagined as the greatest threat to the industry of IVF (see Bender 2006). Furthermore, given the cost, these technologies are primarily available to middle- and upper-class women, most of whom are white. It is not just that racial mixing is imagined as impure or abject and therefore taboo, but also that white women are exhorted to reproduce, while women of color are seen as reproducing too much. Recall Sylvia Ann Hewlett's manifesto *Baby Hunger*, in which she warns young, middle-class, college-educated—read white—women not to wait to have babies until it is too late. As we have seen, she concludes that these "superior" women have a duty to have children, not only for themselves but also for the nation (2002:266). Hewlett's book suggests that college-educated white women have a duty to contribute their genetic material to the gene pool for the good of everyone. The underside of her argument is that lower-class, uneducated women do not have a duty to reproduce, that their reproduction is not good for the nation. Indeed, following Hewlett's eugenics argument to its logical conclusion, perhaps they have a duty not to reproduce; it may even lead to the racist reactionary conclusion that white, educated, middle-class health-care professionals and lawmakers have a duty to regulate the reproduction of those whose reproduction is imagined as undesirable.

## "OCTOMOM," "BABY HUNGER," AND OUR INSATIABLE APPETITE FOR BABIES

Although not necessarily always explicit in Hollywood films and popular culture, by subjecting them to analysis and to interpretation we can see disguised forms of these ideas. Sometimes these messages are masquerading as science and medicine, as comedy or entertainment, or as scandal and spectacle. For example, media coverage of the birth of Nadya Suleman's octuplets brings together many of the anxieties over race, class, and sex that we have been discussing. Suleman was dubbed "Octomom," a designation that she embraced. She gave birth to the octuplets in January 2009 after her fertility doctor implanted twelve frozen embryos and eight attached. Suleman already had six children as a result of IVF (twins and four singletons). The public outcry against Suleman was targeted at her on many fronts: she was a poor woman who lived off of welfare and disability; she had too many children (fourteen altogether); she was an Angelina Jolie wannabe; she was a welfare queen who took advantage of the system; she was like an animal, a breeder; she was of questionable race, possibly even black. Suleman was represented in one online cartoon as an octopus with eight tentacles dangling a baby at each end (fig. 5.1). The caption sums up reactions to her: "The Nadya Suleman Octomom is a new species recently discovered in the Los Angeles area. Her mating habit consists of visiting fertility clinics and impregnating herself with as many spawn that will fit into her capacious womb. She uses her well-manicured eight tentacles to juggle her 14 children while flipping through the pages of any magazine featuring Angelina Jolie. The suckers located underneath each tentacle allow the Octomom to grab as much taxpayer money as possible and to also seek out lucrative endorsement deals, expensive makeup, and maybe even grab Oprah's attention or get her own Bravo/Discovery/TLC/blah blah blah show like the other famous Duggar-esque families out there" (14:2009).

The Gosselin family became the stars of the reality television show *Jon & Kate Plus 8*, about another poor woman who had had eight babies as a result of IVF and became a reviled celebrity too. In her transition from lower-class mother to celebrity cover girl, the public and the media also excoriated Kate Gosselin. Some magazines called her a "monster" and claimed that she was too concerned with her makeover to take care of her children (*US Weekly* 2009).

The description of Suleman as an octopus and the comparison to an animal points to anxieties over women having "litters"

**FIGURE 5.1** Nadya Suleman rendered as an octopus with manicured tenticles, grasping her fourteen children. (Courtesy of 14, at fourteencelebs@yahoo. com. Reprinted by permission)

or "broods" of babies through ARTs and IVF rather than the single births common until now. When she announced that she was getting a pig and a dog to add to her family, tabloid magazines had a field day expanding their remarks about Suleman's animality. Calling Suleman a "new species" signals fears that ARTs and IVF may lead to a new species of animal, not-quite or beyond human. This worry is echoed in the academy by philosophers such as Leon Kass, Michael Sandel, and especially Jürgen Habermas, who argues that genetic engineering may lead to the end of the human race as we know it (Habermas 2003; cf. Kass 2003 and Sandel 2007). As we have seen, these fears fuel horror and science fiction fantasies about women giving birth to new species that threaten the extinction of humanity. But the association between Suleman and animality runs astray into even more vexing territory in terms of race. As Jennifer Morgan argues, "Suleman—and the confusing misrecognition of her as a woman of color—draws critical fire precisely because of the tension around the legitimate use of assisted reproductive technologies by women who apparently embody the problems of the American underclass—women who are, at the very least, as Suleman is, blackened by their status as reproductive outlaws" (Morgan 2010). Certainly the Suleman case has caused some lawmakers to propose legislation on ARTs that would limit access to women deemed more desirable for reproduction (see Johnston 2009; Otto & Pinch 2009; Robertson 2009). Although some of these arguments are couched in language of protecting children, they come dangerously close to eugenics policies that encourage women with "good genes" to procreate and discourage women with "bad genes" from doing so. The internet blogosphere saw many comments that women like her should be sterilized. In other words, some of the responses to Suleman suggest that poor women should not have access to ARTs. In fact, most do not have access because of the expense of fertility treatment and ARTs themselves.

The problem is more complicated insofar as Suleman's dependence on welfare, her status as a single mother, and what many saw as her irresponsible reproduction connect her with the reviled figure of the welfare queen, who is typically seen as black. Insofar as this figure is seen as black, so is Suleman. Again, in the words of Morgan: "What Nadya Suleman does is to repeatedly assault whiteness, the singularity of her case—the extraordinary rarity of the octuplets birth, the complicity of her racial indeterminacy; the questionable nature of her will to emulate Hollywood royalty. . . . Her racial ambiguity would be enough, but her effort to subvert racially coded heteronormativity through ARTs closes the door on her white citizenship. She has become indelibly raced by her far too close association with the iconic welfare queen" (Morgan 2010). One irony is that the very characteristics of Angelina Jolie that Nadya Suleman emulates are the ones that apparently signal her racial ambiguity, especially her lips. Further irony is that the Jolie-Pitt family, a racially mixed family, has become an American icon of family values, while Suleman's imitation is misrecognized as racially mixed and therefore seen as illegitimate.

Diane Negra's analysis of the "Brangelina family" points to the problematic of race and class differences in these two cases as evidence of conflicting family values in American popular culture. As Negra argues, "the celebrity driven 'family values' representational regime suggests that forms of social, racial, class, and even international inequality can be resolved through the assembling of families in the ultimate 'privatizing' gesture. . . . It is this version of wealthy celebrity family that is symbolically positioned to solve economic and social justice problems" (Negra 2010:60). So, while super-wealthy celebrities are seen as solving problems, race and class inequities, and injustice through their embrace of alternative families that include adopted poor children of color from various parts of the world, poor women like Suleman, particularly women of color, in the United States are seen as causing the problem and bringing their poverty on themselves by having too many babies and abusing the system. As we have seen, in pregnancy films the "welfare queen" and "white trash" are familiar tropes, from *Baby Mama*'s Angie and *The Brothers Solomon*'s Janine to *Precious* and *Just Another Girl on the I.R.T.* We have also seen that even white "welfare queens" are racialized by their proximity to poverty: Angie is called a "baby mama"; Janine gives birth to a black baby; and Nayda Suleman's whiteness is called into question (for a discussion of stereotypes of welfare queens as welfare cheats, see Ortiz & Briggs 2003).

While Suleman's use of IVF seems excessive, the extreme measures used by middle-class and wealthy women to have babies through ARTs remain hidden behind the closed doors of fertility clinics. Their "baby hunger" is legitimate, even encouraged, while poor women, especially women of color, are not only denied access because of the cost but also seen as excessive when they use ARTs, especially when they have multiple babies as a result. For middle-class white women, then, it seems that the worst that can happen is that they end up childless because they didn't listen to their biological clocks, while for poor women, especially women of color, the worst that can happen is that they have too many babies "to get the welfare," in the words of Precious's mother (cf. Ortiz & Briggs 2003, on "crack babies" and "welfare cheats"). The response to Suleman shows that while 30-something, middle-class white women feel an urgent need to reproduce, others feel an urgent need to legislate the reproduction of the "lower classes," which has resurfaced with a vengeance in debates over restricting access to new reproductive technologies.

## NOT OF WOMAN BORN?

These debates take us back to our earlier discussion of choice. Who has the right to choose reproduction? Who has the right to choose what type of reproduction they will use? How far does reproductive choice extend? New reproductive technologies complicate these discussions in ways that outstrip our understanding of ourselves as a species, for these technologies not only make it possible for women and men previously considered infertile to reproduce, they also make it possible to choose what to reproduce. Genetic engineering and cloning technologies make it possible to design offspring in ways unimaginable just a few decades ago except in science fiction. Do parents have the right, even the obligation, to choose to genetically enhance their children (cf. Harris 2010; cf. Oliver 2010)? Or does this type of choice undermine the freedom to choose their offspring (cf. Habermas 2003; cf. Oliver

2010)? While answers to these ethical questions are beyond the scope of this book, recent Hollywood representations of cloning and genetic engineering technologies manifest some of the fears and desires over the continuation of the human species and take up these contemporary debates. Although cloning films are not technically pregnancy films, they do rehabilitate pregnant bodies and wombs in interesting ways.

Like pregnancy films, many cloning and genetic engineering films also recuperate heterosexual sex and the good "old-fashioned" way of having babies. Remember the hero Vincent Freeman (Ethan Hawke) in *Gattaca* (1997), who is not genetically engineered in a genetically engineered world and makes it nonetheless; even his name, "Free-man," suggests that he is the real human living amongst technological products who have become more like sterile machines than people. Like the pregnancy films, many genetic engineering and cloning films feature longing for "real" experience rather than technologically mediated, enhanced, or artificial experience, along with idealizations of the nuclear family, if not of woman born. For example, Adam's clone (Arnold Schwarzenegger) in *The 6th Day* (2000) joins forces with the "real" Adam to fight the evil corporation that illegally cloned him and to save his family. As the title of the film suggests, cloning is represented as hubris or playing God, which is represented as evil. It is noteworthy that in this film, and in other cloning films, the evil is associated with the capitalist desire to make money through exploitation. In this way, these films are also morality tales about the dangers of greedy capitalists using and abusing people for their own gains. From the film's "re-pet" commercials that promise new pets better than the old (i.e., designer pets wherein nasty characteristics are deleted), to the illegal cloning of human beings, *The 6th Day* presents a world in which cloning is immoral not only because it is playing God but also because it turns living beings into products.

This signals another anxiety of many cloning films, namely that humans are produced rather than reproduced. As Susan Squier puts it: "While current techniques in assisted reproduction challenge the boundaries of gender and species, the technique of cloning challenges another boundary, perhaps even more funda-mental to our thinking than either generation or species, although implicated in both of them: the boundary between reproduction and replication" (1999:112). So, if assisted reproduction challenges the hetero-normative ideals of reproduction, cloning goes further in that it requires neither heterosexual sex nor two genetic contri-butions (one from a male and one from a female). Yet it does still require a womb in which to gestate the cloned embryo.

It is telling that it is necessary to point out that, regardless of the technologies involved, including genetic engineering and cloning, women's wombs are still necessary for gestation. Why is that fact so easily forgotten or imagined away? Is it because the maternal body is imagined as merely the maternal environment or a container that can easily be replaced by a prosthetic womb or container? The erasure of the maternal body in these films once again signals an ambivalence, even a contradiction, in our fantasies regarding reproduction and reproductive technologies. On the one hand, we can easily do without the pregnant body, but on the other, we want natural human reproduction through sex rather than technologically assisted reproduction. We want good old-fashioned sex without the problematic expanding, leaky bodies of pregnant women. Discussing our preference for sexual origins rather than technological ones, Anne O'Byrne reminds us that, "We are all gestated in the body of another, and it will be no different for the clone, who will not be a 'homunculus in a retort' any more than test-tube babies are born out of test tubes" (O'Byrne 2010:162).

This fact is erased in recent representations of cloning, which are all imagined as clones "born" fully grown from factories or laboratories. In *The 6th Day*, *The Island*, *Moon*, *Surrogates*, and *Splice*, no woman's womb is required for the gestation of the clones or offspring. These are clearly fantasies of reproduction/replication without women. *The 6th Day*, *The Island*, and *Surrogates* all fea-ture evil father figures who establish their wealthy cloning enterprises by reproducing human beings without the need for women, which not only gives them more quality control in terms of their products but also less emotional attachments and more expedient means of production. In *The 6th Day*, Adam appears immediately after his genetically identical and unsuspecting genetic donor supposedly dies in a helicopter crash; he apparently requires no gestation at all. In *Surrogates* (2009), Lionel Canter (James Cromwell) repeatedly re-creates his wife against her wishes and she repeatedly dies of cancer. In *The Island* (2005), Dr. Bernard Merrick (Sean Bean) heads a corporation that creates clones to provide spare body parts for wealthy clients. Here, adults are "born" fully grown from womblike envelopes, and like big babies have to learn everything once they are removed. This film even features a pregnant clone whose water breaking requires cleanup by an emergency anti-contamination crew, suggesting that the pregnant body contaminates the fantasy of male-controlled reproduction sans women. All of the other clones look on in wonder since they have never seen a baby. The clone is killed immediately after she gives birth, and her baby is given to the genetically identical rich—and presumably infertile or just too busy—couple in the next room.

Images of adult clones as new infants entails fantasies of giving birth to oneself in a world without children, where pregnancy is both celebrated and anomalous (think too of *Children of Men*). Recent genetic engineering and cloning films display anxieties about the end of human existence as we know it. They sometimes present an odd dystopian mix of new forms of discrimination or racism against those who don't measure up genetically, at one pole, and, at the other, the commoditization of genetically enhanced or cloned "people" who become products. In all of these films, clones represent a new underclass that is exploited, enslaved, and denied any human rights. Yet in all of these films, the clones are sympathetic characters, often innocents, who have been duped into believing they are "real." Of course, they *are* real and they *are* human (for a discussion of clones as natal and therefore "like us," see O'Byrne 2010; for a discussion of why clones are imagined as "monsters," see Hartouni 1997). Yet in these films they are treated as if they are artificial and therefore somehow less human than their originals.

Like the pregnancy films discussed here, these science fiction thrillers display anxieties over technological interventions into reproduction that threaten to change humanity by changing how we reproduce. As in other films about assisted reproductive technologies, these films prefer the real deal, "good old-fashioned" sex as the means of reproduction. In sum, these cloning films manifest the same anxieties as pregnancy films—namely, the preference for the "real" over the "artificial" and the "natural" over "the technological," worries about the speed of reproduction, concerns over the commoditization of human beings, and perhaps most vexing, the separation of sex, love, and reproduction. For example, *The Island* ends with two clones falling in love, discovering sex, escaping from their "masters," and sailing off into the sunset, the new romantic couple. Love triumphs over technology and sets them free. In *Gattaca*, Vincent finds sex and love, also forbidden, similarly liberating.

## LOVE BABIES VERSUS TECHNO-BABIES

Throughout this book, we have seen how the possible uncoupling of sex and reproduction leads to fantasies of techno-babies replacing real ones, and sterile laboratories or factories replacing the warm embrace of sex and more romantic pregnancies. One of the threats of technologically mediated reproduction seems to be the fear that if our babies are not created in or out of love then they will not be loved. If they are not created through sex and human passion, then we cannot feel as passionately about them. The fear is that if reproduction is controlled by technology, then we will lose our humanity, which is based in good old-fashioned sexual reproduction and women giving birth to babies as nature intended. This fear of technology undermining love and the bond between mother and child is at the center of the 2008 documentary featuring Ricki Lake, *The Business of Being Born*. This documentary, unlike most of the other pregnancy films discussed here, is by and about women. It is about women giving birth and not about how they got pregnant or their romance with "the one" that made it all possible. Still, it is about another sort of romance, the romance between mother and newborn infant. And it is about more romantic births as an antidote to alienating, technologically mediated ones. In this regard, *The Business of Being Born* takes us back to arguments by feminist philosophers such as Iris Young who describe the ways in which doctors and the medical establishment can alienate a pregnant woman from her own body and her experience of it. Indeed, the documentary presents itself as a feminist film intended to educate women about the dangers of medicalized childbirth and the alienating effects of hospital protocols.

Taking on the medical establishment with its high-tech births, in *The Business of Being Born*, Ricki Lake urges women to opt for at-home natural childbirth because, if they don't, women will miss out on the real experience of birth; the drugs given in hospitals and the sterile atmosphere with doctors controlling the scene alienate women from the true authentic experience of giving birth. Moreover, the film warns, these drugs and hospital protocols not only alienate the woman from her own body and the experience of childbirth but also from her newborn baby. This is really the "worst that can happen." The mother-child bond is destroyed by drugs and medical technology. The documentary is haunted by the specter of so-called "love hormones" released during natural birth that are impeded if women choose to use technology or chemicals to deaden the painful experience of birth. The insinuation is that babies born in hospitals are technologically mediated to the point that the "natural love" that a mother feels for her baby disappears. Like the feature films already discussed, this documentary suggests that women should opt for more romantic babies rather than high-tech babies because the experience and therefore the babies are more "real."

Since the release of *The Business of Being Born*, home birth has increased dramatically, especially in urban areas. As a counterpoint to high-tech births, there is a renewed interest in home births and a revival of "natural" childbirth. This movement resists technological intervention in childbirth, which it contends both diminishes the true "experience" of birth and makes labor more difficult for the mother and is not healthy for the child. It is interesting that in *The Business of Being Born* low-tech home birth is not advocated just because it is more "natural" but also because it is less alienating than high-tech hospital birth. The message of the film is that women in hospitals do not have any choice about their birth experience, while women at home have more choice and more control. Again, the issue of choice is emphasized and redeployed from familiar pro-choice discourse into the childbirth arena. As Janelle Taylor points out, however, "the ideological opposition between 'wholistic' and 'technocratic' models of pregnancy and childbirth plays itself out against the backdrop of a consumer culture and a class structure that remain fundamentally unchallenged" (Taylor 2000:406). Because they are expensive and insurance may not cover them, at-home births are by far more accessible to middle-class women. And women are held responsible for making the right choice for their babies. Although the explicit message of the documentary is that women should choose home birth for the sake of their babies, the implicit message is that home birth is agonizing (e.g., by showing women screaming in pain and begging for drugs), which suggests that home birth may not be all that it is cracked up to be.

Throughout *The Business of Being Born*, doctors and midwives and various women who have given birth at home argue that low-tech birth promotes bonding between mother and child, bonding that is interrupted by technology and drugs in the hospital. The so-called "love hormones" supposedly released during a drug-free birth are repeatedly invoked as the primary reason women should give birth at home. The film ends on a sad note when the filmmaker, Abby Epstein, laments that complications during birth

forced her to go to the hospital and, as a result, she did not experience the bond produced by those "love hormones." Epstein was
pregnant during the making of the film. It is clear that, after she
has to be rushed to the hospital, she feels like a failure, responsible
for losing out on the "love hormones" that home birth is supposed
to provide, and jeopardizing the bond with her baby. The film
romanticizes home birth as a more loving and authentic experience for mother and child. While we watch various women begging for help and in agony, saying that they can't do it, we are told
that they must do it for the sake of their baby and their future bond
with it. We might ask at what point does this demand for bonding becomes bondage to an ideology of love born against technology and the medical establishment? Like the Hollywood films
that romanticize conception and pregnancy, this documentary film
romanticizes birth and gives us a more "authentic love" born of
pain and at-home designer births whose rhetoric harkens back to
expectations of maternal sacrifice.

*The Business of Being Born* presents a stark contrast between
high-tech alienated births in hospitals and more "authentic natural" births at home. Whereas the natural childbirth movement of
the late 1960s and '70s evokes hippies and earth-mothers rejecting
"the establishment," these new high-end if not high-tech urban
births primarily are marketed to career women who are powerful
consumers because they are financially independent. The argument
is not just that home birth is more natural, but also that it makes
labor and birth easier on mother and child and fosters bonding
between them. Moreover, pregnant consumers are urged to choose
home birth over hospital birth so that they will be more in control
of their birthing process by refusing to relinquish their power to
doctors and give in to drugs that numb them to the experience. In
this film, the argument against hospital birth turns on the rhetoric of choice and control, which the film contends is taken away
from women and given to doctors. Home birth, then, appears as
yet another way for women to assert their "right to choose" to have
babies in the face of threatening and alienating technologies. The

film "sells" home birth by suggesting that through it women have more control, a message that is clearly undermined by the repeated images of women screaming in agony and begging for drugs and the few that have complications and have to be rushed to the hospital to save them and their babies. Like the pregnancy feature films, this documentary signals anxieties about women's choices, responsibility, and control in the face of changing technologies.

# CONCLUSION

## *TWILIGHT* FAMILY VALUES

THE *TWILIGHT* SERIES is immensely popular, especially with girls and young women, the "Twihards" and "Twimoms." The latest installment in the film series, *Twilight: Breaking Dawn* (2011), is a pregnancy film that brings together many of the themes discussed throughout this book. For that reason, and because it is the latest pregnancy film as of this writing, we end with issues of romance, choice, excess, teen pregnancy, abject pregnant bodies, the fetus versus maternal body, fears of hybridity, and the cult of maternity as they manifest themselves in this blockbuster gothic romance franchise.

Although the fourth installment in the franchise, *Twilight*: *Breaking Dawn*, continues a long line of horror films featuring women giving birth to otherworldly creatures, it is also part of a romance between a beautiful human teenage girl, Bella (Kristen Stewart), and a smoldering, eternally 17-year-old vampire, Edward

(Robert Pattinson). In some ways, the *Twilight* series fits into the standard romantic comedy genre of boy-meets-girl from the other side of the tracks—obstacles keep them apart, but witty banter and lots of music video moments bring them together, and eventually they overcome the obstacles through personal transformation and maturation. In addition to the obvious species difference between Bella and Edward, which must be overcome, there is also class difference, since apparently vampires are really rich and Bella comes from a working-class family—her dad is a cop in the small town of Forks, Washington (think *Twin Peaks*). Also, Bella is an only child while Edward has a large family of blood-sucking siblings who have a hard time resisting Bella's blood every time she cuts herself, which is often. Needless to say, there are huge hurdles to be jumped before this romance gets off the ground; luckily, Edward can jump across canyons and fly Bella around the world on his back.

Although much of the humor in the series is dark, as in other comedies the foibles of one person trying to "pass" in the world of the other provide the laughs. From a feminist perspective, however, much of the humor is unintentional—watching it with other feminists, we found ourselves the only people in the theater laughing throughout the movie. There are plenty of examples of awkward moments when Edward and his family try to pass as human and when Bella starts to hang out with vampires. For example, at a vampire baseball game, when the bad vampires show up, Edward tells Bella to pull her hair out of her cap so she will look more like a vamp than a snack. And to pass as human, Edward drives a sports car really fast, when he could just fly really fast; and he laughs when Bella asks him to put on his seatbelt (before she knows he is immortal). Edward's family continues to adjust to his romance with a human, while Bella (all too quickly) comes to terms with her lover's undead condition.

Ultimately, however, the transformations that enable their unlikely romance to last forever are Bella's pregnancy, birth, and becoming an immortal vampire. Bella becomes a mother and an immortal in the same scene, in which her daughter is born and

Bella dies, but is reborn (thanks to Edward's venom) as a vampire. What does it mean, in terms of our analysis of pregnancy as the transformation that unites unlikely couples in romcoms, that in this romance-horror film, pregnancy, birth, and the transformation from human to inhuman are all part of the same process?

While the transformation from human to vampire—necessitated by her death during childbirth—is the one that will allow Edward and Bella to stay together literally forever, Bella's pregnancy acts as a bonding agent for other characters in the story. Her pregnancy brings sworn enemies—vampires and wolves—together by first bonding Jacob (her werewolf friend and enemy of all vampires, played by a beefed-up Taylor Lautner) and Edward in their common goal of protecting Bella; and second by bonding Jacob and Bella's newborn daughter Renesme when Jacob "imprints" on her, which in the world of *Twilight* means that his "genes" are bound to hers and that he will protect her at all costs. It also means that any wolves, which until then wanted to kill her, cannot harm her. As Edward says at the end of *Breaking Dawn*, reading Jacob's mind—yes, another of his many superhuman abilities—Jacob has imprinted on the vampire-human hybrid baby, and imprinting is the most sacred law of the wolves. So, Bella's pregnancy not only brings her everlasting life with Edward but also brings together the warring wolves and vampires, particularly the boys who have been fighting over her since the beginning, Edward and Jacob. As in other films we have discussed, pregnancy is a vehicle for transformation that enables unlikely couples and characters to unite and bond.

Bella's pregnancy also forges an unlikely alliance between Edward's vampire sister Rosalie (Nikki Reed) and Bella, who have not gotten along until now. Rosalie wanted a family when she was human, and now she can fulfill her maternal longings with Bella's baby. When Edward demands that they return from their honeymoon so that Carlisle Cullen (Peter Facinelli), Edward's father (and a doctor), can "take care of it," Bella calls Rosalie for help. In *Twilight: Eclipse* (2010), Rosalie told Bella the traumatic story of her death and her wish that she hadn't been changed; she wanted a normal life as a wife and mother. Rosalie is adamant that while she didn't have a choice about becoming a vampire, Bella does. This scene foreshadows the rhetoric of reproductive choice in *Breaking Dawn*, and suggests that while decades ago women like Rosalie did not have a choice, Bella does. Furthermore, as we will see, Bella's choice can and should be used to embrace the traditional family values lost to Rosalie.

## BELLA'S BABY: EXTREME HOME BIRTH

While the *Twilight* series shares some characteristics with romantic comedy, it also mixes romance with science fiction in ways that are familiar to gothic romance with its haunted houses and suggestions of otherworldliness, and a few crazed vampire women, now liberated from the attic. *Breaking Dawn*, like its *Twilight* predecessors, has superhuman werewolves and vampires that make it a sci-fi film, but it is noteworthy that it is Bella's horrific pregnancy with something monstrous—or at least something imagined as monstrous—that turns the franchise toward horror. *Breaking Dawn* mixes gothic romance, comedy, science fiction, and horror to create a venomous cocktail for its heroine.

Breaking with genre traditions, like Polanski's 1968 horror classic *Rosemary's Baby*, where supposedly the most "natural" transformation that a woman can undergo—that of pregnancy, childbirth, and motherhood—becomes threatening, *Breaking Dawn* gives us an updated cautionary tale about the dangers of pregnancy and childbirth for women. Just as Lucy Fischer argued that *Rosemary's Baby* is a realistic representation of women's alienation during pregnancy at the hands of the medical establishment, Sarah Blackwood argues that *Breaking Dawn* is a realistic representation of the fear women experience when pregnant and facing the real dangers of childbirth (Blackwood 2011). Yet, as we will see, despite significant similarities, there are major differences between the treatment of pregnancy in Polanski's 1968 nightmare and Bill Condon's nightmare-turned-fairytale—or, we could say, fairytale-turned-nightmare. Both the similarities and the differences tell us something about the changing attitudes toward pregnancy and birth that we have been tracking throughout this book.

In *Breaking Dawn*, Bella Swan is a modern-day Rosemary, whose pregnancy with a "demon" leaves her wasting away. While Rosemary drinks vile potions prepared by witches, Bella drinks blood out of kiddie Styrofoam cups complete with straw. She is further infantilized cuddled up on the couch under her childhood quilt, reminiscent of the childlike Rosemary. Whereas *Rosemary's Baby* ends with a close-up of the demon baby's glowing red eyes, *Breaking Dawn* ends with a close-up of Bella's glowing red eyes, signaling her transformation into a vampire.

Another nod to *Rosemary's Baby*, the birth scene is nightmarish, with flashing images of a screaming Bella being drugged so that vampires can remove the baby. Talk about extreme home birth! Rosalie starts the C-section but rushes from the room at the sight of human blood, presumably because she cannot control her desires to taste it, which is a recurring theme throughout the series. So, Edward completes the C-section and delivers the baby by chewing through the amniotic sac—not a very sterile operation, but it does the trick. Still, don't try this at home! While Edward is chewing from the outside, the vampire baby is chewing from the inside. Covered with blood, but not the monstrously incomplete hybrid demon they all fear, the baby looks adorable after Rosalie cleans her up . . . perhaps by licking off all that blood in the next room?

## BELLA'S BLOOD

Blood is, of course, a central character in the *Twilight* series. Obviously, the vampires drink blood, although you rarely see the Cullens doing so; only the bad vampires kill people to drink their blood (the Cullens are "vegetarian vampires" who only kill animals). It is not just any blood, however, that figures prominently throughout the series—it is Bella's blood. In fact, it is remarkable that, given how many deaths there are in each installment of the series, there is not much blood. The bloodless vampires are beheaded and burned without so much as a drop of blood. And even when the bad vamps suck human blood, very little of it is seen (maybe a blood mustache around the lips here and there). Bella, on the other hand, bleeds in every film. She is either cutting herself accidentally and driving her vampire friends to distraction, or she is cutting herself on purpose to distract her vampire enemies. In *Twilight: Eclipse*, she slits her arm to distract the vampire who is about to kill Edward. And she pricks her finger so that she can smear her blood around the forest and lead them astray.

It is in *Breaking Dawn*'s birth scene, however, that we see the most Bella blood—so much so that all of the vampires leave the room, except for Edward whose love for Bella by this time makes him immune to the smell and sight of her blood. By the end of the scene, her white gown and bed sheets are soaked with blood; and the baby taken from her womb is covered with blood—as is Edward's face after performing the C-section with his teeth. In a series about vampires, it is telling that the most blood we ever see is associated with birth and women's role in reproduction. Not coincidentally, it is Bella's abject pregnancy and bloody birth that moves the series from sci-fi or gothic romance to horror. The bloodstains between Bella's legs suggest that we have more fascination with—or anxiety over—blood associated with women's menstruation and reproduction than with blood-sucking vampires.

Bella's bleeding body recalls other leaky female bodies in pregnancy films, from the comic water-breaking scenes in romcoms like *Baby Mama* to the suspense-drama of Stephanie Delany's bloody footprints. The fact that Bella bleeds in every film not only confirms her humanity but also her femininity; it reminds us that she is a post-pubescent young woman who bleeds. It is noteworthy that from the very first film Bella asks (then bargains, even pleads with) Edward to change her into a vampire to escape her human body, her woman's body. Rather than face the changes that come with puberty, Bella would rather be changed into a bloodless vampire. She would rather suck the blood of others than bleed herself because, within the world of *Twilight*, to bleed is to be weak and fragile. Bella's vulnerability, then, comes not just from the fact that she is human but also from the fact that she is a woman who bleeds.

## BELLA'S CHOICE

Bella's insistence that it is her choice to have the baby echoes recent Hollywood pregnancy films that shun abortion and endorse family values (*Nine Months*, *Fools Rush In*, *Knocked Up*). In these films, whatever the sacrifices and dangers involved, babies and motherhood are true sources of women's happiness, even if, as in *Rosemary's Baby* and *Breaking Dawn*, the monster baby may kill its mother and threaten humanity. Although most of Edward's vampire family, including his father Carlisle, warn her against going through with it, Bella is insistent. She is told that she will die and yet she wants to have her baby anyway. Although the vampires are stronger than she is and could force her, everyone respects her decision, her choice, no matter how much they disagree with it or fear for her life. It is clear that the choice is hers, all hers, and no one else's. At one point Edward complains that they should be partners in the choice and that she has shut him out, but she maintains her position and he accepts it.

In another scene, when Edward is begging her not to become pregnant because he doesn't want to lose her, she tells him that he will have a little piece of her in the baby. He is not consoled by this and claims that he can never love a baby whose existence killed her. Yet, later, when he can hear the loving thoughts of the fetus, he comes around. This scene operates in much the same way as the ultrasound scenes in other films (e.g., *Nine Months*) wherein the reluctant father bonds with the fetus only after seeing it. Edward bonds with the fetus only after hearing it with his vampire telepathy. The fact that the fetus is endowed with thoughts and emotions while in the womb suggests that it is already a person, even if it may be a monstrous one. Like other films we have analyzed, *Breaking Dawn* rejects the possibility of abortion, even in the most extreme case when the mother's life is at stake (no pun intended), and sides with the fetus over the mother, who sacrifices herself for the sake of her child, a decision that ultimately everyone respects, including the general viewing audience.

Even when Edward and his vampy doctor father explain to her that they can't save her by changing her at the last minute if she dies in childbirth or if her heart stops before they deliver the baby, she still insists on having it. Once again, we have a film where the fetus is at odds with the mother—not just insofar as it is literally killing her and taking all of her nutrients, but also insofar as, according to vampire lore, Bella can't be turned while pregnant without killing the baby. To save Bella is to kill the baby and to save the baby is to kill Bella. This is not merely the plot twist that drives *Breaking Dawn*, but, as we will see, the association between death and reproduction that drives Bella's sexual desires.

## BLOOD MIXING: NASTY NIGHTMARE OR UTOPIAN EUGENICS?

For most of the film, Edward is repulsed by the fetus, which is growing at breakneck speed inside Bella. In one scene he recoils after an internet search reveals horrible images of hybrid human-vampire monsters. As in its horror sisters (*Species*, *The Astronaut's Wife*, *Grace*, *Splice*), the threat posed by this fetus is not that it is an alien or a vampire, but rather that it is a hybrid. Because of its mixed blood, it contaminates the human species, a threat even greater than its thirst for blood. Throughout the *Twilight* series it is clear that vampires, wolves, and humans must not mix, especially through sex or reproduction.

Miscegenation or blood mixing is presented as the greatest danger and is seemingly punishable by death—at least it is this hybridity that causes Bella's death. But Bella's baby doesn't just threaten her life. It threatens all of humanity with something superhuman, like the super-beautiful, super-smart, super-strong vampires, but now mixed with human blood. And it is this mixing that makes Bella's baby more dangerous than any of the vampires. After all, vampires and wolves alike see this hybrid baby as a threat and want to dispose of it or kill it. In the plot, it is described as a threat to the humans, to the wolves, and perhaps even to the vampires insofar as it also will pollute their pure bloodline.

The end of *Breaking Dawn* suggests that there may there be more species mixing in the future between Bella's vampire baby and her wolf pal Jake, who has imprinted on Renesme—the wolf version of love at first sight. We have to wonder whether Edward and Bella's species mixing will lead to "better race relations," so to speak. Or is the "miracle" baby (as Bella calls it) born from the union between an extraordinarily beautiful white teen and her superman, super-wealthy vampire lover an argument for eugenics? Is this a case where only the best of the gene pool should reproduce? As Bella's schoolmate remarks at the wedding when he sees the beautiful vampire cousins from Alaska, "that must be some gene pool!" And it is true that all of Edward's family are white, beautiful, strong, cultured, and seemingly highly educated—at least insofar as that is signaled by their tastes in classical music and art, not to mention the wall full of diplomas. Edward's family is different from the rest of the townspeople not just because they are vampires but also because their "gene pool" makes them the ideal family that Bella hopes to join.

Bella wants to get herself some of those genes! She wants to be rich, beautiful, and immortal like the vampires. Of course she chooses Edward over Jacob. Of course she chooses the rich, sophisticated, cosmopolitan vampire over the poor half-clothed wolfboy who has spent his entire life on the reservation! Bella has been begging and bargaining with Edward to change her into a vampire from the first installment of the series. She agreed to marry him only if he agreed to change her. Bella doesn't just love Edward, she wants to be him, and she wants to reproduce him (she decides, early on, that her baby is a boy). At the end of the third installment, *Eclipse*, she admits to Edward that she wants to be part of his world as much as she wants him; and she has made it pretty clear throughout the series that she really wants him—the only thing she begs for as much as she pleads to be changed is sex. We might say that Bella "gets her cake and eats it too" by becoming a mother and a vampire in the same scene. In a sense, motherhood makes her immortal. She knows what she wants, and she gets it, because Bella is the North Star in the world of *Twilight*.

## BELLA'S BABY HUNGER

Bella Swan could be the poster-girl for Sylvia Ann Hewlett's book *Baby Hunger*, which advises white, educated women to marry young and start having babies before devotion to their careers leaves them childless and bitter—those with the best genes have a duty to the nation to reproduce. With Edward, Bella produces a superhuman creature, stronger than human or vampire. But *Breaking Dawn* also gives a new meaning to "baby hunger," not only in Bella's desire to have her baby but also in the baby's hunger for blood and the fact that it chews its way out of her from the inside. Just as much as its mother is hungry for it, this baby is hungry for its mother. And, in the still-to-come *Breaking Dawn: Part Two*, when Bella's vampire hunger is awakened, she may suffer from yet another type of baby hunger—the thirst for blood that is nearly uncontrollable in newly minted vampires, called "newborns" in the world of *Twilight*. The sequel promises lots of baby hunger and hungry babies; Edward will have two newborns on his hands!

## RECKLESS SEX AND THE EXCESSES OF FEMALE SEXUALITY

Bella has been begging for dangerous vampire sex and venom from the start. Indeed, she courts danger in every episode and is repeatedly saved by Edward or Jacob. In *Twilight: New Moon* (2009; the second in the series), after Edward leaves town to remove himself and the danger of the vampire world from her life, Bella soon discovers that if she puts herself in harm's way by behaving recklessly, she has visions of Edward warning her to turn back. After speeding away on the back of an obviously lecherous man's Harley while her stunned friend looks on, Bella says, "It was fun!" (using the same tone she will use later when she says, with a glint in her eye, that the blood she drinks to nourish her vampire fetus "tastes good"). She wants to be bad so badly that she can taste it. And the adrenaline rush she gets from her continued recklessness is consistent with her constant pleading that Edward turn her into a vampire and give her more dangerous vampire sex. At the end of *Twilight: Eclipse*, she tells Edward that although she has almost died countless times in his world, it is where she belongs. She belongs to a world of death. She wants to experience dangerous vampire sex while she is still human, with her human desire for Edward intact, before he changes her. Bella wants risky sex almost as much as she wants to be changed into a vampire—in other words, almost as much as she wants death itself.

At the wedding, when Jacob learns that Bella plans to have honeymoon nookie with Edward while she is still human, he screams that sex with Edward will kill her. Throughout her pregnancy, everyone, including the vampire doctor, is certain that having the baby will kill her. And it does. To say that Bella has a death wish is an understatement. The entire saga revolves around her being almost killed and saved at the last minute or being killed and being brought back to life by Edward. She begs to be killed so that she can experience for herself the superhuman rush of the vampire lifestyle. She at once pleads with the self-controlled Edward to lose control and tells him that she trusts him not to lose complete control. She wants to keep Edward on the edge of his ability to control his desires, and only then can she satisfy hers.

Throughout the series, Bella repeatedly tells everyone, especially Edward, that she is not afraid. She faces vampires and wolves more easily than she does her high school friends. She thrives on the adrenaline rush of the vampire lifestyle, but more than that, on the adrenaline rush of her own human recklessness, which forces vampires and wolves alike to save and protect her over and over again. Everyone's desires are both fueled and checked by Bella's desires. There are the vampires that want to kill her and those that want to save her, the vampires that want to feed on her and those that almost starve in order to protect her. Edward is the epitome of repressed desires, the ultimate super-ego reigning in the bloodthirsty id, the superman who has overcome his animality to become a cold one who does what is required and asked of him, usually by Bella.

If Edward is the model of cool chastity, Bella is an all-American warm-blooded girl who wants sex, and more than that, dangerous unprotected sex. Somewhere in between the cold ones and the animal wolves whose sexuality is ultimately controlled by instinctual "imprinting," Bella's human passions are inflamed. She wants both Jacob's warmth and Edward's cool. In a sense she sucks the life out of both of them in her fragile human form, driving them both crazy with her demands and her recklessness. In other words, they too are turned on by her dangerous desires, her desire for death.

The sex scene between Edward and Bella in *Breaking Dawn* is the most anticipated in this saga of teenage longing and abstinence. After four installments of pent-up libido, is it any wonder that the 100-year-old virgin vampire breaks the bed during sex?

And, either vampire semen is especially potent, or Bella, like other recent pregnant Hollywood teens (Juno aka "Fertile Myrtle") is hyper-fertile and gets pregnant immediately. Indeed, she gets pregnant after sex with a bloodless immortal with crystal in his veins and presumably crystal for semen. Some of the vampires are as baffled by this as the audience, but thanks to an internet search, Edward confirms that it is possible.

Bella is not just knocked up by a little vampire sex; she's knocked around. The ultrasensitive Edward refuses to continue bruising his beloved, and again Bella has to beg him for more dangerous violent sex. Within the world of *Twilight*, feminine sexuality is driven by risky, even masochistic, behaviors that repeatedly leave Bella bruised, bleeding, and on the edge of death. In this sense, her risky pregnancy is yet another manifestation of her desire for dangerous sex. For young girls, pregnancy is always a risk associated with sex. And *Breaking Dawn* does indeed hit a nerve when it portrays the danger associated with sex as part of its lure. Akin to unprotected sex with HIV-positive partners, or what is called "barebacking" in gay culture, for some hetero-girls the risk of pregnancy becomes part of the fantasy associated with unprotected sex. The risk of becoming pregnant makes the sex more exciting. And the risk of pregnancy also always brings with it the risk of sickness and death. This is certainly the case with Bella. The sex she craves is violent, dangerous, and eventually leads to her death. In *Twilight* young feminine sexuality in the figure of Bella is driven by this death wish. The danger and risk of death make life—and sex—more exciting.

## *TWILIGHT*'S NEW CULT OF MOTHERHOOD

Unlike Rosemary's abject pregnancy, which some critics claim is the result of her repressed and ambivalent sexual desires for a more powerful lover, Bella's abject pregnancy is a result of sex with a super-powerful lover and her desires for him seem far from repressed. Yet if Rosemary's ambivalent relation to her own body is manifest in her wasting away and debilitation during pregnancy, the same could be said of Bella. Unlike Rosemary, however, Bella's ambivalence to her body also seems less repressed. In other words, over forty years later, this young woman openly hates her body. Bella complains that her body is awkward and clumsy, that she is "literally stumbling" through life, and that she wants to be a vampire so that she will have a stronger, better body. She is pale and has a taste for blood even before she becomes a vampire (or pregnant with one). It is clear that Bella wants to exchange her old inferior body for a new superior one.

This is a central difference between Roman Polanski's 1968 *Rosemary's Baby* with its insecure and possibly crazy protagonist and what director Bill Condon calls the "heroic female sacrifice" by his self-assured, no-nonsense protagonist in *Breaking Dawn*. Like Rosemary, Bella wants to protect her baby. But unlike Rosemary, who is manipulated and manhandled by those around her, Bella is in control of those around her. Even if other characters think that she does not understand the threat posed by her hybrid baby, she knows better. She is sure of herself in a way that Rosemary is not. She knows what she wants and knows how to get it, whereas Rosemary turns out to be a pawn in a game played between her husband and a group of devil-worshipping witches. In spite of all of the drama and angst around her, Bella knows that her baby will be okay. And, ignoring warnings from others, she seems confident that Edward will once again find a way to save her, and to give her what she has wanted all along, to be reborn as a vampire. Whereas Rosemary is all alone and afraid, Bella is surrounded by people (okay vampires, wolves, and a couple of people) who love and support her, who bring her everything she needs, and who live to protect her. Bella is the center of the *Twilight* universe whereas Rosemary is alienated from her own world, especially during her pregnancy.

Another telling difference between pregnancy as imagined in *Rosemary's Baby* and in 2011's *Breaking Dawn* is that Rosemary's husband is selfish and exchanges their baby's soul for his career, while Edward is the epitome of thoughtfulness who devotes himself to his wife's well-being, even if that means controlling his vampire urges to taste her sweet-smelling blood, and his teenage hormones that want more bed-breaking sex. If Rosemary's husband is every woman's nightmare, Bella's is every woman's dream. Although she may seem passive, even whiny—a depressed Juno McDuff—unlike Rosemary, Bella is in control, knows what she wants, and gets it from everyone around her, especially Edward who is under her spell—or is it her smell?

Along with new images of pregnancy come new images of the sensitive partner, the man who worships his beloved, or at least supports her choices and stays with her during her pregnancy. If *Rosemary's Baby* is a warning against the alienating aspects of pregnancy and childbirth just as women were making social demands in the women's liberation movement, *Breaking Dawn* is a post-feminist reassurance that in spite of the sickness, pain, and risks, pregnancy and childbirth bring people closer together and lead not only to the birth of a beautiful baby but also to the rebirth of a woman as mother. With *Breaking Dawn*, *Twilight* has become a dark endorsement for the cult of motherhood.


## THE PREGNANT BELLY AS SCREEN

In conclusion, Hollywood continues to provide us with entertaining depictions of women's role in reproduction that, on the one hand, romanticize pregnancy and childbirth, and, on the other, render that process grotesque. Whether pregnancy through "good old-fashioned" sex is made desirable yet funny in pregnant romantic comedies, or technological reproduction without sex is made threatening and monstrous in horror or science fiction films, Hollywood displays a strong preference for non-technologically mediated "romantic" pregnancies that deliver non-technologically

mediated "romantic" babies. Across the genres of Hollywood pregnancy films in the first decade of the new century, we see our fears
and desires played out on the bellies of pregnant women. From the
crazy pathologized pregnant women in horror, to the monstrous
interspecies pregnancies of science fiction, through the spunky teen
moms and baby-hungry career women who will stop at nothing
to get a baby, pregnancy is exploding onto the screen. Even as the
pregnant body has "come out of the closet" in Hollywood, these
films reiterate images of abject maternal bodies along with conservative notions of family values and familiar anxieties over women's
role in reproduction, especially fears of miscegenation. Even if it is
gross, and possibly dangerous, pregnancy is represented as attractive, cute, or sexy. Even the crazy ladies of horror (Jillian and Elsa),
and some of the baby-hungry aliens of science fiction (Sil and
Dren), are "hot" (perhaps even "in heat" in the case of Sil).

Since the appearance of Demi Moore's glistening, heavily pregnant belly on the cover of *Vanity Fair* in 1991, Hollywood screens
have capitalized on images of cute and sexy mothers-to-be. This
apparent liberation of pregnancy from the shroud of shame that
cloaked it until the late twentieth century is a new form of objectification of the female body and a regression to traditional family values in the face of shifting demographics which indicate that
college-educated white women are having fewer babies. In a sense,
these Hollywood films act as advertisements for white career
women choosing to have babies in order to fulfill their lives and
their destinies, so that they can "have it all." Even as these images
valorize the pregnant body (oftentimes while making fun of it),
they also continue a history of cultural ambivalence about wom-
en's bodies and pregnancy in particular.

The pregnant body, specifically the swollen belly, can be interpreted as a screen for contemporary fantasies, fears, and desires
about ourselves as human beings and about humanity itself. Many
films we discussed function to reassure us that, despite shifting
cultural paradigms that empower women and new reproductive
technologies that offer more choices for reproduction, traditional

values of heterosexual coupling and sexual reproduction remain the path to true love. These films often employ, to great comic effect, hyperbolic images of modern existence—career women, one-night-stands, IVF—to illustrate the necessary and felicitous return to a traditional family structure. As we have seen, the rhetoric of feminism and women's right to choose is co-opted and redeployed to turn accidental pregnancies into chosen babies in ways that actually foreclose women's options, especially to abortion, and "resolve" the complexities of pregnancy and childbirth with happy endings.

Tracing the meanings of pregnancy and its representations in film from classic cinema of the 1940s when the Hays Code banned using the word *pregnancy*, to contemporary popular film where the swollen belly becomes the butt of the joke in raunchy comedies and a graphically violent spawn-spewing generatrix in science fiction and horror genres, it becomes obvious that the ubiquity of these images tells us something about our fears and desires. These pregnant bellies have become screens onto which some of the most dramatic concerns of our age are projected. The expanding pregnant belly has become a cipher for issues of race, humanity, technology, nation, family, and religion. As one of the most significant changes that a human body can undergo, and the ability of this body to produce another life, the pregnant body has become a visual metaphor for other types of transformations. As we have seen, pregnancy films send multiple and sometimes contradictory messages about pregnancy and women's role in reproduction, especially in light of new reproductive technologies. By examining Hollywood film, we have learned that images of pregnancy in popular cinema, even and perhaps especially comedies, are serious indexes of social norms. As we have seen, our preoccupation with the natural and biological processes of pregnancy and childbirth cover over deeper anxieties about the ways in which these processes are mediated not only by technology but also and moreover by politics, particularly the politics of race. Although pregnancy is as old as the species of man, the pregnant body has become the bio-political exemplar of struggles over ideals of nationalism, cultural authenticity, domesticity, and patriarchal norms as they are inflected by changing technologies that make it possible to imagine reproducing the species in laboratories.

New reproductive technologies are coming out of the fertility clinics and into theaters near you, where the hippest new art film may be an ART film. With recent advances in reproductive technology outstripping our public policies and laws governing them, not to mention our ethical attitudes toward them, it is no wonder that Hollywood has stepped in to fuel our imaginations with both romantic and cautionary tales. The moral of these stories is that real babies are born from real romance, real love, and real sex (not necessarily in that order). Even as they raise the specter of a world peopled by test-tube babies and unfeeling automatons or monstrosities created though technology, these films also reassure us that technology will never replace love. Even if the pregnant body is an ambiguous cipher for our unspoken fears and desires, somehow its appearance on the big screen reassures us it is bigger than life. And, in light of the fantasy of its disappearance, we need it now more than ever.

# NOTES

## 2. MOMCOM AS ROMCOM: PREGNANCY AS A VEHICLE FOR ROMANCE

1. Ed Sikov argues that "screwball" came from the baseball pitch that is fast and curves in. In addition, he explains that "screwy" was used to describe drunkenness and lunacy. Therefore, "screwball" conjures speed, unpredictability, drunkenness, and giddiness (see Sikov 1989:19).

2. For a discussion of the difference between screwball comedies and romantic comedies, see Wes Gehring's *Romantic vs. Screwball Comedy* (2002). There, he argues that screwball emphasizes the zany and funny whereas romantic comedy emphasizes love. For a discussion of screwball films and their directors, see *Romantic Comedy in Hollywood: From Lubitsch to Sturges* (Harvey 1987).

3. For a discussion of the relationship between screwball and the Depression, see the introduction to *The Screwball Comedy Films: A History and Filmography, 1934–1952* by Duane Byrge and Robert Milton Miller (1991). This book also chronicles the films of this period and their stars. See also Wes Gehring's *Romantic vs. Screwball Comedy* (2002) and Nicholas Laham's *Currents of Comedy on the American Screen: How Film and Television Deliver Different Laughs for Changing Times* (2009).

4. For a discussion of "Boss-Ladies and Other Liberated Types" in early Hollywood romantic comedies, see Ted Sennett's *Lunatics and Lovers: A Tribute to the Giddy and Glittering Era of the Screen's "Screwball" and Romantic Comedies* (1973). Sennett concludes: "These, then, were the forceful ladies who made their mark and cut their professional niche in Hollywood's Never-Never-Land, only to discover that in this land at least, love and marriage were the only real goals, and the men who brought them both were the only true necessities. . . . [I]n Never-Never-Land, Women's Liberation is the stuff of farce" (224).

5. For a discussion of class in Hollywood comedies, see Beach (2002).

6. Sigmund Freud describes the fort-da in relation to his grandson, who throws a spool from his cot and pulls it back over and over again, reenacting, according to Freud, the child's mother leaving and coming back. Perhaps it is not merely coincidental that this Freudian trope becomes popular in Hollywood at a time when other Freudian notions are being imported by directors such as Fritz Lang and Alfred Hitchcock among others.

7. For discussion of the changes that led to the separation of sex and romance, see Neale (1992) and Seidman (1991).

8. For discussions of the split between sex and romance in *My Best Friend's Wedding*, see McDonald (2007), Krutnik (1990), and Evans and Deleyto (1998, introduction).

9. See McDonald (2007, conclusion); see also Claire Mortimer (2010, ch. 3); Mortimer discusses *Knocked Up* as a case study of the new male hero of romantic comedies, particularly in regard to "bromance."

10. For an excellent analysis of the ways in which Hollywood's romantic comedies reinforce patriarchal ideology, see Mark Rubinfeld's *Bound to Bond: Gender, Genre, and the Hollywood Romantic Comedy* (2001). Although Rubinfeld does not discuss pregnancy in romcom, he does analyze the ways in which various common narratives in these films perpetuate gender norms that rein in unruly women and men and in the end make women subordinate to men (2001).

11. In *Film Comedy*, Geoff King diagnoses humor in gross-out comedies in terms of an overflow or transgression of boundaries. Using Mikhail Bakhtin's theory of carnival based on the body as a source of the grotesque and Kristeva's theory of abjection as that which calls into question borders, King argues that Hollywood raunchy humor makes manifest bodily borders as it transgresses them (2002:63–65). For both Bakhtin and Kristeva, conception, pregnancy, and birth are the quintessential human experiences that call into question boundaries—boundaries between inside and outside, between one individual and another, between mother and child, between man and woman, etc. As Kristeva points out, how do we determine whether a pregnant woman is one person or two?

12. In a more general context, Mary Ann Doane gives a Freudian interpretation of women as both the object of the gaze and the butt of the joke in "Film and the Masquerade: Theorising the Female Spectator" (1982:418–36).

13. News media blamed the romantization of pregnancy, especially teenage pregnancy, in films such as *Juno* and within celebrity culture (with the pregnancies of Jamie Lynn Spears and Bristol Palin) for the so-called "pregnancy pact" in Massachusetts and for rising rates of pregnancy among teenagers. For a sociological study of the impact of romantic comedies on our expectations in relationships, see Johnson (2009). There the researchers investigate the ideals of relationships presented in Hollywood romances and their impact on viewers. It would be interesting to make a similar study of recent representations of pregnancy on viewers.

## 3. ACCIDENT AND EXCESS: THE "CHOICE"
## TO HAVE A BABY

1. For discussions of the effects of ultrasound imaging on our conceptions of the fetus as an individual with rights, see Petchesky (1987), Berlant (1994), and Franklin (2007).
2. For an interesting feminist discussion of *Look Who's Talking,* see Berlant (1994).
3. "The birth rate last year [2009] for U.S. girls 15 to 19 was the lowest since the government began tracking the statistic in 1940" (Stobbe 2010:4A).
4. For example, see the *New York Times* online (www.nyt.com) for June 20, 2008: "Hollywood Films *Juno* and *Knocked Up* Blamed as Teenagers Race to Become Mothers" by Jane Bone. MSNBC.com calls it the "Juno–Jamie Lynn effect": see "Teen 'Pregnancy Pact' Has 17 Girls Expecting" (MSNBC News Service, June 20, 2008).

# FILMOGRAPHY

*4 Months, 3 Weeks, and 2 Days* (Cristian Mungiu, 2007)
*The 6th Day* (Roger Spottiswoode, 2000)
*Alien* (Ridley Scott, 1979)
*Aliens* (James Cameron, 1986)
*Along Came Polly* (John Hamburg, 2004)
*American Pie* (Paul Weitz, 1999)
*Annie Hall* (Woody Allen, 1977)
*The Astronaut's Wife* (Rand Ravich, 1999)
*Away We Go* (Sam Mendes, 2009)
*Baby Mama* (Michael McCullers, 2008)
*Baby on Board* (Brian Herzlinger, 2009)
*The Back-up Plan* (Alan Poul, 2010)
*Basket Case* (Frank Henenlotter, 1982)
*Basket Case 2* (Frank Henenlotter, 1990)
*Bella* (Alejandro Gomez Monteverde, 2006)
*The Birds* (Alfred Hitchcock, 1963)
*Bringing Up Baby* (Howard Hawks, 1938)
*Broadcast News* (James L. Brooks, 1987)
*The Brood* (David Cronenberg, 1979)
*The Brothers Solomon* (Bob Odenkirk, 2007)
*The Business of Being Born* (Abby Epstein, 2008)
*Children of Men* (Alfonso Cuarón, 2006)
*Citizen Ruth* (Alexander Payne, 1996)
*Deadly Twins* (Joe Oaks, 1985)
*Demon Seed* (Donald Cammell, 1977)
*Due Date* (Todd Phillips, 2010)

*Expecting Mary* (Dan Gordon, 2010)
*Father of the Bride II* (Charles Shyer, 1995)
*Fool's Gold* (Andy Tennant, 2008)
*Fools Rush In* (Andy Tennant, 1997)
*Gattaca* (Andrew Niccol, 1997)
*Ghosts of Girlfriends Past* (Mark Waters, 2009)
*Grace* (Paul Solet, 2009)
*Head of Family* (Charles Band, 1996)
*Home Fries* (Dean Parisot, 1998)
*How to Lose a Guy in 10 Days* (Donald Petrie, 2003)
*If These Walls Could Talk* (HBO, Cher and Nancy Savoca, 1996)
*The Incubus* (John Hough, 1982)
*The Island* (Michael Bay, 2005)
*It Happened One Night* (Frank Capra, 1934)
*I Was a Male War Bride* (Howard Hawks, 1949)
*Junior* (Ivan Reitman, 1994)
*Juno* (Jason Reitman, 2007)
*Just Another Girl on the I.R.T.* (Leslie Harris, 1992)
*Kick-Ass* (Matthew Vaughn, 2010)
*The Kids Are All Right* (Lisa Cholodenko, 2010)
*Knocked Up* (Judd Apatow, 2007)
*Labor Pains* (Lara Shapiro, 2009)
*Leap Year* (Anand Tucker, 2009)
*Lebensborn* (David Stephens, 1997)
*Leave Her to Heaven,* (John Stahl, 1945)
*Look Who's Talking* (Amy Heckerling, 1989)
*Look Who's Talking Too* (Amy Heckerling, 1990)
*Lover Come Back* (Delbert Mann, 1961)
*Manny & Lo* (Lisa Krueger, 1996)
*Marnie* (Alfred Hitchcock, 1964)
*The Miracle of Morgan's Creek* (Preston Sturges, 1944)
*Miss Conception* (Eric Styles, 2008)
*Moon* (Duncan Jones, 2009)
*My Best Friend's Wedding* (P. J. Hogan, 1997)
*My Man Godfrey* (Gregory La Cava, 1936)
*My Sister's Keeper* (Nick Cassavetes, 2009)
*New in Town* (Jonas Elmer, 2009)
*Nine Months* (Chris Columbus, 1995)
*Once Around* (Lasse Hallström, 1991)
*The Opposite of Sex* (Don Roos, 1998)
*Palindromes* (Todd Solondz, 2004)
*Pan's Labyrinth* (Guillermo del Toro, 2006)
*People Will Talk* (Joseph L. Mankiewicz, 1951)
*Pillow Talk* (Michael Gordon, 1959)

*Precious* (Lee Daniels, 2009)
*The Pregnancy Pact* (TV, Rosemary Rodriguez, 2010)
*The Proposal* (Anne Fletcher, 2009)
*Psycho* (Alfred Hitchcock, 1960)
*Quinceañera* (Richard Glatzer, 2006)
*Revolutionary Road* (Sam Mendes, 2008)
*Riding in Cars with Boys* (Penny Marshall, 2001)
*Rosemary's Baby* (Roman Polanski, 1968)
*Saved!* (Brian Dannelly, 2004)
*Send Me No Flowers* (Norman Jewison, 1964)
*The Seven Year Itch* (Billy Wilder, 1955)
*Sex and the Single Girl* (Richard Quine, 1964)
*She's Having a Baby* (John Hughes, 1988)
*Some Like it Hot* (Billy Wilder, 1959)
*Species* (Roger Donaldson, 1995)
*Splice* (Vincenzo Natali, 2009)
*Stephanie Daley* (Hilary Brougher, 2006)
*Sullivan's Travels* (Preston Sturges, 1941)
*Surrogates* (Jonathan Mostow, 2009)
*Suture* (Scott McGhee and David Siegel, 1993)
*The Switch* (Josh Gordon and Will Speck, 2010)
*There's Something About Mary* (Bobby Farrelly and Peter Farrelly, 1998)
*To Save a Life* (Brian Baugh, 2009)
*The Twilight Saga: Breaking Dawn: Part One* (Bill Condon, 2011)
*The Twilight Saga: Eclipse* (David Slade, 2010)
*The Twilight Saga: New Moon* (Chris Weitz, 2009)
*The Ugly Truth* (Robert Luketic, 2009)
*The Unborn* (David S. Goyer, 2009)
*Vera Drake* (Mike Leigh, 2004)
*Waitress* (Adrienne Shelly, 2007)
*Wedding Crashers* (David Dobkin, 2005)
*Where the Heart Is* (Matt Williams, 2000)
*X-tro* (Harry Bromley Davenport, 1983)

# TEXTS CITED

14 (pseudonym). 2009. "The Nadya Suleman Octomom." *Gallery of the Absurd*. February 18; see www.galleryoftheabsurd.com/2009/02/the-nadya-suleman-octomom.html.

Adams, Sarah LaChance. 2009. "Becoming with Child: Pregnancy as Provocation to Authenticity." In Adrian Mirvish and Adrian van den Hoven, eds., *New Perspectives on Sartre*, 25–36. Cambridge, Eng.: Cambridge Scholars Press.

Beach, Christopher. 2002. *Class, Language and American Film Comedy*. New York: Cambridge University Press.

Beauvoir, de, Simone. 1949. *The Second Sex*. Trans. H. M. Parshley. New York: Vintage.

Bell-Metereau, Rebecca. 1985. *Hollywood Androgyny*. New York: Columbia University Press.

Bender, Leslie. 2006. " 'To err is Human' ART Mix-ups: A Labor-Based, Relational Proposal." *Journal of Gender, Race and Justice* 9: 443–508.

Benfer, Amy. 2009. "Single and Knocked Up." *Salon*, March 26; see www.salon.com/life/broadsheet/feature/2009/03/26/self_magazine_on_single_mothers/index.html.

Berenstein, Rhona. 1990. "Mommie Dearest: *Aliens*, *Rosemary's Baby*, and Mothering." *Journal of Popular Culture* 24.2: 55–73.

Berlant, Lauren. 1994. "America, 'Fat,' the Fetus." *Boundary 2* 21.3: 145–95.

Bewell, Alan. 1988. "An Issue of Monstrous Desire." *Yale Journal of Criticism* 2.1: 105–128.

Blackwood, Sarah. 2011. "Our Bella, Ourselves." *The Hairpin*, November 16 (last accessed January 1, 2012); see http://thehairpin.com/2011/11/our-bella-ourselves.

Braidotti, Rosi. 2002. *Metamorphoses: Towards a Materialist Theory of Becoming*. Cambridge, Eng.: Polity Press.

Byrge, Duane and Robert Milton Miller. 1991. *The Screwball Comedy Films: A History and Filmography, 1934–1952*. Jefferson, NC: McFarland.

Candies Foundation, 2008. "America, Wake-Up!" Advertisement. *New York Times*, October 27, A9.

Carroll, Noël. 1990. *The Philosophy of Horror or Paradoxes of the Heart*. New York: Routledge.

Chambers, Ross. 1997. "The Unexamined." In Mike Hill, ed., *Whiteness: A Critical Reader*, 187–203. New York: New York University Press.

Chanter, Tina. 2008. *The Picture of Abjection: Film, Fetish, and the Nature of Difference*. Bloomington: Indiana University Press.

Chappetta, Robert. 1969. "Review [*Rosemary's Baby*]." *Film Quarterly* 22.3 (Spring): 35–38.

Creed, Barbara. 1993. *The Monstrous-Feminine: Film, Feminism, Psychoanalysis*. New York: Routledge.

Cussins, Charis. 1998. "Quit Sniveling, Cryo-Baby. We'll Work Out Which One Is Your Mama!" In Davis-Floyd and Dumit, eds., *Cyborg Babies: From Techno-Sex to Techo-Tots*, 40–66.

Davis, Angela Y. 2000. "Outcast Mothers and Surrogates: Racism and Reproductive Politics in the Nineties" (1991). In Wendy Kolmar and Frances Bartkowski, eds., *Feminist Theory: A Reader*, 478–84. Mountain View, CA: Mayfield.

Davis-Floyd, Robbie. 1993. *Birth as an American Rite of Passage*. Berkeley: University of California Press.

Davis-Floyd, Robbie and Joseph Dumit, eds. 1998. *Cyborg Babies: From Techno-Sex to Techo-Tots*. New York: Routledge.

Doane, Mary Ann. 1982. "Film and the Masquerade: Theorising the Female Spectator." In E. Ann Kaplan, ed., *Feminism and Film*, 418–36. Oxford: Oxford University Press.

Donchin, Anne. 1996. "Feminist Critiques of New Fertility Technologies: Implications for Social Policy." *Journal of Medicine and Philosophy* 21: 475–98.

Evans, Peter William and Celestino Deleyto. 1998. *Terms of Endearment: Hollywood Romantic Comedy of the 1980's and 1990's*. Edinburgh: Edinburgh University Press.

Fischer, Lucy. 1992. "Birth Trauma: Parturition and Horror in *Rosemary's Baby*." *Cinema Journal* 31.3 (Spring): 3–18.

Ford, Clellan Stearns. 1945. *A Comparative Study of Human Reproduction*. New Haven: Yale University Publications in Anthropology, no. 32.

Franklin, Sarah. 2007. "Fetal Fascinations: New Dimensions to the Medical-Scientific Construction of Fetal Personhood." In Sarah Franklin, Celia Lury, and Jackie Stacey, eds., *Off-Centre: Feminism and Cultural Studies*, 190–205. London: Routledge.

Freeland, Cynthia. 2000. *The Naked and the Undead: Evil and the Appeal of Horror*. Boulder, CO: Westview.

Freud, Sigmund. 1990. *Totem and Taboo* (1913). The Standard Edition, vol. 13, *The Complete Psychological Works of Sigmund Freud*. Translated from the German under the General Editorship of James Strachey. New York: Norton.

———. 2001a. "The Theme of the Three Caskets" (1913), in *The Case of Schreber, Papers on Technique and Other Works*. The Standard Edition, vol. 12, *The Complete Psychological Works of Sigmund Freud*. Translated from the German under the General Editorship of James Strachey. New York: Vintage.

———. 2001b. *An Infantile Neurosis and Other Works*. The Standard Edition, vol. 17, *The Complete Psychological Works of Sigmund Freud*. Translated from the German under the General Editorship of James Strachey. New York: Vintage.

Gehring, Wes. 2002. *Romantic Versus Screwball Comedy*. Lanham, MD: Scarecrow Press.

Gordon, Linda. 1973. "Voluntary Motherhood: The Beginnings of Feminist Birth Control Ideas in the United States." *Feminist Studies* 1: 5–22.

Grant, Barry Keith, ed. 1996. *The Dread of Difference*. Austin: University of Texas Press.

Grossbart, Sarah and Rachel Paula Abrahamson. 2010. "Teen Mom: Inside Their Brave Struggle." *US Weekly*, August 30, 38–45.

Habermas, Jürgen. 2003. *The Future of Human Nature*. Malden, MA: Polity Press.

Hanson, Clare. 2004. *A Cultural History of Pregnancy*. New York: Palgrave Press.

Hardy, Quentin. 1996. "Idaho County Tests a New Way to Curb Teen Sex: Prosecute." *Wall Street Journal*, July 8, A1.

Harris, John. 2010. *Enhancing Evolution: The Ethical Case for Making Better People*. Princeton: Princeton University Press.

Hartouni, Valerie. 1997. *Cultural Conceptions: On Reproductive Technologies + The Remaking of Life*. Minneapolis: University of Minnesota Press.

Harvey, James. 1987. *Romantic Comedy in Hollywood: From Lubitsch to Sturges*. New York: Knopf.

Hewlett, Sylvia Ann. 2002. *Baby Hunger: The New Battle for Motherhood*. London: Atlanta Books.

Houston, Beverly and Marsha Kinder. 1968–69. "Rosemary's Baby." *Sight and Sound* 38 (Winter): 17–19.

Ikemoto, Lisa. 1995–96. "The In/Fertile, the Too Fertile, and the Dysfertile." *Hastings Law Journal* 47: 1007–1061.

Irigaray, Luce. 1993a. *An Ethics of Sexual Difference*. Trans. Carolyn Burke and Gillian Gill. Ithaca: Cornell University Press.

———. 1993b. *Sexes and Genealogies*. Trans. Gillian Gill. New York: Columbia University Press.

Johnson, Kimberly and Bjarne Holmes. 2009. "Contradictory Messages: A Content Analysis of Hollywood-Produced Romantic Comedy Feature Films." *Communication Quarterly* 57.3: 352–73.

Johnston, Josephine. 2009. "Judging Octomom." *The Hastings Center Report* 39.3 (May–June): 23–26.

Jong, Erica. 2010. "Mother Madness." *Wall Street Journal*, November 6, The Saturday Essay.

Kant, Immanuel. 1993. *Grounding for the Metaphysics of Morals* (1785). 3d ed. Indianapolis, IN: Hackett.

Kass, Leon. 2003. "Ageless Bodies, Happy Souls." *The New Atlantis* 1 (Spring): 9–28.

King, Geoff. 2002. *Film Comedy*. London: Wallflower Press.

Kristeva, Julia. 1980. *Powers of Horror*. Trans. Leon Roudiez. New York: Columbia University Press.

——. 1983. "Stabat Mater" (1976). Reprinted in *Tales of Love*. Trans. Leon Roudiez. New York: Columbia University Press.

——. 1989. *The Black Sun: Depression and Melancholia*. Trans. Leon Roudiez. New York: Columbia University Press.

——. 2002. *The Portable Kristeva*. Edited by Kelly Oliver. New York: Columbia University Press.

——. 2010. *Hatred and Forgiveness*. Trans. Jeanine Herman. New York: Columbia University Press.

Krutnik, Frank. 1990. "The Faint Aroma of Performing Seals: The 'Nervous' Romance and the Comedy of the Sexes." *The Velvet Light Trap* 26: 57–72.

Kushner, Eve. 2000. "Go Forth and Multiply: Abortion in Hollywood Movies of the '90s." *Bitch: Feminist Response to Popular Culture* 11.29: 34–37, 81–82.

Laham, Nicholas. 2009. *Currents of Comedy on the American Screen: How Film and Television Deliver Different Laughs for Changing Times*. Jefferson, NC: McFarland.

Longhurst, Robyn. 2000. "'Corporeographies' of pregnancy: 'bikini babes,'" *Environment and Planning D: Society and Space* 18: 453–72.

Lundquist, Caroline. 2008. "On Being Torn: Toward a Phenomenology of Unwanted Pregnancy." *Hypatia: A Journal of Feminist Philosophy* 23.3: 136–55.

——. 2011. "Recovering the Tragic: Exploring the Ethical Dimensions of Rape-Related Pregnancy." In Michael Barber, Lester Embree, and Thomas Nenon, eds., *Phenomenology 2010*, vol. 5, part 1. Bucharest, Romania: Zeta Books.

Matthews, Sandra and Laura Wexler. 2000. *Pregnant Pictures*. New York: Routledge.

Meltzer, Marisa. 2011. "WombTube: The Odd and Addictive Videos of Women Who Reveal Their Pregnancy Test Results Online." *Slate*, March 14; see www.slate.com/id/2286434/.

McDonald, Tamar. 2007. *Romantic Comedy: Boy Meets Girl Meets Genre*. London: Wallflower Press.

McWhorter, Ladelle. 2009. *Racism and Sexual Oppression in Anglo-America: A Genealogy*. Bloomington: Indiana University Press.

Monk, Katherine. 2010. "The Switch Works Better as a Bromance Than a Chick Flick." *Vancouver Sun*, August 20.

Morgan, Jennifer. 2010. "Echoes of Slavery? 'Race,' 'Nature,' and Reproductive Technologies." Paper presented at the PhiloSophia Conference, March 25, CUNY Graduate Center, New York.

Morrone, Wenda Wardell. 1984. *Pregnant While You Work*. New York: Macmillian.

Mortimer, Claire. 2010. *Romantic Comedy*. New York: Routledge.

Mulvey, Laura. 2009. "Visual Pleasure and Narrative Cinema." In *Visual and Other Pleasures*, 14–30. 2d ed. New York: Palgrave Macmillan.

Mundy, Liza. 2008. *Everything Conceivable: How Assisted Reproduction Is Changing Our World*. New York: Random House.

Neale, Steve. 1992. "The Big Romance or Something Wild? Romantic Comedy Today." *Screen* 33.3: 284–99.

Negra, Diane. 2010. "Brangelina: The Fertile Valley of Celebrity." *The Velvet Light Trap* 65 (Spring): 60–61.

New England Free Press. 1971. *Our Bodies, Ourselves*. New York: Simon and Schuster.

Newton, Niles. 1996. "Emotions of Pregnancy." In Philip K. Wilson, ed., *Diseases of Pregnancy and Childbirth*, 349–69. New York: Garland.

O'Byrne, Anne. 2010. *Natality and Finitude*. Bloomington: Indiana University Press.

Oliver, Kelly. 1995. *Womanizing Nietzsche: Philosophy's Relation to "the Feminine."* New York: Routledge.

——. 1997. *Family Values: Subjects Between Nature and Culture*. New York: Routledge.

——. 1998. *Subjectivity Without Subjects*. Rowman and Littlefield Press.

—— (with Benigno Trigo). 2002. *Noir Anxiety*. Minneapolis: University of Minnesota Press.

——. 2008. "Alfred Hitchcock: Fowl Play and the Domestication of Horror." In James Phillips, ed., *Cinematic Thinking: Philosophical Approaches to New Cinema*, 11–26. Stanford, CA: Stanford University Press.

——. 2010. "Whose Body? Whose Choice? Enhancing Evolution." *Southern Journal of Philosophy*. Special Issue: *Spindel Supplement: The Sexes of Evolution: Continental Philosophy, Feminist Philosophy, and Evolutionary Theory* 48, Issue Supplement s1.

Ortiz, Ana Teresa and Laura Briggs. 2003. "The Culture of Poverty, Crack Babies, and Welfare Cheats: The Making of the 'Healthy White Baby Crisis.'" *Social Text* 21.3: 39–57.

Otto, Sheila and Winifred J. E. Pinch. 2009. "Ethical Dimensions in the Case of the 'Octomom': Two Perspectives." *Pediatric Nursing* 35.6 (November–December): 389–92.

Petchesky, Rosalind. 1987. "Fetal Images: The Power of Visual Culture in the Politics of Reproduction." *Feminist Studies* 13.2: 263–92.

Quiroga, Seline Szkupinski. 2007. "Blood Is Thicker Than Water: Policing Donor Insemination and the Reproduction of Whiteness." *Hypatia* 22.2 (Spring): 143–61.

Rich, Adrienne. 1976. *Of Woman Born*. New York: Norton.

Roberts, Dorothy. 1997. *Killing the Black Body: Race, Reproduction, and the Meaning of Liberty*. New York: Pantheon.

——. 2009. "Race, Gender and Genetic Technologies: A New Reproductive Dystopia?" *Signs: Journal of Women in Culture and Society* 34: 783–805.

Robertson, John. 2009. "The Octuplet Case—Why More Regulation Is Not Likely." *Hasting Center Report* 39.3 (May–June): 26–28.

Rubinfeld, Mark. 2001. *Bound to Bond: Gender, Genre, and the Hollywood Romantic Comedy*. Westport, CT: Praeger.

Ruddick, Sara. 1989. *Maternal Thinking: Toward a Politics of Peace*. Boston: Beacon Press.

Sandel, Michael. 2007. *The Case Against Perfection: Ethics in the Age of Genetic Engineering*. Cambridge: Harvard University Press.

Sarris, Andrew. 1968. "Films." *Village Voice* 13.41 (July 25).

Seshadri-Crooks, Kalpana. 2000. *Desiring Whiteness: A Lacanian Analysis of Race*. New York: Routledge.

Seidman, Steve. 1991. *Romantic Longings: Love in America, 1830–1980*. New York: Routledge.

Sennett, Ted. 1973. *Lunatics and Lovers: A Tribute to the Giddy and Glittering Era of the Screen's "Screwball" and Romantic Comedies*. New York: Limelight Editions.

Sharpley-Whiting and T. Denean. 1999. *Black Venus: Sexualized Savages, Primal Fears, and Primitive Narratives in French*. Durham, NC: Duke University Press.

Sikov, Ed. 1989. *Screwball: Hollywood's Madcap Romantic Comedies*. New York: Crown.

Simons, Margaret. 1984. "Motherhood, Feminism and Identity." *Women's Studies International Forum* 2: 349–59.

Sobchack, Vivian. 1996. "Bringing It All Back Home: Family Economy and Generic Exchange." In Barry Keith Grant, ed., *The Dread of Difference*, 143–63, Austin: University of Texas Press.

Squier, Susan. 1999. "Negotiating Boundaries: From Assisted Reproduction to Assisted Replication," in E. Ann Kaplan and Susan Squier, eds., *Playing Dolly: Technocultural Formations, Fantasies, and Fictions of Assisted Reproduction*, 101–115. New Brunswick, NJ: Rutgers University Press.

Stobbe, Mike. 2010. "U.S. Teen Birth Rate Is Higher Than in Western Europe." *The (Nashville) Tennessean*. December 31, 4A.

Sullivan, Shannon. 2006. *Revealing Whiteness: The Unconscious Habits of Racial Privilege*. Bloomington: Indiana University Press.

Sundstrom, Ronald R. 2008. *The Browning of America and the Evasion of Social Justice*. Albany: State University of New York Press.

Taylor, Janelle. 2000. "Of Sonograms and Baby Prams: Prenatal Diagnosis, Pregnancy, and Consumption." *Feminist Studies* 2 (Summer): 391–418.

Thompson, Mary. 2010. "Juno or Just Another Girl?" In Andrea O'Reilly, ed., *Twenty-First-Century Motherhood: Experience, Identity, Agency*. New York: Columbia University Press.

Tyler, Imogen. 2001. "Skin-Tight: Celebrity, Pregnancy and Subjectivity." In Sara Ahmed and Jackie Stacey, eds., *Thinking Through the Skin*, 69–83. New York: Routledge.

*US Weekly*. 2009. "Kate Gosselin: Mom to Monster." June 1.

Valerius, Karyn. 2005. "Rosemary's Baby, Gothic Pregnancy, and Fetal Subjects." *College Literature* 32.3 (Summer): 116–35.

Waldman, Diane. 1981. "Horror and Domesticity: The Modern Gothic Romance Film of the 1940s." Ph.D. diss., University of Wisconsin, Madison.

Wiegman, Robyn. 2002. "Intimate Publics: Race, Property, and Personhood." *American Literature* 74.4: 859–85.

Westfall, Sandra. 2009. "Bristol Palin: Life Comes Second Now." *People Magazine*, June 1, 59–65.

Wexman, Virginia. 1987. "The Trauma of Infancy in Roman Polanski's *Rosemary's Baby*." In Gregory Waller, ed., *American Horrors: Essays on the Modern American Horror Film*, 30–43. Urbana: University of Illinois Press.

Willett, Cynthia. 1995. *Maternal Ethics and Other Slave Moralities*. New York: Routledge.

Wood, Robin. 2004. "An Introduction to the American Horror Film." In Barry Keith Grant and Christopher Sharrett, eds., *Planks of Reason: Essays on the Horror Film*, 107–141. Lanham, MD: Scarecrow Press.

Young, Iris Marion. 1990. *Throwing Like a Girl and Other Essays in Feminist Philosophy and Social Theory*. Bloomington: Indiana University Press.

——. 2005. *On Female Body Experience*. New York: Oxford University Press.

# INDEX